Difference Unbound
The Rise of Pluralism in Literature and Criticism

Reviews of <u>Difference Unbound: The Rise of Pluralism in Literature and Criticism</u>:

"Metzidakis has written an erudite, ambitious, and intentionally provocative work addressing the ways in which we respond to a plurality of readings of both literary and critical texts, and offering what he terms a 'three-fold polemic against literary criticism'." --Rosemary Lloyd, <u>The French Review</u>

"The strength of the book lies in Metzidakis' approach(es). He combines, juxtaposes and synthesizes the history of ideas, theory of literature, and the practical criticism of texts. He does all three, and all three well. I see at work a fine, subtle, comprehensive mind, a philosophical mind. Metzidakis treats authors and books in a number of languages (French, German, English, also Italian; he *knows* literature and criticism from 1750 to the present. This is one of a relatively small number of books on critical and theoretical questions that takes ideas seriously yet is also couched in clear, comprehensible English."--William Calin, <u>South Atlantic Review</u>

"Metzidakis … reveals many of the ambiguities, half-truths and uneasy compromises that lie at the heart of critical endeavor today. These pages are both enjoyable to read, and, at the same time, disturbing in their implications …He is always careful to point out that he is not making moral judgments on the phenomena that he examines. He merely points out their inherent dangers, and particularly those attached to the contemporary love of the new and original." --David J. Bond, <u>French Forum</u>

FAUX TITRE

94

Etudes de langue et littérature françaises
publiées sous la direction de

Keith Busby, M.J. Freeman,
Sjef Houppermans, Paul Pelckmans et Co Vet

Difference Unbound
The Rise of Pluralism in Literature and Criticism

Second Enlarged Edition

Preface by Mary Ann Caws

Stamos Metzidakis

AMSTERDAM · NEW YORK, NY 2012

The paper on which this book is printed meets the requirements of 'ISO 9706: 1994, Information and documentation - Paper for documents - Requirements for permanence'.

Le papier sur lequel le présent ouvrage est imprimé remplit les prescriptions de 'ISO 9706: 1994, Information et documentation - Papier pour documents - Prescriptions pour la permanence'.

Second Enlarged Edition
ISBN: 978-90-420-3626-0
Trefw.: pluralisme en literatuur / pluralisme en literaire kritiek.
© Editions Rodopi B.V., Amsterdam - New York, NY 2012
Printed in The Netherlands

Table of Contents

Mary Ann Caws

In this interesting book, Metzidakis takes up the issue of plural interpretations of various classic and modern works. He makes, right at the start, an essential point about the "admittedly Gallic slant" of his study, despite its more general title. That seems to me to make no *difference* to his argument, for it seems to me far preferable to have a firm place upon which to stand – such as that of his specific field – for any discussion such as this, which he entitles "literary pluralism."

Metzidakis has both a basic and an advanced knowledge of the individual players in the history and scope of this pluralism which makes up the foundation of his study. For those who are to some or even a large extent familiar with these participants – say, Paul de Man, Geoffrey Hartman, and Michael Riffaterre in one instance -- the discussion will be all the more interesting as X focuses on what Y *could* have been saying about a text, as opposed to what Y was indeed saying. This scheme of things and critics concerns some of us a good deal, given our bias toward a practical textual analysis, during which it is what we *are* in fact talking about that seems to us to matter greatly, and not what we *might* be talking about. In many cases, the details singled out by Metzidakis are such that we find ourselves involved in the issues. Now that, I submit, is exactly what a theoretical study should do: involve us in the issues as they are presented, argued, summed up, and contextualized.

I could take quite a few exemplary cases here, some as celebrated as the various interpretations of Baudelaire's sonnet "Les Chats," about which Riffaterre took on the structuralist interpretations of Claude Lévi-Strauss and Roman Jakobson: when that debate echoed in the august halls of the Collège de France, the amphitheatres were closed to latecomers, who watched the entire procedure with its witty repartee on television screens. Involved or not, depending on our various métiers and stances about textual interpretation -- I was, as were many others in the audience -- we are all (whoever "we" might possibly be) intrigued by the cases that call for examination. No ultimate answers, fine. However, the author believes that giving up the search for a potential answer, however provisional, for a potential conclusion, however tentative, constitutes a danger.

That danger, expressed the length of this confessedly structuralist study, is one of closing off a possible openness. Umberto Eco's advocacy of the *opera aperta* or the "open work" has taught us all how pluralistic points of view weave a complex story, of ultimate fascination. The procedure is not about choosing sides, but rather about seeing what each camp has to offer. Now that's practical openness, and it works.

The non-exclusionary wins out, when we are lucky, over the clique-ness of academia and institutions of authority. But ah yes, Riffaterre believed in the "proper" and correct interpretation of certain texts – and of their literariness. About literariness: one of the most interesting discussions in these pages has to do with the prose poem and its singular quality, its absolute particularity. Metzidakis takes the case of Max Jacob's "Poème," called just that, its development of the uncanny as it is recognized by the reader, and its strange similarity to Baudelaire's text "L'Etranger." He then brings up the problem, which is of course the substance of this book, of plural interpretations, the continuum of different readings that, "in practice, renders the very possibility of an ontologically 'whole' text nil." Nice touch. Now the issue is not that many of us never believed in an ontologically "whole" text – true as that may be – but that this pluralism, often under attack, calls forth all sorts of formerly hidden agendas and problematic worries.

Of course, this pluralism permits not only our so differing styles, adapted or not to their objects, but all sorts of theoretical stances potentially stirring to our often lazy minds. I was delighted to see the pages, in the penultimate chapter, on my own professor René Girard and his theory of mimetic desire (A desires B, which furnishes a model for C's own desire of B, thus increased, the whole structure enabling a kind of violence, the struggle for authority or winning out.) So a reading of any text does violence to the preceding reading, in a system prevalent in what Metzidakis terms a "typical modern-day analysis of a literary work." The new reading has to cleanse or purify the ground of the previous reading: where is the progress, if the sense of a tradition is thereby lost? It finally comes down, or up, to a concern about value and evaluation, a concern in which all of us as readers share.

Mary Ann Caws
Graduate School, City University of New York

AUTHOR'S NOTE ON THE SECOND EDITION
Stamos Metzidakis

Much has occurred since this book first appeared in the mid-1990s at the height of the so-called "culture wars" in the United States. Among the most prominent events for the context here are the bloody attacks of 9/11; the subsequent war(s) on primarily Islamic terrorists or supposed terrorist states; the election of an African-American to the presidency; the extreme polarization of our recent politics; and finally, a nearly devastating economic crisis. The point these five events drive home is that we can never again pretend to live in some imagined homogeneous world where a majority of people live, act or think in more or less the same manner. Over this same time period what has not changed, however, is that societies all over the globe continue to grapple--often violently--with questions about what kind of world they want to create and inhabit, given our many dissimilarities.

Diversity, heterogeneity, multiculturalism, and finally, *difference* are words that evoke these very socio-political, artistic, biological, religious, ethnic and gender-based traits that distinguish people from one another throughout the world. Most anyone also knows that terms like these frequently appear in all sorts of contemporary discourses, and represent ideals to which large numbers of citizens in the West, at least, aspire. Difference Unbound (DU) fully recognizes and supports the appropriateness, intrinsic desirability and widespread reality of these terms and their underlying concepts. In the most pragmatic sense, the second edition of this book, no more than the first, does not therefore dispute the belief that the promotion of diversity, heterogeneity, multiculturalism and difference itself is a very good thing indeed for the greatest number of people today, as well as in the future. In that regard, its aim could not be any more utilitarian.

Nonetheless, for the sake of the arguments presented here, and for reasons I explain in the pages that follow, I have placed all these and related concepts under the general sign or rubric of pluralism. What sets DU apart from more complete and far stricter anthropological, sociological or political studies of this same widespread cultural phenomenon is that it seeks to provide a concise history and analysis of this belief in regard to literary studies in particular. This history is little more than two centuries old. Still, DU does not, indeed cannot, attempt to address the entire spectrum of issues surrounding the notion of cultural pluralism. It aims instead merely to counteract a slight hesitation or fear I and others have felt that was best expressed perhaps by a leading Marxist critic nearly fifty years ago, Herbert Marcuse. The latter wrote that whenever it is not examined closely, "the reality of pluralism becomes ideological, deceptive."[1] The study of what I call here a two-fold "literary pluralism," heuristically divided up here into its aesthetic and critical domains, therefore demands, first and foremost, the type of historicization and re-thinking found in the pages that follow.[2] It demands this because, failing such an historical reassessment, pluralism threatens to become an entrenched, hypostasized kind of dogma within the entire literary field; to establish, in other words, a potentially insidious form of authoritarianism among readers and writers alike.

Professor Mary Ann Caws, the distinguished critic who has graced this new edition with a kind preface (for which I thank her warmly here), would also seem to concur with this point of view. Endowed with encyclopedic knowledge of both these and so many other areas of literary scholarship, Caws recently provided me with the following reference, "to bear out" further, in her words, the following investigation of pluralism of mine. The reference she shared with me comes from a telling remark she isolated while reading a recent piece on Marcel Duchamp in a new study of Game theory:

> "To spell it out again, I am arguing that rather than throwing further interpretations on the pile, we might now reflect on the existence of the pile itself; we might take the top-heaviness of the Duchamp business as a cue to interpret interpretation in our discipline."[3]

So, rather than dismiss or downplay my re-examination of this ubiquitous contemporary concept on the flimsy basis that such an investigation is somehow antagonistic to some particular person's idea of "proper" or "true" pluralistic inquiry (as a few earlier reviewers tried to do), closer readers of this second edition would do well to keep in mind something else Marcuse wrote awhile ago; to wit, that a "new totalitarianism manifests itself precisely in a harmonizing pluralism, where the most contradictory works and truths peacefully coexist in indifference."[4]

In addition, given my book's claims about the powerful influence played by the notions of *originality* and *progress* in generating literary pluralism over the last few centuries, new readers might wonder how modernism and, especially, postmodernism fit into the theoretical model advanced here. Is it not true, for instance, that much modernist art and literature strives not for thematic or formal novelty (one of the major claims of <u>DU</u>), thereby exhibiting what I call "forward-looking" originality, but relies instead on earlier themes or forms, as suggested by a recent show at the Guggenheim Museum in New York City?[5] Don't such "exceptions" invalidate some of the points made ahead regarding the continuing quest for novelty and originality? Indeed, the main argument of that museum show's organizers was that in the wake of oftentimes chaotic experimentation of earlier Modernists, like the Italian Futurists, Dadaists and Surrealists--many of whom are also examined in <u>DU</u>--, "a powerful desire for regenerative order and classical beauty emerged in Europe."[6]

    In response, let me first insist that I do not dispute this last assertion. One need only consider the rise of fascism, with its concomitant valorization of the kind of cold symmetry, impersonal grandeur and eerily inhuman harmony noticeable in so much of that particular time's painting (by Donghi, Picasso), public architecture (Le Corbusier), even cinema (Riefensthal) to realize that the 20th-century avant-garde sometimes appeared most "original" when it in fact looked "backwards." But, for terminological reasons explained later in my book, it is important to realize that one can also effectively translate such a return to classical aesthetics in terms of a "backwards-looking" originality. The notion of originality is, after all, fundamentally <u>ambivalent</u>, since it is derived from the word "origin." In this sense, many quests for originality are more properly seen as "backward-looking" gestures, since on some level they often seek to recover some forgotten or occulted *origin*. Similarly, the notion of "revolution" always already implies a return to an origin of its own, i.e., a revolving-around-to where it too began. Rather than belabor this point anymore here, however, I suggest that readers consult the new concept-index added to this edition, where they will find more specific examples and references to understand this argument even better.

    As for the infamously elusive notion of postmodernism and its relation to the analysis found here, I am convinced that much about this same reasoning applies. That is because what distinguishes postmodernism from modernism perhaps most of all is the so-called disappearance of trust in or reliance on concepts like progress and originality. Caught up in a web of intertextuality, with no definitive beginning or end, postmodern works of art in general, and literary texts in particular, are said to admit to no privileging of any particular order, structure and meaning. Often in flux, and ludic by nature, many such works eschew any and all classifications as purposeful or teleological. At best, many of them appear <u>auto-telic</u>. Yet, even as recently as 2010, in an extensive review article on postmodern life and its literature written by one of our most distinguished literary critics, Michiko Kakutani, of the <u>New York Times</u>, it is clear that for many people a firm belief in certain purposes or values, like the disinterested search for new ideas and configurations for their own sake, or the exploration of our innermost selves or psyches, persists. The operative word here, of course, is the adjective "new" and all the diversity and novelty it implies. In the words of Kakutani, it is never enough just to juggle things around that have been around since time immemorial, not even for the best artists or wordsmiths:

> The very value of artistic imagination and originality, along with the primacy of the individual, is increasingly being questioned in our copy-mad, post-modern digital world
> [...] All too often, however, the recycling and cut-and-paste esthetic has resulted in tired imitations; cheap, lazy re-dos; or works of "appropriation" designed to generate controversy ..."[7]

Re-combining bits and pieces of our cultural heritage, with no regard for a sense of an appropriate, maybe even exemplary, arrangement of them ultimately leads us nowhere, therefore; except perhaps to despair, to nihilism. And I for one, along with many of you readers of this second edition, no doubt, am loath to continue down that path.

Since the first printing of this book led to a certain amount of controversy, then, I can only hope that this second edition will stir up still more debate. For, in the absence of a no-holds barred discussion about the true purposes of and rationale for ever-different readings, my continued concern, like one expressed back in 1980 by Gerald Graff, is that academic literary criticism remains

> rootless and inconsequential, though not without influence. It remains governed by a series of fads, each of which generates newly mythical readings. The succession of these readings lends credibility to the doctrine that all readings are myths. While this situation persists, criticism has less and less claim to be a mode of serious inquiry. Though outwardly it seems to prosper, criticism expires from within.[8]

And more than anything else, the expiration of serious literary studies is precisely what <u>Difference Unbound</u> aims to help us prevent.

***

A few final notes of thanks go to my former research assistant and current doctoral student, Ms. Amanda Lee, for her excellent work on the detailed concept-index published for the first time here in this edition. Amanda also provided much appreciated help with several other aspects of the manuscript's preparation. Thanks to her new index, which richly complements and extends the reappearing name index, readers should have much less difficulty finding information of interest and use to them. Second, I must acknowledge the Saint Louis Art Museum which, once again, has given me permission to reproduce one of its wonderful paintings for a book cover, Joan Mitchell's glorious "Ici." Through sheer serendipity, it happens that a new biography of Mitchell[9] has recently renewed interest in Mitchell's work; something I had no idea would happen when I first decided to use her painting for my front cover. Yet, as with so many other significant events and actions I have noted over the years, this coincidence makes me once again accept the role that Surrealist "objective chance" seems to play in all of our lives. For more often than not, it is what we do not yet know, or not yet realize we are doing, that frequently turns out to be what was <u>really</u> occurring all along. The same likely holds true for whatever other unsuspected intentions lie behind this second edition as well.

Stamos Metzidakis, New York City, Spring 2012

Notes

---

[1] Herbert Marcuse, <u>One-Dimensional Man</u>. Boston: Beacon Press, 1964, p. 51.

[2] For a longer apology of my atypical perspective on pluralism vis-à-vis modern literature, see Stamos Metzidakis, "Why the Study of Pluralism Demands Pluralistic Approaches," <u>Nineteenth-Century French Studies</u> 27 (Fall 1997), 324-26. This essay appeared in the form of a "Letter to the Editor" in response to an earlier review in that same journal of my <u>Difference Unbound</u>.

[3] From Gavin Parkinson, "The Duchamp Code" in <u>Diversion to Subversion Games, Play, and Twentieth-Century Art</u>, ed. David J. Getsy, (University Park, PA: Pennsylvania State Press, 2011), n. 83, p. 187.

[4] Marcuse, p. 61.

[5] The show, which ran from Oct. 1, 2010 to January 9, 2011, was called "Chaos and Classicism: Art in France, Italy and Germany, 1918-1936."

[6] Quoted from the short brochure for the Guggenheim show. n.p..

[7] Michiko Kakutani, "Texts without Contexts," <u>New York Times</u>, Sunday, March 21, 2010, p. 23A.

[8] Gerald Graff, "Who killed Criticism?" <u>The American Scholar</u>. Vol. 49, no. 3 (Summer 1980), p. 355.

[9] Patricia Albers, <u>Joan Mitchell: Lady Painter, A Life</u>. New York: Knopf, 2011.

INTRODUCTION

In a book that appeared in 1985, the political scientist Stanislaw Ehrlich states that the phenomenon of pluralism

> should be the object of research on the level of political structure, economic structure and in the field of cultural life.[1]

Because he limits himself in his book to an analysis of the first two levels only, Ehrlich implicitly extends an open invitation to future researchers who would concentrate instead on the third field mentioned in this quotation. The present essay represents an acceptance of the invitation thus extended. It examines the particular cultural field known as literature from a pluralistic perspective. To be more specific, this book examines the historical importance of the concepts of difference, originality, and progress in relation to the production and interpretation of literature, to the rise of what I shall call "literary pluralism." It is the *historical* perspective of this book then, rather than a primarily *epistemological* one, that distinguishes it most from other recent attempts to study the subject of pluralism and literature.[2]

By arguing that the contemporary critical emphasis on *difference* results from the nineteenth century's fusion of the concepts of originality and progress, I shall seek to redefine cultural pluralism in its various literary manifestations. Given the scope of such a project, few readers will be surprised to learn that the background material for this study has been gathered from the philosophic and literary traditions of many different countries. What all these traditions have in common is the profound influence they have had on the ways literature has been produced as well as described in most economically advanced Western countries. The countries most important for my purposes here happen to be France, England, Germany, and the United States. The reason for this lies not in any deliberate Eurocentric bias on my part, but rather in the realization that these countries, rightly or wrongly, have been the most highly

instrumental in the creation and understanding of Western Literature
as it is generally known today in the Anglo-American context.

The reader will also notice that the following pages contain many
different styles and discourses. At certain times, for example, one
finds passages whose tone recalls an older, more traditional form of
literary history. On other occasions, the book reads like a series of
close textual analyses. At still other moments, a more generalized
type of theoretical argument and statement is favored. One will even
discover a few pages which are best described as quasi-
autobiographical, confessional perhaps. In all of these instances, it
is hoped that the reader understands why such a discursive potpourri
or stylistic admixture should not be considered a fundamental flaw
in the analysis of the problem at hand. Instead, this "weakness"
serves as a kind of icon of our problem. Consequently, insofar as we
shall be examining the phenomenon of pluralism as it relates to
literature, one should expect a *plurality* of tones and approaches, foci
and emphases. As will be suggested in chapter four, the mimetic
impulse of all critics (not to mention all people) to copy their
subject-matter may very well be unavoidable anyway.

The majority of specifically "literary" examples used in this
analysis—by which adjective is meant certain linguistic phenomena
whose ontological differentiation from theoretical statements is, for
the moment, assumed—are taken from the works of several paradigmatic French writers (especially poets) of the eighteenth, nineteenth,
and twentieth centuries. To this extent, some may think that it would
have been better to give the present book a more restrictive subtitle
like "The Rise of Pluralism in *French* Literature and Criticism"
rather than the more inclusive title, "The Rise of Pluralism in
Literature and Criticism." Since the former subtitle underscores the
national specificity of a large number of my examples, in a certain
sense, it may indeed be more accurate. One would, therefore, be
well advised to keep it in the back of one's mind throughout a
reading of this book.

In spite of the admittedly Gallic slant of this study, i.e. despite
the specific ties that I, like most other students of literature, have to
a specialized subject-matter, I have nevertheless chosen to retain the

more ambitious title. To say that the various language and literature sections of established Western universities today are places where diverse critical influences meet and interact daily is, after all, hardly an exaggeration. Indeed, the very sections in question distinguish themselves from each other not so much by selecting a specific kind of methodology or theoretical perspective over others as by focusing their critical energies and attention on texts written in one language, and one language only.

Though this study is in some sense limited then by the (a?) literary canon which forms my personal academic specialty, it is my firm belief that it has much wider theoretical implications of use to specialists in other domains as well. For the phrase "literary pluralism" as it is conceived here is a term which covers both the production *and* interpretation of literature in Western countries since the eighteenth century, irrespective of the particular language isolated. Within the term "literary pluralism" I thus include both *aesthetic* and *critical* manifestations of pluralism or pluralistic thought. My book does not limit itself then *merely* to "critical pluralism," even if fundamentally critical issues are raised throughout. The goal of chapter one is precisely to delimit these two facets of our problem and to set the stage for my later development of them.

The main thrust of this essay is to explain and justify the need for a more limited view of pluralism, of the ways in which it actually benefits or hinders people working in the literary field. The reason we require such an apology now is that not very many people in the profession believe in the idea of aesthetic or hermeneutic limitations. That is, while *in practice* many writers and critics of literature accept limits (notwithstanding some of their dearest beliefs about themselves and their work), few appear comfortable in admitting that this is the case. No doubt because of our society's collective sense of ideological, or even "political" correctness vis-à-vis all forms of cultural pluralism and diversity, most artists and intellectuals nowadays seem inclined instead to act as if their true preferences were to live and to let live, to accept different kinds of literary texts and different readings of texts, provided that sufficient justification or "evidence" be presented to support their existence. In this respect, my apology for a limited or more restricted view of literary pluralism will inevitably reveal the degree to which modern writers and critics have unwittingly supported, and contributed to, the widespread acceptance of pluralism, through their desire for palatable *self*-perceptions.

As it turns out though, their own practice has not always meshed with this desire to be "pluralistic." To pick a particularly telling example, in an earlier essay,[3] I tried to show how the influential critic, Roland Barthes, remained much more of a structuralist throughout his career than he himself was willing to admit. To grasp how important this question of *self-image* was to Barthes—and, by extension, to many other modern critics—it suffices to trace the obsessive usage of the term "image" throughout the various phases of his evolving work. From the so-called structuralist beginning of his career to the post-structuralist, autobiographical end, images are what continually come to the fore in Barthes' essays. Images of countless varieties, from poetic to photographic, always seem to attract his critical eye.

Yet, if we are to understand fully the significance of Barthes' obsession with the word/concept "image," we must first of all remember that the term itself derives from the Latin verb *imitare*, "to imitate." This fact, insignificant by itself, takes on special meaning if we remember that when he first defined "structuralist activity" in the early 1960s, this form of cognitive activity meant nothing less to Barthes than the symbolic elaboration of perceived *imitations* or recurrences in target texts. As my essay indicates, Barthes continued nonetheless to favor this term well after 1963. Although it is true that he applied it more and more to *himself* in his later works, and less and less to other "texts," one can argue (as I did) that this transformation signals not so much a change in the logic and/or procedures subtending his critical *activity* as it does a change in his critical *focus* or perspective. This change can most succinctly be described as a shift in Barthes' interpretive focus from the "text itself" to the reader-of-the-text. In chapter two, we shall examine more closely how this personal shift in focus came to be standard operating procedure in many other critical writings of the time as well, not just Barthes', and why, from the point of view of literary pluralism, this shift turns out to be both a necessary and epistemologically valid change of perspective.

However, the crucial point regarding Barthes' (and our) hermeneutic *practice* that my article tried to emphasize is this: changing the set of textual "data" to be analyzed, from the text itself to the reader, as Barthes and so many others have done, does not necessarily mean changing the analytical means of "explicating" these data. The particular choice of "texts" or textual features may change, but it is not clear whether, cognitively, critics ever significantly modify their individual practices of analyzing them. In this sense, we can say that for Barthes, and probably for most other readers as well, the perception of imitation remained the procedural key to his critical practice; and this, even though the objects he sought to understand through such perception varied constantly. So, while he and many other contemporary critics appeared to be more and more "pluralistic" in their modern quest for textual *difference*, it is a fact worth noting from the very beginning of this study that his writings consistently relied on the hermeneutic stability and pragmatic *identity* afforded by the models and copies created whenever a reader perceives an imitation, a repetition. Without perceiving these "images," he, like others, might have had, literally, *nothing to say*.

My central thesis, therefore, constitutes a three-fold polemic against contemporary literary pluralism. One part argues that most critics, despite any dramatic pronouncements they may make, usually choose one textual interpretation, or one type of interpretation, over others. They thereby limit their own, sometimes professed, theoretical receptiveness to pluralism. A second part insists that all writers have always written within various kinds of boundaries, despite the incontestable fact that they often make a point of trying radically to break "out" of such boundaries. The last part of my polemic advances the idea that because of certain trans-historical factors discussed in chapter four, writers and critics will most likely never cease behaving in the manner to which we have grown accustomed. By means of the present argument, my hope is merely that some of them might at least be persuaded to modify ever so slightly their *perception* of their respective activities. For, modifying these perceptions is surely one way to help future poets, critics, and students view literature in a truly different light, not *just* in the light of difference.

Before concluding these introductory remarks, let me emphasize how much we must all begin to recognize our practice for what it is, and to stop living under various illusions perpetrated by certain powerful poetic and critical precursors. The major illusion to which I refer is the all-encompassing one of "literary pluralism" that my first chapter aims to define. It is time for us to stop acting as if we were perfectly open to the literary styles, techniques, or methods of others when, in fact, we are far more limited *in our practice* than we realize. No longer should we give mere lip-service to the notion of pluralism when, in reality, no such complete acceptance of the phenomenon has ever really existed. In a word, it is time to change our views concerning the causes and effects of literary pluralism so that we might better understand exactly what is being done when we "do" literary criticism and/or theory, or when we "make" verbal art.

* * *

In order to facilitate the extrapolation from my examples to those of other literary traditions, English translations of materials published originally in other languages are provided. Unless otherwise indicated, translations from the French are my own. Whenever the original text contains certain stylistic features whose translation is open to considerable debate—as will often be the case for versified poems—the original appears before the translation. If, however, in a given context, the non-English text's form matters much less than the thought(s) it conveys, only a translation is used.

For their generous support at the start of this long project, I would like to thank the trustees of the Camargo Foundation in Cassis, France, and especially the foundation's director, Mr. Michael

Pretina. Thanks to these individuals, as well as to the Graduate School of Arts and Sciences of Washington University in Saint Louis, I was able to spend a semester on leave as a Fellow of the Foundation several years ago. I should also like to acknowledge my warm appreciation to Professor Norris J. Lacy, the present chair of Romance Languages and Literatures at Washington University, for his sustained help with the project, as well as to my former chair, Professor James F. Jones, Jr., for his early encouragement. My editorial assistant, Ms. Donna Nix, was extraordinarily helpful, as always, in putting together the final manuscript. I would also like to acknowledge the editors of the journals *Rivista di letterature moderne e comparate* and *Dada/Surrealism* for their kind permission to reprint in chapters 3 and 4 certain parts of articles previously published in their journals.

In addition, I wish to thank Professors Roger Little of Trinity College in Dublin, and Gerald Rabkin of Rutgers University, with whom I spent innumerable hours in Cassis discussing our respective projects. Without their important input into my developing ideas (an input which, thankfully, often went against the grain of my own ideas), I would probably still be trying to tie them all together. I also want to acknowledge the help of my wife Sara who, as always, has been my best and most patient critic throughout. I thank her and my two children, Katina and Willie, for many things that, since they could only be understated here, are better left unsaid.

Finaliy, I wish to dedicate this study to the memory of my late father, Steve Metzidakis. His sense of duty, in all its forms, kept me focused when many distractions, including his prolonged illness, threatened to dampen my enthusiasm for the project. In many subtle ways, this book reflects my understanding of, and respect for, the positive pluralistic model he and the rest of my Greek-American family have provided me over the years.

NOTES

[1] Stansilaw Ehrlich, *Pluralism On and Off Course* (Oxford: Pergamon, 1985), p. 233.

[2] Three other recent books on the subject of pluralism and literature, written by Wayne Booth, Ellen Rooney, and K. M. Newton, tacitly respond to Ehrlich's invitation as well, though in ways dissimilar from mine. I shall have numerous occasions to cite these works later on, and to show more completely how the present book differs from them.

[3] See my article, "Barthes' Image," *Neophilologus*, 71 (1987), 489-495.

Chapter I
THE "PROBLEM" OF LITERARY PLURALISM

Following a heated debate over a lecture I delivered a few years ago, a colleague asked me a question that he surely thought—as, I confess, I myself and others in the hall at the time also thought—was perfectly simple and appropriate to the issue at hand. His question was this: "What is *wrong* with one more new reading of *Hamlet*?" To appreciate fully the sense and effect of his inquiry, it is necessary to realize that earlier in the discussion I had advanced the apparently bizarre idea that perhaps nothing of real value was to be gained by producing an indefinite number of new readings or interpretations of the same work of art. In this respect, the simplicity of his question derived from a direct assessment of what he had taken to be the main thrust of my initial argument.

After some reflection, I finally saw that the problem was not so much the reaction of my friend or my audience as it was the form of his question. Rephrasing his question, I thus responded in the following way: While having 2001 interpretations of *Hamlet* was certainly not, to my mind, "bad" in any transcendental or metaphysical way,[1] the more important question was rather why it seemed so *correct* to almost everyone there, and, one might add, elsewhere, that this be the (desired) case in literary criticism and theory. What I wanted to convey was my uneasiness with the knowledge that modern literary studies as a whole appeared permeated by just such a pluralistic attitude. For it seemed to me then only normal, indeed indispensable (as it still does), to ask why no one else wondered whether this unquestioned faith in pluralism constituted a positive sign of modern critical activity or not. It was as if pluralism was, by definition, not only desirable, but possibly even *necessary*; that to doubt this fact was tantamount to my being either a fascist, or, at the very least, a reactionary anachronism in aesthetic circles.

Since I never considered myself to exemplify either of these unsavory options, I, of course, felt that a legitimate defense was in order. My defense has taken the form of this book. In the process of defending my own critical positions, I have become ever so slightly sympathetic, as more "progressive" thinkers might fear, to the repeated attempts by E.D. Hirsch and a host of others in the United States and Europe to valorize the notion of interpretative validity, of critical acceptability. Lest there be any misunderstanding, however, I must confess right away that my moderate sympathy with Hirsch's arguments has in no way translated into acquiescence. I still harbor very serious doubts about the actual success he and his defenders have had in proving the many intriguing points they try to make concerning an author's intention, the notion of a "correct" interpretation, and the supposed existence of a shared body of knowledge whose proper assimilation leads to "cultural literacy." It is not so much the idea of shared knowledge that bothers me, but rather the formulation of any and all *specific* canons or dictionaries that would presume to serve everyone, and for all time.

Yet, in spite of these important reservations, I feel that the time has come for us in the literary profession to examine some of the reasons why so much controversy has surrounded not just Hirsch's seminal work on the subject,[2] but more importantly, his *type* of research. My intention is not to serve as apologist for Hirsch or any one thinker in particular; nor to return us to "the good old days" of even earlier criticism, when critics were white males of European descent, and their truth was The Truth. Rather, I would like to analyze our ever-increasing collective resistance to the very *possibility* of critical determinacy in general. The issue is not whether critics and theorists possess a set number of criteria for interpretative validity, but instead whether, as a recent critic has stated, "such coherent criteria are even possible in theory."[3]

This book attempts to provide some answers to questions that derive logically from an extended consideration of the situation just described. The questions are: 1) Why do the vast majority of modern[4] readers and writers think that artistic works in general, and literary works in particular must, at all costs, be different somehow from those produced before?, 2) By what means do texts and interpretations distinguish themselves from others?, and finally, 3) How has it happened that pluralism has become so acceptable in Western intellectual circles? Why, in other words, does anyone pondering its suitability as a guiding principle in criticism, and more generally, in things literary, provoke disbelief, impatience, even resentment on the part of individuals who are sometimes barely even aware of the tacit support they give thereby to the ideological hegemony of pluralism?

The expression "ideological hegemony" needs to be emphasized here because of how widespread the ostensibly blind acceptance of pluralism—or what might more accurately be described as the need or demand for *difference* in all cultural spheres—has become. Indeed, in the United States, at least, it has become so entrenched and reified that it has turned into a kind of absolute article of intellectual and quasi-political faith of our time. As an article of faith, the acceptance of pluralism has taken the form of an all-too-natural belief, a belief that most people think is not just shared by large "interpretative communities" (to use Stanley Fish's term), but more disturbingly perhaps, *must* be shared by all. Questioning the legitimacy of this belief, as I intend to do in the pages that follow, is thus equivalent, or so it would seem, to flying in the face of one of modern society's most solid, if relatively new, conceptual foundations. Questioning pluralism amounts to undermining the authority of this concept/phenomenon to determine the very way people regard any cultural productions whatsoever, and in particular, literary ones.

To hazard a preliminary response to the question of *why* people react so strongly against an interrogation of pluralism, let me advance an idea that it will be my task to prove a little later on. Critical attempts to denigrate pluralism nowadays go against Western society's epistemological grain mainly because they contradict or otherwise undermine two contemporary myths under whose spell we have lived unawares for almost two hundred years. The two myths in question are those of *originality* and *progress*. Any questioning of pluralism provokes negative reactions because it is seen as an attack on the following commonly-held idea: Whenever someone creates something original, e.g. a new poem or a different reading, one adds something new to the general pool of valuable literary art that, as such, is "significant." What makes this creation so significant is that it represents, as it were, something one step beyond that which has already existed.

The really important aspect of the process, however, is that somewhere along the way the creator[5] of this originality, of this *difference*, as well as the (literary) society around the creator, are assumed to have made some type of human or humanistic "progress." Progress results from precisely that move "forward" and away from, that which has already been accomplished, said, or done elsewhere. To deny anyone the right to be, find, or make something new (which, after all, constitutes the gesture of the writer or critic who poses fundamental questions about the desirability of the simultaneous co-existence of *dissimilar* literary texts or readings, respectively) is therefore seen by die-hard supporters of pluralism as a potentially dangerous attempt to deny everyone the same possibility. Such a gesture is regarded as a threat to, or undermining of, the possibility of difference, a possibility which most people today, of course, scarcely even question. In other words, the gesture involved in questioning one's legitimate right-to-difference constitutes a temporary freezing of the universal praise and acceptance that are otherwise generously bestowed upon the author who purports to have presented, discovered, or produced something new in the midst of the already-there, i.e. previous literature and criticism.

From this point of view, it is ironic that all would-be enemies of those who question pluralism are in a very real sense more "reactionary" than any debunkers of pluralism could ever hope to be. It is important to emphasize the reactionary nature of these potential negative responses which the present critical inquiry (and any others that follow) may generate. The apparent unwillingness of most critics and theorists to ask many serious questions about pluralism can only be understood as a determined effort on all their parts to hold on to one of our culture's central mythologies. This mythology, an essentially uncontested faith in the intrinsic worth and value of pluralism, is promulgated throughout the West. It would have those of us who work in the literary domain believe that we are open to suggestion and to innovation, when, in fact, we are far less magnanimous with respect to "difference" than such a auto-fiction implies.

The important question, therefore, is not whether modern literary institutions like universities, publishing houses, academic journals, as well as literary "schools" from the early German Romantic *Athenaeum* group of Jena (1798-1800) to twentieth-century "avant-garde" movements have had the unalienable *right* to exercise authority. Once again, it is not a matter here of speculation on metaphysical rights or wrongs. Rather it is a question of ascertaining whether these same institutions, in the words of K. M. Newton, have not actually sought "to disguise through [an] attempt at mystification the fact that [they] control interpretation by force."[6] Since my very contention is that pluralism exists more in words than in reality, what we have to determine is whether or not pluralism exists as something other than a kind of password to literary acceptability.[7] We need to figure out whether it constitutes anything more than an ideologically-laden mystification of what is *really* happening.

On the other hand, it is crucial to understand how contemporary versions of the myths of originality and progress have also contributed significantly to the said mystification. As one shall see in the second half of this book, these two hitherto separate concepts began to merge at the end of the eighteenth century, and formed an important conceptual hybrid of the two. In turn, this hybrid or unquestioned overlapping of two theoretically distinct notions formed the seed of the modern predilection for pluralism. For the moment, however, I should perhaps leave these last ideas in the form of hypotheses, since much needs to be examined before they can be proved.

In any event, it is difficult to dispute the fact that originality and progress merit even more critical attention than they appear to have received, especially as they relate to literature and literary studies. That these myths continue to seduce poets and critics alike into believing a disturbing, perhaps even dangerous, fallacy about themselves and about their work has, to my mind, not been sufficiently examined. This fallacy deludes them into thinking that what they can, and moreover, *should* do within their respective areas of expertise is to seek out, almost indiscriminately, some kind of difference that would justify their practice. Put succinctly, difference is, from the point of view of these individuals, that which helps them and their colleagues *progress*. The critical search for difference or originality has become thereby the primary vocational responsibility of many creative academic types (but only after it enjoyed equal success amongst poets, from the Romantic period to the present). The assumption subtending most activities undertaken by modern critics, from feminists to deconstructionists, is that thanks to the unquestioned, and uniformly positive, nature of novelty itself, any differences they may discover will somehow permit them to say things that are in one way or another significant to someone. An important aim of this book is to prove that it is precisely the modern *will-* or *need-to-create-difference* which explains better than anything else why the same canonical texts have generated so many diverse readings over the years.

In returning to the point of departure for these preliminary reflections, the reader can now see why the more apt question my colleague should have asked a few years ago is, "What is so wrong with finding the *definitive* reading of *Hamlet?*" Let me once again be clear on this important point before going any further. In seeking an answer to this question, my purpose will *not* be to arrive at the "proper" interpretation of various literary texts. I *categorically deny the existence and/or eventuality of any universally acceptable reading or universal literary "classic."* Such a denial, however, does not in the least contradict what has been suggested until now about the pragmatic need to limit pluralism; and this, for two reasons. First, to say that no single correct interpretation or perfect work of art exists once and for all time is not to say that an individual interpretation or literary innovation does not *practically* function that way as long as it dazzles, convinces, or impresses more people in powerful, literary institutional positions than its rivals do. The great reading or great play has always existed, and surely will always exist, whether or not idealized, platonic literary forms exist somewhere else.

Second, we have to realize that the way most students and creators of literature have come to regard the object of their different energies has changed dramatically over the last twenty years or so.

This collective shift in focus from the notion of the "text itself" to the "reader of the text" implies a fundamental shift in the locus of aesthetic and critical worth or value. Thus, in admitting, provisionally, the existence of a "greatest" English play, or the *definitive* reading of *Hamlet*, one is only accepting the reality of literary history, of the apparent pragmatic need for aesthetic comparisons. This admission in no way suggests that such judgments are blindly accepted or etched in stone, nor that their "universality" might not suddenly vanish.

My final preliminary task is to give a more complete description of what I mean by the term "literary pluralism." As was mentioned already in the preface, literary pluralism is a concept that underscores the ever-increasing diversity of both aesthetic and critical texts. These texts, considered together, form a field called "literature." The question of the boundaries between this field and that of "non-literature" is irrelevant in the present context since the question itself re-emphasizes the modern critical propensity to accept more and more written matter as "literary," thereby pluralizing the entire field. One must insist on the phrase "more and more," rather than "less and less" because for all the recent talk of literature's "death," of theory's demise, terms like "poem," "text," "poet," "novelist," "critic," "theorist," and a host of others continue to serve as common critical currency, even if the definitional boundaries between many of them appear ever more hazy.

In this sense, the field of acceptable literature and literary study has been expanding for so long that we cannot help but compare it to the more general cultural phenomenon of pluralism encountered in political, sociological, and demographic contexts. Hence the need to coin the term "literary pluralism." To summarize then, this study will be devoted to a close examination of the specific diachronic and synchronic origins of the two-sided brand of pluralism found in the field of literature. In other words, it will seek to describe the historically-specific, as well as trans-historical, reasons for the present state of literary production and theory.[8]

* * *

Most literary critics and theorists are either uninterested in, or else incapable of, stating exactly why they believe that certain readings of texts should be universally preferred over others. To be sure, sometimes they take other critics or critical schools to task, and try to show how their adversaries are mistaken, or otherwise misguided in one way or another. But, rarely, if ever, do they set out to show systematically why certain choices, exclusions, and summations they themselves make at different points of their respective analyses are universally justifiable hermeneutic acts. Roland Barthes recognized this from the start of that most systematic reading of readings that we know as *S/Z*. From the very start, he admits that his textual segmentation of Balzac's short story *Sarrazine* (a segmentation that is the sine qua non of *any* interpretation) "could not be more arbitrary."[9] In other words, before moving on to his actual analysis, not even so masterly a reader as Barthes is able to justify his fundamental, hence, consequence-laden choices over others.

To cite another example, we would do well to consider Geoffrey Hartman's attack on a brand of textual criticism, structural stylistics, perfected by the critic Michael Riffaterre. Instead of telling us *why* we should prefer his type of analysis (hermeneutics) over Riffaterre's, or why the stylistic aspects the latter critic observes in a work are not valid, Hartman spends his time commenting more on those textual features Riffaterre has overlooked than on those he actually saw.[10] Like his Yale colleague, Paul de Man, Hartman seems to put more stock in what other critics *could* have extracted from a piece of literature than on what they really *did* extract.[11] The simple problem here is that both of Riffaterre's opponents appear able only to propose solutions to textual enigmas other than those proposed by Riffaterre. Even so, they do not seem particularly anxious to explain just *why* one set is necessarily preferable to the other. Hartman, in fact, admits as much in the same article when he states that all methods, not just his, "are unable to determine, qua method, what find is to be emphasized."[12]

In principle, however, the reticence to confront this problem should disturb anyone involved in the business of explicating texts for a living. Whether critics describe the status of their practice in these terms or not changes nothing, of course, in regard to the exclusionary gesture implicit in the selection of their *own* interpretations over someone else's. Yet, with only a few notable exceptions, a lack of common or collective interpretative standards has forced us all, paradoxically, to accept—as a more or less homogeneous institutional group—a plurality of analytic methods and results. One of the primary goals of most modern critical practice, in fact, has been to underscore the polysemic nature of texts (cf. Barthes' infamous *pluriel* of which a text is made[13]); to accommodate, in theory, at least, other readings, and to avoid thereby appearing too reductive. The point I am trying to make is that one might very well have expected a more defensive and defensible reaction on the part of critics. One might have anticipated a more visible, firm rejection of interpretations that, by their very existence, call into question the unjustified grounding of their earlier ones.

Instead, what we have been witnessing for some time now is a kind of laissez-faire attitude within the ranks of professional critics, an attitude that, in essence, says this: the fundamental assumptions, procedures, and conclusions of different approaches to literature vary so much that we can never hope to agree with anything other than, perhaps, our legitimate right to disagree. This, however, has not meant that all readings are acceptable to all critics. Certain criteria, which have been diversely described over the years by innumerable scholars, have been posited or advanced as being necessary qualities intrinsic to all literature. With varying degrees of success, scholars armed with such criteria have all tried to reduce texts in one way or another to some kind of quintessence, and, in the process, to disqualify some readings as faulty or deficient.

But so many different sets of criteria, "simple forms" (a term introduced by the neo-formalist theorist André Jolles several years ago) or other schemata have been proposed in the last forty years that, in the final analysis, they all begin to appear hopelessly arbitrary to most other theorists and critics. In spite of themselves, most people in the profession have started to believe that one group of readers can think and say one thing about a text, while another group can, and *should*, say something else, regardless of any fortuitous overlapping. That different critical schools and approaches have come to be called merely so many "stories of reading"[14] undermines, however, the authority of anyone's claim to a particular validity for his or her commentary. If everyone's reading can be "called into question" (which, as we saw earlier, often merely means that someone else can *add* something to what has already been noted), then no one can claim to have said the so-called final word on anything. The very idea of the "final word" is dismissed as a utopian dream at best, a dangerous lie at worst.

Yet, without some notion of an *end* in the production of an aesthetic or critical text, all hope for critical or methodological legitimacy would itself have to be abandoned. No one to my knowledge has gone this far in opposing the very idea of those acts of legitimation that literary institutions, in and of themselves, perform with and on texts. No one, in other words, is willing to state in unambiguous terms that *whatever* anyone else wants to say about literary works is valid, in spite of the obvious fact that innumerable readings of these same works have been proposed.[15] To this extent, we must assume that an arbiter, or perhaps a set of unwritten standards, exists somewhere, in some form or other. Without this standard, it is difficult to see how so many intelligent people could have accepted the existence of so many things that they did not perceive themselves. To persist in acting as if there were no "problem" with literary pluralism is, therefore, tantamount to maintaining the illusion of a presumed universal value of originality. To accept blindly the idea that it is somehow "good" or, at least, appropriate, that different people demonstrate their originality by producing different kinds of literary works or analyses is to ignore the egregious reality that most people nonetheless *choose certain ones over others*.

It does not suffice to say that for different readings to be acceptable they must, at least, be logically compatible ones, as I.A. Richards has suggested.[16] In this kind of cumulative or additive argument, one would have us believe that the reason it is appropriate to have yet another reading of *Hamlet* is that such a reading does not refute or deny what an earlier one proposed or discovered. It merely adds to, or supplements (Derrida's term) what was already there. But, how often does a critic or writer really let on as if s/he is *merely* adding a small piece to what, in some instances, is already a huge pie? Is it not instead the case that, in the modern world, an ideological emphasis has been placed more and more on the purported originality, path-breaking, or ground-breaking quality of a piece of art or criticism? The simple fact is that to the detriment of a textual tradition or history, we have witnessed an increased privileging of all that is perceived as new and different, however small this difference may be.

Given this reality, it is time to reconsider the value to scholars, teachers, and students alike of what one might call "critical reductionism." Critical reductionism can be defined as the tendency to reduce a text's formal and semantic particularity to a more manageable (to a *specific* critic, anyway) unity. It represents not so much a desirable cognitive process as an inevitable one. Here I am less interested in attacking the notion of critical pluralism per se than in showing how it is the logical result of our collective ignorance. The ignorance in question concerns the conclusions we need to draw from the various purposes for which we readers use a literary text's words-on-the-page.

Let us consider the remarkable case of the recent interpretation(s) of Charles Baudelaire's famous sonnet, "Les Chats"/ "The Cats." Ever since the now classic debate over this poem, which was initiated over twenty years ago when Michael Riffaterre published his formidable objections to the earlier reading of the poem by Roman Jakobson and Claude Lévi-Strauss, the text has generated enough opposing analyses to form several so-called "methodological" anthologies.[17] From our perspective, the most striking aspect about these anthologies is the common editorial reluctance one notes to do anything other than catalogue the different approaches under various epistemological rubrics. In reading the introductory remarks in one of the more important collections, one gets the distinct impression that the editors are content to classify types of literary analyses without ever daring to deduce from them some commonly-shared practice, or to select the "best" one from among them:

> [Our mission] is to present the work of others. In order to introduce the different contributions, we will group them together by family, never forgetting however the chronological order of their publication ... It is important to situate the essential contribution of each in the "school" [*courant*] in which it can stand to be classified or, for certain ones, in the general economy of its own textual theory.[18]

Since the word "critic" itself evokes, etymologically, the idea of judging or choosing, it is immediately clear that such editorial activity can hardly be considered critically important at all. One ends up with the uneasy feeling that anything and everything goes in the formal study of this, and, by extension, any other poem under scrutiny, on the condition that certain initial criteria be met in the eyes of "true" critics. However, these criteria are never fully articulated, since they are apparently thought of as self-evident by these same critics.

Yet, significantly, whenever validation criteria are presented as such, that is, whenever a critic sets out to put together his or her reading with the help of certain textual elements, the elements in question do, in fact, share a similar quality. This quality has been noticed since the time when Aristotle and Quintillian were writing about writing, but has not been sufficiently emphasized, it seems to me, in recent years.[19] I am talking about the *iterativeness* of all critically located textual traits. Provided one perceives the repetition of a given image, theme, word, or phrase, one begins to construct patterns that, by (unexamined) definition, are significant. Once these smaller patterns combine to form larger units critics begin to feel that they have put their individual fingers on something. This "something" becomes synonymous with the "text itself," with what Hirsch suggests is the text's "meaning." At very least, this "something" co-exists with many of a text's words-on-the-page. In this way, everyone stands ready to accept different readings of the same work so long as one can substantiate a particular analysis on the basis of iterative details. So, while each reading varies according to individual idiosyncracies of a reader, each is subtended by an uncritically accepted belief in the validation-capacity of repetition.

From this point of view, it should be easy, theoretically speaking, to resolve the whole debate over which method or reading is the "best." The entire issue could be reduced to a simple matter of choice, the choice of one set of repeated features over another. Criticism would thus be transformed into a self-conscious game of *one's choosing.*[20] In theory, no one would have the right any longer to assert that one set should be universally preferred to another, because all sets would be on the same epistemological footing. Any attempt to prove one set necessarily more "pertinent" to all readers than another—such as we often find in some early forms of structuralist analysis—would thus be doomed to failure. As Paul de Man correctly indicates, the very existence of alternative readings implies, on the contrary, that texts never force anyone to read them in one way, and only one way. To that extent, literary texts are, according to de Man, precisely those philosophical, historical, as well as "aesthetic" writings whose figurativeness occasions the most conflicting, heterogeneous reactions in the minds of readers.[21]

But, instead of following through with the latter argument concerning the rhetorical figurality of "literature," which leads de Man to conclude that texts self-destruct or, more precisely, self-*deconstruct*, it should be noted how the wide-range of modern reader responses also bespeaks a certain *desire* for difference, for interpretative originality, on the part of the readers themselves. If the early structuralist dream of reducing a text to a fixed series of primary "narrative structures," "functions" or "forms" failed to materialize, it seems to me that this was not because of the text's actual *inability* to yield up such structures, but rather because of the unwillingness of most modern critics to tolerate the eventuality of such ultimate, transcendental structures. After all, the very existence of countless "structural" readings proves that certain structures are *present*, in some sense anyway, within the fabric of texts.

However, dissatisfied with the idea that one critic's structure was no more methodologically or epistemologically definitive than that of another critic, it is apparent that literary scholars have gradually abandoned hope for this kind of formalistic solution to the problem of interpretation. Because no one solution satisfied everyone's practical needs and personal desires, the notion of critical consensus, so important to an earlier "practical critic" like I. A. Richards or a stylistician like Leo Spitzer, seems in and of itself to have lost out to individual choices and preferences. To be sure, formalists and structuralists posited intriguing, and oftentimes, effective, rules and sets of forms. But the question one must ask is this: Just *whose* rules were they when, as frequently happened, others disagreed with what was posited, claiming that this was not what "we" did? Terry Eagleton makes a similar point to the one being made here when he writes:

> Structuralism may examine and appeal to existing practice [i.e. certain rules]; but what is its answer to those who say, 'Do something else?'[22]

The only answer to this question until now has been simply to give up the search for common interpretative standards, to live and let live, as was said earlier. Unable to come to grips with the arbitrariness of formalist solutions, the University in particular has not insisted that its various representatives agree with each other with regards to things literary. As Eagleton says,

> All that is being demanded is that you manipulate a particular language in acceptable ways. Literary studies [...] are a question of the signifier, not of the signified.[23]

In other words, it apparently does not matter any longer exactly *what* one says about a text as long as "it" is *well* said, as long as it exhibits persuasiveness, and, yes, even *originality*. (Witness the proliferation of this last substantive in any kind of positive artistic review.) The wish to disagree, to discover meanings other than those already found, appears within the modern critical arena to have thereby outweighed the wish to concur.

Wishing for something (disagreement), however, does not necessarily make it correct. If one considers that the New Criticism was founded on the firm belief that critical agreement was both possible and desirable, the prevalent contemporary belief in the opposite, i.e. the necessity of disagreement, of differing points of view, could not be more ironic, indeed, perverse. From all appearances, the hermeneutic tradition, which originally derived from biblical exegesis, has been stood on its head by many recent reformers. Often called post-structuralists, these critics and theorists reject the notion of a "proper" or final interpretation of a text, opting instead for (merely) *an* interpretation, *a* reading that neither aspires to Truth, nor pretends to be a closed system of any sort.[24] With respect to one of the more influential of these recent reformers, Jacques Derrida, one is even tempted to say that the traditional need to trust what a text says has been replaced by a need *not* to trust it. Norman Holland expresses the situation thus:

> Derrida, I think, writes out of a need not to believe, a need to *dis*trust ... [But] Disbelief is itself a belief in disbelief ... Such disbelief I would expect to mask a disappointed need to believe.[25]

Of course, what should concern us most here is not the ethical or moral propriety of this gesture, but its practicality. To prefer one's own set of significant textual features over another just because one is "disappointed" or dissatisfied with the absolute truth and/or persuasiveness of the other (and, more importantly, to do so without ever bothering to explain exactly why everyone else should make the same choice) thus constitutes nothing more or less than a value judgment. In no way does it represent the logical assertion of a kind of universal hermeneutic primacy of one reading over another. Just the same, this choice or value judgment could not be made were there not an underlying belief on the critic's part in the possibility, indeed necessity, of saying something beyond what has already been said critically (or creatively, in the case of a poet) elsewhere. If certain readers did not think themselves obliged, or, at least, able to bring something new and perforce "illuminating" to the discussion of a work, there would be no good reason to have critics and theorists among us at all. About the most one could say about one reading's superiority over another's is what Derrida said in a 1980 interview:

> I would not say that some interpretations are truer than others.
> I would say that some are more powerful than others.[26]

Yet, in spite of this assertion, one continues to find an unspoken need in most modern literary circles to believe in critical and aesthetic progress. This need is illustrated within these circles by a common faith in pluralism. Since the tasteful imitation of the Ancients and other later models was considered until the eighteenth century to be, by and large, the only proper manner of proceeding both amongst commentators and poets, the question that arises is thus: How did such a contrary idea suddenly emerge? For what reasons did writers begin to search less for imitation than for originality whenever they tried to write poetry or criticism? The example of modern methodological confrontation occasioned by Baudelaire's sonnet, or by a notoriously polyvalent text like Kafka's *The Metamorphosis*, makes the answers to these questions all the more pressing, for, to a large extent, most critics have viewed the debate surrounding "Les Chats" as an essentially arbitrary one. That is, they do not necessarily think that this poem is, in fact, more evocative or provocative than others on which they could have chosen to wage their methodological wars. As the editors of the anthology mentioned above state,

> True Baudelairean scholars will have to pardon us [for producing this anthology]. Baudelaire was *not* the principal stake in this debate (my emphasis).[27]

But if Baudelaire wasn't/isn't the "principal stake in this debate," who or what is? How can the editors legitimately say this and, at the same time, provide no guidelines whatsoever for determining which of the proposed readings are "better" or "worse"? They say this, obviously, because they, too, are under the "spell" of pluralism, and honestly believe that merely by providing more and more readings they are doing someone, or perhaps some literary institution, a service. It is neither their responsibility, nor place, nor right, to do any more than *add* to an already vaste plurality (of readings).

Thus, the collective pluralistic will of all critics (of "Les Chats" or of any other privileged literary text) to say something original about it seems emblematic of our contemporary obsession with originality. This obsession takes the form of a drive to replace, at all costs, the old with the new. Rimbaud's famous statement, *Il faut être absolument moderne/* "One must be absolutely modern," is very telling in this regard. It makes explicit the will to originality found at the heart of all modern literature, as well as of modern theory and critical practice.

Because of this, one has the right to think that, in general, poets and critics in the West have increasingly aspired to be "absolutely modern" for the last two hundred years or so. Their so-called modernity, which we attribute to them *a posteriori*, is the direct result of their *and* our comprehension of originality as an intrinsically positive, *progressive* "quality" inherent in their work. Moreover, whether it is true or not, many people assume that "progress" occurs whenever one writes about something, or in some way, that does not appear to have been tried before. Thus, if one chooses to approach the "problem" of a ever-growing number of different kinds of works and of different interpretations of works from the perspective of this will to originality, one no longer needs to be forced (as I myself and others have been) into the all-too-limiting procedure of establishing an ultimately inexhaustible typology of different reading conventions, strategies, techniques, frames, and rules. One need not look only at very subtle linguistic details in order to understand where and how one reading stopped, and another started.

Nor is it necessary to catalogue different approaches, methodologies, and theories on the basis of similar descriptions and interpretations of the same verses or words in a poem, as so many editors have done. My working hypothesis from here on is precisely that differences among various literary theories and readings point much more to critics and poets than they do to the texts themselves. That is, the former choose to create something new or different in places where they insist on finding something old or in need of revision. To account for the ever-growing number of readings of the same texts involves, therefore, a necessary act of reduction. It requires that one locate and describe a common cause for the many literary approaches now in use. The different chapters of my essay will sketch out the contours of this cause, displacing the problematics of different readings from the text's formal characteristics back to the context formed by the needs and desires of modern poets and critics. Edward Said dubs this context their "intention to write."[28] As my second chapter will show, the words-on-the-page of a piece of literature will no longer be as important an issue as they were in earlier formalist and structuralist times, since their very existence depends on their being perceived as significant by particular readers. They have no effective life outside of our perception, not because they are not, in fact, *there*, but because they can only be there insofar as we ourselves decide to know them (to be there).

What we have decided to do for the last two hundred years or so, however, constitutes an intriguing story in its own right, one whose articulation, I hope, will go far in helping us to understand better the reasons why we do not always agree on specifics whenever we talk about, or try to write, something "literary." It is perhaps time, finally, to abandon once and for all a certain (early) structuralist dream of discovering final solutions to literature's specificity within the boundaries of the text itself. One needs to recognize that with every new interpretation of *Hamlet*, *Madame Bovary*, or *The Metamorphosis*, a different, individual reading *will* is at work, a will that literally transforms the text into a personalized experience that can never be fully duplicated or shared.

After a closer examination of the limitations of a purely formalist approach to literature in chapter two, I shall thereafter dispense with an exclusive isolation of the formal properties of a given piece of literature, and pinpoint instead the desires and needs that actualize those same properties. For the critic, the text will thereby begin to reveal its "true" character. This character involves playing the role of a pre-text with which an individual's psyche operates, and onto which the latter projects itself, leaving behind it a kind of mutation. Like all mutations, the "post-text," i.e. that which remains or stands out after a critical operation, will, by definition, then seem "new."

The question one still has to ask oneself, however, is this: Should such a mutant text be prized just because of its originality? Surely certain mutations are, in some fashion or other, "bad," or, if one prefers a less moral register, worthless. Surely all original readings are not equally effective or relevant just because they derive from what I might call the critic's "perceptual repetition compulsion," i.e. one's innate heuristic capacity to find patterns and other types of iterative phenomena.

Or are they? Are we really ready to accept any *believable* "story of reading?" What about the poet in regard to this thirst for originality? When Baudelaire insists on plunging into the unknown in order to find the "new," are not at least some of his discoveries doomed to be grotesque, like the poetic flowers he calls, provocatively, *Flowers of Evil?* Does everything grotesque merit our societal praise or even attention? Let me hasten to reply to my own rhetorical questions. I am not trying to suggest that this irresistible slippage from novelty to monstrosity must somehow be avoided, much less condemned. What I mean rather is that since there is such a fine line between good and bad "monsters," as in the case of the line between fools and geniuses, one has to pay close attention to the delicate act of producing an original poem or reading. If "original" implies, as it sometimes does, that an object's origin lies within itself, that it arises *ex nihilo*, then the will to create something out of nothing resembles closely a divine act. Indeed, the idea of the poet as a kind of God-like figure certainly represents an important topos throughout European literary history.

Yet, perhaps the best expression of this topos appears in Romantic literature, with Wordsworth's "the child is father of the man," or Goethe's Faust, or Hugo's poet/magi, or finally, Rimbaud's poet/alchemist/seer. Significantly, these characters appear at a time when the institution of modern criticism itself comes into being, mostly because of the literary productions of these very same poets. Historically speaking then, the critic seems to have followed the path taken by the poet. In his turn (I purposely use the masculine pronoun), he, too, had to assume a God-like role in fabricating original material out of which his "new" interpretation could rise. In order for this to happen, it was, and continues to be, necessary for him to: 1) desire this newness, difference, or originality, then 2) eliminate the old to make room for the new, and finally, 3) create the original by various means, all of which we shall have to examine in detail in the next three chapters. The longer this three-step process goes on, the less likely it is that critical agreement or interpretative consensus will ever occur again.

Some may scoff at this apparently paranoid fear of hermeneutic anarchy on the grounds that Nietzschean free-play and Derridean deconstruction have once and for all done away with any such logocentric nostalgia for transcendent truths or meanings. Perhaps they have. The important point to note, however, is that while the search for an *ultimate* answer to, and correct reading of, a text is most assuredly destined to fail, the deliberate abandonment of each *provisional* search, of each *tentative* conclusion, constitutes a much more dangerous act. After all, to say that texts can express an increasing number of meanings does nothing to the historical fact of there being more or less fixed, individual readings of texts.

Therefore, we owe it to ourselves as writers and critics to rethink our contemporary place in relation to texts. If our modern sensibility makes us relentless in our quest to make texts say practically everything we, as a society and/or profession, ever wanted them to say (and more), then we have essentially lost any interest in genuine communication, in the truest sense of the word. The work of art no longer "speaks" to or with us; rather, we talk to or play with it.[29] By this curious twist, the very theorists most concerned with reducing the "authority" of a certain kind of critical discourse, as well as of most "literary" works, run the risk—which, perhaps, is precisely what they want?—of usurping this same authority. If our modern penchant for discovering and valuing the new within or below the old goes unchecked, then the only real object of value left will be that of the new itself. Therein no doubt lies the explanation for why a host of critical and theoretical currents would have us place those discourses on the same epistemological and ontological planes as literature itself.

But this newness or originality is highly ephemeral indeed, since it can only be known through, and thanks to, the old. One might even say that without the authority of always-already-given texts, neither poets nor critics would have sufficient authority to submit in turn their own so-called original creations. Like Jonathan Culler in regard to Paul De Man, one is led

> to suspect that a certain faith in the [classic] text and the truth of its most fundamental and surprising implications is the blindness that makes possible the insights of deconstructive criticism, or the methodological necessity that cannot be justified but is tolerated for the power of its results.[30]

In other words, we have reached a point in the history of literary criticism and theory when every new reading, and every new poem reeks of arbitrariness. When we start expanding critical labels that, in the beginning, had a certain utility—consider terms like "structuralist," "modernist," "New Criticism," "New Novel," etc.—and then, begin adding the prefixes "post" or "new," even going so far as to compound them, as in the extraordinarily convoluted phrase "Beyond post-structuralism" recently used at an important academic conference, it becomes obvious that our over-riding desire for transcendence and originality, so constitutive of our modernity, has created monsters of incomprehensibility. As Murray Krieger has indicated quite rightly,[31] one wonders why nobody ever cares to use the prefix "pre" anymore. No one wants to think of him/herself as "merely" pre-figuring or re-figuring something else that is *really* important.

Either we stop, therefore, and ask ourselves how this will- to-originality has emerged as a dominant force in the literary domain, or else we continue to multiply our different readings until such time that the poems and novels we scrutinize will disappear under the sheer weight of the commentary. This is not to say that we may no longer read *Moby Dick* and enjoy it for its "own" merits. But it does mean that, as a pluralistic society, we have grown increasingly unwilling, sometimes even unable, to react naïvely to a work of art. It is useful in this regard to contemplate those contemporary students of ours who do not seem willing to think anything at all about a given passage in a great book because they know that their teacher has a "better" opinion than they; or the museum visitors who cannot understand why a painting is so famous since no one ever gave them a "good" reason to believe in its intrinsic aesthetic worth. Both sets of individuals are victims of a society whose vested interest in originality has prevented its members from staying in touch with their own, genuine feelings about art. I say "genuine" for lack of a better term, even though in most cases, the feelings in question are not at all "original" when they finally are articulated. For better or for worse, the words used to describe one's feelings are usually replete with discursive bits and pieces of earlier experiences had by others, and expressed by others, that are simply re-invoked, *intertextually*, as it were, by the present circumstance.

Yet, in spite of the manifestly *un*original nature of many of these expressed sentiments, expressing them forms the very experiential social fabric permitting human communication itself. It is unfortunate that this uninspired discourse is all too often inhibited in professional conferences, classrooms, even cocktail parties, presumably because of its iterative character. I say "unfortunate" because many people today are inhibited from profiting from, or otherwise deriving pleasure from, some of humanity's best artistic productions. From all appearances, nothing else better explains this phenomenon than our society's contemporary obsession with difference, our collective lack of interest in any critical comment, or artistic production, that does not immediately strike us as new.

In this light, several other related philosophic questions immediately come to mind that will have to be addressed in the following chapters. They are: Whence this common feeling in Western intellectual circles that previous literary works, or previous interpretations of literary works, always need to be surpassed? Why is it that anyone caught repeating a previous art, or a previous analytic approach to a text for the purpose of communicating in a direct, all-too-familiar or simple way, is condemned to the boring ranks of the uninspired? Even worse, why has an artist or scholar's "originality" become an indispensable criterion for either commercial success, critical authority, or academic success? With obfuscation and other forms of oblique communication slowly but surely becoming the orders of the day, it would appear crucial for us to begin questioning the legitimacy of literary pluralism, of the seemingly obsessive need, in other words, to say things *differently* from ways they have already been said or thought before.

This, then, is the type of reflection that informs the rest of my analysis. In order to answer more fully the many questions about pluralism raised in this opening chapter, the next chapter examines the precise methodological and epistemological reasons why the "text itself" can no longer be seen as the primary (or better, exclusive) source of differences in critical opinion. These opinions concern the value and meaning of a piece of literature. After doing this, I shall look more carefully at the evolution of the notions of originality and progress. In the process, one shall see how the historical fusion of these concepts has created a monolithic conceptual force which, probably more than any other factor, has helped generate the rise of literary pluralism. In the final stage of my inquiry, it will be necessary to determine to what extent *trans-historical* factors have encouraged the appearance and, indeed, dominance of, pluralistic thought in all (modern) things literary. Only then will the reader be in a position to understand better the rise of literary pluralism in modern Western countries, and to see why it may now be appropriate, as well as desirable, to temper its extraordinary growth, specifically, its *critical* dimension.

NOTES

[1] Ever since Nietzsche, many of us in the literary field try, anyway, to be beyond *good* and *evil*.

[2] I refer here to Hirsch's early work, *Validity in Interpretation* (New Haven: Yale University Press, 1967), although his later work, especially *Cultural Literacy* (Boston: Houghton-Mifflin, 1987) also exemplifies this same conviction of a common, *proper* interpretative stance toward the world in general, and toward the world of literature in particular.

[3] K. M. Newton, *In Defense of Literary Interpretation* (London: Macmillan, 1986), p. 17.

[4] By "modern" I mean poets and critics of the last two hundred years or so, from the French Revolution on. That is generally what I shall mean in my essay when using this adjective, unless otherwise indicated.

[5] If we were to talk more generally about *cultural* and not just *literary* pluralism, the creator of difference could be replaced the "embodiment" of it. In this case, a significant "other" might be someone from a minority, one whose differences from more historically powerful groups have not been adequately appreciated and/or understood, especially as these differences reflect other types of human progress. The reader is well-advised in this regard to compare continually what I state about literary pluralism in particular to what one could infer from, and about, the more general phenomenon of cultural pluralism.

[6] K. M. Newton, *In Defense*, p. 224.

[7] The newest password in the Academy now is the term "politically correct," which the media and countless individuals have gone to great lengths to try to define.

[8] In this respect it aims to go further than Ellen Rooney goes in her recent study of the philosophical relations between pluralism and contemporary theory alone. It seems to me that the situation is more complex, and much older, than her otherwise fascinating study suggests. See her *Seductive Reasoning: Pluralism as the Problematic of Contemporary Literary Theory* (Ithaca: Cornell University Press, 1989).

[9] *S\Z* (Paris: Seuil, 1970), p. 24.

[10] Hartman, "The Use and Abuse of Structural Analysis: Riffaterre's Interpretation of Wordsworth's 'Yew Trees,'" *New Literary History*, 7, 1 (1975), 168-69.

[11] Cf. Paul de Man's comment, "We can hardly believe in Riffaterre's assertion that the literary work consists of an "inimitable code" bound to elicit a definite response in the reader if we can *legitimately* put into question all the readings he suggests ..." (my emphasis) in "Literature and Language: A Commentary," *New Literary History*, 4, 1 (1972), 185. The question, of course, is what this "legitimately" really means.

[12] "Use and Abuse," 166.

[13] *S\Z*, p. 11.

[14] See the section titled thus in Jonathan Culler's *On Deconstruction* (Ithaca: Cornell University Press, 1983), pp. 64-83.

[15] Certainly there have been many opponents of widely divergent theories and methodologies, but no one appears ready to discard entirely that general practice we could call "textual commentary."

[16] See his "Variant Readings and Misreading," as well as his "Poetic Process and Literary Analysis" both in *Style in Language*, ed. Thomas A. Sebeok (Cambridge, MA: MIT Press, 1960), pp. 241-252 and pp. 9-23, respectively for a development of this idea.

[17] The reading that started the debate was Roman Jakobson and Claude Lévi-Strauss, "'Les Chats' de Charles Baudelaire," *L'Homme*, 2, 1 (1962), 5-21. Riffaterre then responded with his "Describing Poetic Structures; Two Approaches to Baudelaire's 'Les Chats'" in *Yale French Studies*, 36 & 37 (October 1966), pp. 200-42. The methodological "battle" of readings these two approaches led to eventually generated enough material for several anthologies, the first and most important of which was *Les chats de Baudelaire. Une confrontation de méthodes*, eds. Maurice Delcroix et Walter Geerts (Namur: Presses Universitaires de Namur, 1980). This debate, in addition to Norman Holland's now famous *5 Readers Reading* and other Anglo-American works, may very well have spawned the many "handy" collections of so-called *readers' readings* that have recently appeared in the US (from the presses of the MLA, Florida State University, etc.). One is forced to wonder what it means that all of these different readings are suddenly deemed worthy of being bound together as separate volumes, and that these volumes deserve our professional attention.

[18] *Confrontation*, eds. Delcroix et Geerts, p. 10.

[19] With the notable exception of Jacques Derrida, who makes of it a pillar of deconstruction.

[20] Cf. Terry Eagleton's comment in *Literary Theory: An Introduction* (London: Blackwell, 1983), p. 211: "What you choose and reject theoretically [...] depends upon what you are practically trying to do."

[21] A "literary" text is any one that "implicitly or explicitly signifies its own rhetorical mode and prefigures its own misunderstanding as the correlative of its rhetorical nature; that is, of its "rhetoricity." Paul de Man, *Blindness and Insight: Essays in the Rhetoric of Contemporary Criticism* (New York: Oxford University Press, 1971), p. 136.

[22] *Literary Theory*, p. 126.

[23] *Literary Theory*, p. 201.

[24] Jonathan Culler generalizes about the distinction at hand in these terms: "Structuralists are convinced that systematic knowledge is possible; post-structuralists claim to know only the impossibility of this knowledge." *On Deconstruction*, p. 22.

[25] In his "Re-Covering 'The Purloined Letter'" in *The Reader in the Text*, eds. Inge Crosman and Susan Suleiman (Princeton: Princeton Univ. Press, 1980), p. 362.

[26] James Kearn and Ken Newton, "An Interview with Jacques Derrida'" *The Literary Review* (18 April - 1 May 1980), 21, quoted in Ellen Rooney, *Seductive Reasoning*, p. 19.

[27] *Confrontation*, p. 9.

[28] In his *The World, The Text, The Critic* (Cambridge: Harvard University Press, 1983), p. 130.

[29] Cf. the title "How to Speak to Literature" from Julia Kristéva's article "Comment parler à la littérature" which first appeared in *Tel Quel*, 47 (automne 1971) and was reprinted as the title for the whole first half of her book *Polylogue* (Paris: Seuil, 1977).

[30] *On Deconstruction*, p. 280.

[31] In his "Literary Invention and the Impulse to Theoretical Change: 'Or Whether Revolution be the Same,'" *New Literary History*, 18, 1 (Autumn 1986), 205-6.

Chapter II
CHANGING APPROACHES:
FROM TEXTS TO READERS (AND BACK)

Always historicize.
Frederic Jameson[1]

An earlier book of mine[2] established a classificatory system of linguistic categories that described the abstract conceptual apparatus used by most people to read literature critically. Using the prose poems of Baudelaire, Rimbaud, and Breton, my idea was to find what we might call the minimal "literary" aspects of certain influential, albeit historically marginal, texts in order to generalize about similar features found in all literary texts. "Literary" was a term I used in the classic Jakobsonian sense of "literariness"; that is, in a sense that allowed me to to describe stylistic phenomena in terms of a perceived repetition or recurrence of linguistic elements on the paradigmatic and syntagmatic axes of a text's language. Once noted by the reader, these individual minimal literary features were then presumed to be heuristically combined—according to various institutional and ideological conventions,[3] consciously or unconsciously accepted by the reader—to form a work of verbal art.

In proper formalist and semiotic tradition, the underlying assumption of the book was that although different readers produce different interpretations of the same works of verbal art, most critical readers share much of the same language and culture with which other writers and readers of their society are familiar. Using a systematic approach, with its theoretical roots in transformational and generative grammar, as well as in certain reader-response models, my goal was to delineate and relate all the linguistic levels on which a literary text, by dint of various forms of repetition, could be said to signify *something* to *someone*. In spite of this insistence on the commonality of readers' experiences, it was nevertheless assumed that individual readers might very well interpret the same core data in many different ways. In other words, it was a theoretical given that any text's pure *difference*, as a phenomenal object-in-the-world "waiting" to be analyzed, most often generated a plurality of interpretations. The term "pure difference" refers to that quality by virtue of which a text's necessarily unique concatenation of sounds and symbols differs (from), and defers, all other texts. An additional given was that this plurality of interpretations occurred, even though each of these "different" readings seemed to be articulated in a common analytic fashion, a fashion my book went to great pains to define.

At the start of the research for the present book, I still firmly believed that by delving further into the previously established categories, it would be possible to find other formal elements that could help me understand not just *what* people have in common when they read, but also *why* people read differently from each other. On the level of a commonly-noted phrase of a text, for instance, I thought that by further investigating the syntactic and semantic constraints each individual linguistic element added to the given phrasal sequence, it might be possible to figure out exactly *how* different meanings were attributed to the same phrase by many different people. One such possibility emerged when I noticed that, in two very different analyses, the deconstructionist critic Barbara Johnson and I both had directed much of our respective interpretive energies to a consideration of the same phrase found in Baudelaire's prose poem, *Le Mauvais Vitrier/*"The Evil Glazier." The phrase in question was quite short, *casser les verres/*"to break windowpanes" (or, in Johnson's reading of this prose poem, " to break poetic *vers* or "verses").⁴ From my perspective, the interesting point about this coincidence was not just that it had occurred, but, more important, that we had chosen *not* to read this detail (or what I called our commonly-shared textual ground) in the same way.

It will, of course, be suggested that nothing about this difference of opinion, in and of itself, should surprise anyone involved in the serious study of literature. Everyone knows that such disagreements have always occurred, and always will. By temporarily leaving aside the issue of who was the *correct* reader and who misguided in this regard, I nonetheless hoped to gain something of critical value by doing, at the very least, a more thorough analysis of the formal particularities of that peculiar lexical sequence. Since both Barbara Johnson and I had obviously deemed the phrase significant for one reason or other, there was every reason to assume that a closer look would yield still more useful results for literary theory.

As might have been expected, the number of possible directions I could have taken to reduce and/or standardize the various connotations and denotations contained in even the shortest of phrases made such a project untenable, not to mention trivial, almost from the start. Relying solely on formal means, I could not reasonably have expected to accomplish much of anything other than to list every grammatical and syntactical rule of the language logically deduced from the phrase in question. As in the case of one of the most elaborate and purely formal readings of a text ever attempted (the pioneering analysis by Lévi-Strauss and Jakobson of the sonnet "Les Chats" mentioned in chapter one), the most I could have gained from this type of "super-reading" of a poem is a complete linguistic description of it. Such a description would hardly have helped us to understand more adequately how this series of signifiers produces that aesthetic effect we call diversely "literature," "poetry," or "verbal art." As one of the principal critics of Lévi-Strauss and Jakobson's analysis writes:

> [...] the structures described do not explain what establishes contact between poetry and [the] reader. No grammatical analysis can give us more than the grammar of the poem.[5]

Therefore, it quickly became obvious to me that if I had chosen to proceed any further in this formalist direction, I could not honestly have expected to come any closer than I had before to a more complete understanding of how the same texts generate *different* readings. I would merely have become more sensitive to, and more acquainted with, a particular textual grammar than I had been previously. My initial approach to the problem of interpretive differences was thus limited by the very "success" of the earlier project.

For this reason, I am led to believe that any such quasi-maniacal formalism can only add so much to our general appreciation of literary pluralism. After all, considering the definition from chapter one, the *critical* component of literary pluralism refers precisely to the problematic co-existence of dissimilar readings in modern literary studies. If the search for individual differences in literary interpretation were based solely on each and every linguistic aspect of a text (and nothing else), it would thus still be doomed to fail. It would inevitably fail because one would still never know, once and for all, whether every conceivable linguistic trait about a text had been accounted for within the economy of a general theory of textuality, or even within the limits of a particular textual reading. Too many external factors impinge upon the relevance, or lack thereof, of the particular traits that one invariably chooses over others. These factors include such things as the reader's linguistic background, one's knowledge of literary style, and one's memory, all of which vary enormously from one person to another.

As a result, the search for differences in interpretation, for an origin to the critical side of literary pluralism, logically has to be directed elsewhere than exclusively to a text's formal dimensions. To understand this point better, it would be fruitful to examine one of Jorge Luis Borges' more celebrated short stories, "Pierre Menard, Author of the *Quijote.*"[6] In this well-known text, the central character attempts the impossible; he tries to write the *Quijote* in the twentieth century as if he *were* Cervantes. He does not re-write or copy the original novel, as the heros of Flaubert's *Bouvard and Pécuchet* might have done, but presumes instead to *write* it, word for word. What we soon discover in this fantastic tale is an startling passage from Pierre Menard's "new" text, a passage which the narrator comments on at some length. Significantly, the newly commented passage is verbally identical to Cervantes'. Despite this, however, we are told that the later text is "almost infinitely richer"(42).

Here is the "original" passage, which is at the same time its verbally-identical and supposedly "richer" copy:

> ... truth, whose mother is history, rival of time, depository of deeds, witness of the past, exemplar and adviser to the present, and the future's counselor ... (43).

The narrator notes that the seventeenth-century passage is little more than an enumeration. He then states that this enumeration represents "a mere rhetorical phrase of history" invented by the lay genius, Cervantes. The very same words under the contemporary Pierre Menard's pen, on the other hand, are praised for the "astounding idea" they convey. The idea is that of making History into "the *mother* of truth." The reason why this is such an astounding idea turns out to have more to do with the philosophic context of Menard's epoch than it does with any intrinsic meaning of the words *themselves*, or of the text *itself*. In fact, the very notion of any and all intrinsic meanings is one that this re-reading already makes more and more difficult to accept. For the "same" words are shown to mean different things through different meta-linguistic emphases.

Borges' narrator then points out that thanks to Pierre Menard's historical proximity to the philosopher, William James, the re-creator of the *Quijote* (Menard) is now able to redefine history in what he suddenly qualifies as a "bold" new way:

> Menard, a contemporary of William James, does not define history as an inquiry into reality but as its origin. Historical truth is not what has happened; it is what we judge to have happened. The final phrases [of this passage in the short story]—*exemplar and adviser to the present, and the future's counselor*—are brazenly pragmatic (43).

The narrator remarks that the contrast in style between the two supposed versions is also "vivid." Menard is said to be "affected," whereas Cervantes, amazingly, is "comfortably at ease with seventeenth-century Spanish"!

What is implicit in this interpretive gesture by Borges' narrator, however, is that a different reader doing a different reading might very well have chosen to emphasize textual aspects *other* those found here. Another reader may very well have selected the metaphor of history as "rival of time," for example, instead of emphasizing the phrase "the mother of truth." Like the story's narrator, this new reader in his or her turn might then have exclaimed, "What an astounding idea!" This, of course, would have lead in all probability to still another legitimate, if different, interpretation. In the end, however, nothing would have guaranteed our having extracted from this example some general hermeneutic principle that we could have then applied to some *other* phrase from some *other* text. At best, we would have had a thorough, though not very interesting, grammatical analysis of this one line from one novel. Nothing theoretical would have justified our applying its particulars to an appreciation of all other lines in all other novels, as would have been the formalist's hope.

Beyond the obvious humor of this fictional story, its moral has special significance to anyone involved with the complex question of differing literary interpretations, of what we are calling "critical pluralism." First of all, when Borges' narrator discovers in this passage a potential modern "source" for Menard's brazen metaphor of truth, i.e. William James, he alludes, without necessarily realizing it, to perhaps *the* most important, and certainly, earliest American exponent of twentieth-century pluralism. The author of *A Pluralistic Universe* (1909),[7] James could not be better suited to Borges' seemingly paradoxical tale of identical texts. Indeed, the former's views both on reality and, especially, on the historical understanding of reality coincide perfectly with a methodological move I have been tacitly suggesting since the start of this chapter. This move involves the theoretical need to change our approach away from the notion of a fixed or intrinsic materiality of texts to the dynamic reality of readers and writers of texts. Borges' tale coincides with my contention that any modern study of critical pluralism requires a change in focus or approach from the linguistic concreteness of signifiers to the existential heterogeneity of the *interpreters* of signifiers.

To see more precisely how it coincides, one can compare this suggested modification in approach to what William James himself says. Let us take, for example, his summary of the views of the French philosopher Henri Bergson. According to James, one of the great philosophic breakthroughs of modern times came about when Bergson made the following point about the reality of objects:

> What really *exists* is not things [e.g. the *Quijote* original in its unarticulated textual difference] but things in the making. Once

> made, they are dead, and an infinite number of *alternative* [my
> emphasis] conceptual decompositions [like both those of Pierre
> Menard and of Borges' narrator himself] can be used in defining
> them [...] Reality *falls* in passing into conceptual analysis; it *mounts*
> in living its own individual life (263-4).

In another equally significant passage from James' work, the
American philosopher underscores how criticism has an innate drive
to substitute its own metalanguage for that of the text it comments
on. Following his model (Bergson), James once again stresses the
idea that a particular

> form is superimposed [on the same object under investigation, say,
> a text] for *practical* ends only, in order to let us jump about over life
> instead of wading through it (my emphasis 272).

In other words, the "life" of a text is no longer in a text itself once
the reader has, so to speak, "killed" it with commentary. If we then
re-read the words found in Borges' short story, we suddenly realize
that his narrator provides a paradigmatic example of what James via
Bergson says happens with all types of (literary) analysis or
criticism. Whenever analyses "superimpose" their conceptual form
onto any given text's fundamental, theoretically irreducible,
difference, they do so mainly for the practical ends of critics. They
also effectively "kill" the text by erasing its dynamic nature.

But there is still more to say when we return to Borges' text
"itself." First of all, we should remember that the narrator
distinguishes himself, from the very start of the story, from the
created character of Pierre Menard. Menard, after all, attempts to
become Cervantes, inasmuch as he wishes to be the original writer
of the *Quijote*. This critical narrator thereby *makes* his new, "live"
text say what the otherwise "dead" text (Cervantes') supposedly
could not, or did not, say. Yet, we outside of the story cannot fail
to notice that there is, in fact, nothing intrinsically "different" about
either version of the *Quijote*. Linguistically speaking, the only thing
that changes is the *choice* of words selected by the narrator. The
same words, re-combined differently, thus create a "different" text
in a place where, manifestly, the "same" text exists. The fact

remains that the "live" text, re-articulated and re-symbolized meta-linguistically by the narrator, is nothing other than a personally truncated, critically modernized version of the original *Quijote*. The same words have merely been used to say different things, undoubtedly for what James contends are "practical ends" only.

Finding the name of William James in this short story could not be more appropriate, therefore, for our purposes here. The strategic mention of his name indicates just how variable, in Borges's mind, the significance of a text in and of itself can be across (literary) history. Indeed, the notion of a text "in and of itself" becomes problematic. The use of James' name in this context underscores how a text's purely linguistic potential to produce different readings, its textual difference, is routinely co-opted and appropriated by particular readers for their own ends. The story also demonstrates, as well as any other example I can think of, how any study of the critical side of literary pluralism cannot, without considerable theoretical and methodological risk, limit itself to the words-on-the-page themselves.

So, what Borges' story ultimately illustrates is this: Through the imposition of a different context, that is, as a result of "an infinite number of alternative conceptual decompositions" (James), the very same words can mean many different things to many different people. Any purely formal attempt to understand modern critical pluralism, or to locate the source of different readings exclusively among the linguistic elements of a text alone, will always fall short of its goal. Without extensive consideration of certain extratextual practical factors that lead different readers to read the same features differently (and likewise, different writers to see their own writings differently), the most a formalist approach can hope to accomplish is to account for every possible concatenation and permutation of the individual linguistic traits constituting a text. Such an approach to the general question of literary pluralism is, needless to say, utopian. In the final analysis though, it is also, perhaps unfortunately, trivial.

For these reasons, it is impossible not to decide to turn most of our critical attention away from the idea of a "text itself." We shall henceforth focus instead on the reader's (and, later on, author's) reactions to the "itself" of a text. The reason we shall turn "most" and not "all" of our attention in this direction is because the notion of the "text itself" can never be totally dismissed. After all, the same words in *Madame Bovary* or *Hamlet* do still appear on the same page, and in the same order, provided that readers possess the same edition or translation of a given work. These words, this "text itself," thus inevitably demands of any reader desirous of understanding it at least a modicum of linguistic and/or "literary" competence in the particular language. Formalist, structuralist, and semiotic models and typologies that articulate the functioning of this dual competence in the critical act of reading literature thereby still offer certain important insights in the meaning(s) and significance of texts. It would not be inappropriate to suggest that my earlier essay on repetition provides, as have many other studies beyond mine, just such an analytic system for the appreciation of this common, *material* dimension of literature.

Yet, as Borges' story illustrates so well, the same "text itself," the very same words, *when selected and arranged differently*, most often signify differently. In the modern fields of literature and its study, they even appear to do so *more* nowadays than ever before, as was suggested in chapter one. This phenomenon can be partially explained by means of isolating specifically "modern" textual features among works written in the last two hundred years or so. But it will be our particular task to show from here on that an even greater reason for this modern expansion of, or rise in, the critical dimension of literary pluralism lies instead in an important, and historically-situated, extra-textual desire to see this transpire. Only by turning most of our attention away from words "themselves" to the readers of these words, therefore, can we hope to determine what *else* is on-the-page, so to speak, besides just black dots.[8] This will not be accomplished until those who work on texts realize collectively the pragmatic critical need to engage in two related activities. The first consists of a more careful examination of the formal causes or, if one prefers, linguistic sources, of our dissimilar re-articulations of the same text "itself." In this activity, one can continue to ask more and more questions such as, Why does a "critic" like Borges' narrator underline certain words and images to the exclusion of other lexical possibilities from the same passage? Furthermore, what exactly are these other formal features that contain, as it were, semantic and semiotic potential?

The second activity, which in my estimation may be even more crucial at the present time, involves re-reading the precise ways in which the "selves" of readers and writers add something significant to the text itself. This re-reading should clarify Frederic Jameson's point that a text

> never comes to us as "a thing-in-itself." Rather, texts come before us as the always-already-read; we apprehend them through sedimented layers of previous interpretive translation. [Thus] the object of our study is less the text itself than the interpretations through which we attempt to confront and appropriate it (*Unconscious* 9).

Given this theoretical as well as methodological need for *both* of these critical activities, we shall no longer consider then a text's words-on-the-page *exclusively*. We shall also look to the reader and writer for further clues to help us justify different readings of the same text. For it will be assumed hereafter that the first clues form only part of the puzzle of modern critical pluralism, and that the most effective way to proceed in studying this cultural phenomenon involves moving constantly from texts to readers and back.

These assumptions now allow me to posit the following hypothesis: the major cause of interpretive differences among modern readers is found not only *in* the text, but perhaps even more *in* the modern reader and writer. This is so because, without some kind of desire or need for difference on the part of modern readers and writers, one is hard-pressed to explain why contemporary critics seem to have ever greater difficulty in getting others to accept their interpretations as *definitive* readings. If it were thought neither desirable, nor necessary in the modern worlds of criticism and theory to bring out different aspects of the same work of art, one could presume that there already exists a sufficient number of readings of the *Quijote*, or of *Hamlet* and *Madame Bovary*, to suit every possible reader.

But, as was seen in the case of Borges' narrator, such has clearly not been the case for some time now. The standard modern reaction to the proposal that there can or should be one reading of a work of art goes something like this: A great work is so complex, and evokes so many universal ideas and emotions, that it must touch different chords in each and every reader. *This fact cannot be denied.* On the other hand, one must ask how it happens that we have chosen particular texts as being those most capable of functioning that way. To this ancillary question, the natural response is: because there is something special, something intrinsic to that particular combination of words that permits it to act on us in such a fashion. Indeed, many critics and theorists have saught precisely to describe and define this very *je ne sais quoi*. The first group to give a "scientific" name to this special quality was, of course, the Russian Formalists, who invented the essentialist notion of "poeticity" or "literariness" in order to define it.

Yet, the whole of modern criticism demonstrates to us its ultimate failure to locate once and for all this special aesthetic quality so firmly held by many to exist within the text itself. The *practical* impossibility of describing fully and definitively this literary essence appears irrefutable. It is irrefutable if for no other empirical reason than that many *dis*similar theories and analyses have been advanced which try to crystalize or extract this same literariness or poeticity out of a given text, as if it were some sort of ultra-valuable mineral. In spite of this collective failure to grasp fully the notion of literariness, many individual theorists and serious readers persist just the same in believing in it. One might surmise that for such literati, not believing in the quintessence of their favorite object of scrutiny is tantamount to rejecting the idea that with every new reading of a text one "progresses" in some way or other.

What needs to be pointed out here, however, is that the act of holding so dearly (albeit tacitly, in certain cases) to the belief in progress is, in many respects, analogous to a religious leap of faith. It resembles a leap of faith because, just as Saint Augustine believed in God as the result of his actual *in*ability to see or know Him,[9] so, too, do most modern critics imagine a transcendent essence that might explain the reasons behind their otherwise inexplicably *powerful* responses to particular pieces of writing called "literary." The reader eager to express his or her idiosyncratic feelings thereby proposes a new reading of those precise texts that an appropriate literary establishment says contain a certain *je ne sais quoi*. The pluralistic mentality, which appears to be one of the inescapable results of the present day post-structuralist mode, is, therefore, partially logocentric, i.e. counter-productive to one of the epistemological and aesthetic stances it often purports to embody. It is logocentric because by allowing many of the same "canonical" works to be re-read ad infinitum it effectively reinforces the earlier privileging of these very texts.

But it is eminently reasonable to assume that a "lesser" work of art, perhaps even a "non-literary" text, say, a polemical newspaper editorial or some unattributed though provocative bathroom graffiti, could, in theory, generate equally multiple or polyvalent "readings," if society chose to privilege *them*.[10] In his influential *Literary Theory*, Terry Eagleton advances a similar idea, which echoes perfectly that of several other modern critics:

> The context tells me that [a text] is literary; but the language itself has no inherent properties or qualities which might distinguish it from other kinds of discourse (6).

Even more to the point, Eagleton states that

> It [the language of literature] leaves the definition of literature up to how somebody decides to *read* ... (8).

Of course, one might object that this statement does not in any way inform us of the exact reasons why society has chosen to privilege the former over the latter. The objection, however, is circular. Society does not (yet) read graffiti as it does *Hamlet* because *Hamlet* evokes more reactions than do graffiti. But if society *did* read graffiti as it does Shakespeare, then what? To answer my own rhetorical question, I believe that they would find a great deal more in it than they previously thought was "there." Consider, for example, the trick played one day by Stanley Fish on an unsuspecting class, who had mistaken random words on the blackboard as an obscure poem by a Renaissance poet. Fish discovered that the reactions, arguments, and debates generated by this non-text were perfectly analogous to those he had grown accustomed to in more "serious" contexts.[11] This experience illustrates very graphically how "literature," like Beauty, exists in the eye of the beholder/reader before existing on the page.

Let us therefore assume that while texts "themselves" do indeed generate different readings to a certain extent, readers and writers (as readers of themselves) also very much contribute to this interpretive process. In order that this not appear to be a simple truism, I must reemphasize the central thesis advanced here. While it has no doubt always been true that readers affect interpretation in ways often similar to those by which textual stimuli affect it, this situation has been exacerbated in the last two hundred years. For historical and epistemological reasons that it is my major task to explore, literary critics and theorists must sooner or later limit their seemingly endless thirst for different interpretive and reading models, or run the risk of relegating literature to a position not merely equal to, but, in fact, inferior to, commentary. Since texts have, or so it seems, the potential to support the desires and needs of an ever-growing number of readers—whom we might wish to call "appropriators"—then every text will sooner or later become nothing but a pre-text. The very originality or singularity which it was the critic's initial job to uncover fades away in this manner in inverse proportion to the increase in interpretive operations performed on it.

We should not be surprised, therefore, to see that for some contemporary students, Harold Bloom's reading of Wallace Stevens might in a certain way be thought just as *valuable* to us as Stevens' poems themselves. Nor should we be unprepared for the modern day attribution of more cultural significance to a critical essay or critical school that canonizes certain texts over others, than to pieces of literature themselves, (problematic writings that are rapidly becoming mere pre-texts for criticism). For better or for worse, some critics and students of literature have begun to do just that.

I would like to suggest, however, that a middle ground exists, or, at least, should exist, between thinking, on the one hand, that literature has its own irreplacable essence as individual marks on the page, and that, on the other, criticism and commentary are just as valuable as "literary" discourse. In order to support this assertion, one must first examine more closely the manner in which the *formal* search for literariness has been conducted, and describe the many other ways in which it can be said to be inadequate. The purpose of this historical investigation is not to reject once and for all the empirically useful entreprise involved in the *formal* study of literary texts "themselves." Nor is it to re-invent the proverbial wheel of modern literary theory, which, to a large extent, has already accepted this shift from texts to readers (and writers as readers) of texts in the last twenty years or so. Rather, it is to emphasize the need in this pluralistic context to view this type of analysis as only one, albeit one very important, part of the hermeneutic transaction known as the literary phenomenon. Once we have reviewed modern criticism with an eye to its particular relationship with pluralism, we shall then turn our attention to the specific theoretical problems posed by the reading of prose poems. This will allow me to complete the argument for a shift in approach to the question of literary pluralism, as well as to lay the theoretical groundwork for an historical examination of the second, *aesthetic* part of my main "problem," literary pluralism.

Recent Approaches to Critical Pluralism

The history of modern literary criticism is rife with examples of theorists who insist that there must be a way to determine where the aesthetic singularity of, say, Rimbaud's *Illuminations* begins, and where the adequacy of their interpretations ends. As was stated above, Russian Formalism, along with its descendents, New Criticism and Structuralism, are all well-known movements that strove to extract from the "text itself" some essentialist form of literariness. This concept has provided the impetus for innumerable linguistic-based studies of literary style that continue to appear both here and abroad, and which aim to quantify and categorize the "stuff" of literature. Rather than review the entire history of this twentieth-century analytic preoccupation with literariness,[12] I shall direct my attention only to those recent instances of this type of critical approach that strike me as being among the most persuasive and influential.

Over the last few years, there has been a growing rift among critics regarding the present fate of so-called "scientific" criticism. What one usually finds included in this term are all those literary approaches whose primary methodological basis is linguistic. The term thus refers to approaches whose focus is on the formal and semantic traits within a text's own margins, in addition to formal and semantic relations between texts. Scientific criticism considers these linguistic entities as real, distinct objects of inquiry that exist independently in the world. Insofar as the concept of "literariness" or "poeticity" acts as the catch-all for the various essences studied by such criticism, it can rightfully be said to be the ultimate object of scrutiny for this type of scientific literary analysis.

According to some, these kinds of critical objects and methods have suffered irreparable damage from a host of post-structuralist attacks. A recent *PMLA* article encapsulates nicely the general anti-scientific point of view in vogue today, when it states that scientific criticism "at least in its twentieth-century incarnation, is drawing to a close."[13] As the author of this essay indicates, the reasons for this demise are many and varied, and, in fact, require a full-length study all by themselves. Yet, what one finds at the core of the different arguments advanced in this article, which I take to be representative of widespread sentiment among many modern critics, is an insistence on the self-destructing, or, more precisely, self-deconstructing nature of scientific approaches.[14] Opponents of this criticism frequently demonstrate how both the models imported from other disciplines, as well as the application of these models, work against the proposed goal of the scientific enterprise, that is, against a systematic articulation of the structure and/or nature of all literary texts.

A second critical camp, however, exemplified by yet another author of a *PMLA* essay, insists that recent reports of scientific criticism's death have been greatly exaggerated. For this commentator,[15] the latter's supposed death has been occasioned at least as much by its deliberate misunderstanding and distortion as by any fundamental weakness scientific criticism actually possesses. As the author says,

> It now seems clear ... that those who were once the strongest promoters of a linguistic-based reading theory are its most vocal opponents; and literary critics may secretly suspect that they have much to teach philosophers and linguists (448).

When we consider that the majority of these promoters—which include critics like Stanley Fish, Mary Louise Pratt, and Wolfgang Iser—were often labelled "structuralists" in their younger days, we might very well call the reactions of such reformed scientific critics "structuralist confessions." It might thus be asserted that, having renounced the "sins" of their earlier ways, influential literary analysts like Tzvetan Todorov, in his 1984 quasi-confessional *Critique de la Critique: Un Roman d'Apprentissage*,[16] and Naomi Schor, in her *Breaking the Chain*,[17] do nothing less than confess to us, in their own fashion, how they have come to understand the limitations of their previous scientific, structuralist models. In Todorov's case, for example, we find him saying this:

> discovering around me a literature that served politics [communism], I used to believe that I had to break any link and preserve literature

from any contact with what was not literary. But the relation to [extra-textual] values is inherent to literature: not only because it is impossible to speak of existence without referring to it, but also because the act of writing is an act of communication, which implies the possibility of an understanding, in the name of common values (187).

Schor, on the other hand, takes her distance from an essentially formalistic, scientific criticism in order to espouse a more engaged feminist position. In her words, she had to break the "chain" of structuralist analysis before she could "write as a woman."

Lest anyone hastily construe these comments as a criticism of these critics on my part, one should here note that the present book also constitutes a kind of structuralist confession of its own. The reader should understand that in the polemic in which I am here engaged it is not so much a question of "choosing sides" as of determining exactly what each camp, structuralist, anti-structuralist, or poststructuralist, has to offer us now and in the future. The simple fact is that, regardless of which group is more "correct," or more clairvoyant than the other, we have no reason *a priori* to exclude either point of view. To the extent that formal, scientific criticism can still produce results that have some value to literary studies, we can certainly argue for its continued use as a legitimate alternative to other interpretive methods. To assume that it no longer has a place in literary studies because, theoretically speaking, it cannot provide the "last word" in its analysis or appreciation of a given piece of literature, is patently absurd.

Yet, if one does not realize that such an approach does, indeed, have certain limitations, many of which I shall discuss in greater detail later in this chapter, one will quickly find oneself at an important theoretical impasse. The impasse in question involves the very feasability of any scientific model of literature that purports to be universal, but that nevertheless contains within itself the empirically observed *potential* to be rejected by particular critical readers. What then explains this impasse? How can any critics continue to work on what seems to be a utopian, formal system of literature, a system that allows all readers to reach a "proper," i.e. common, understanding of artistic productions? How can theorists pursue such research when those most engaged in it over the last thirty years or so know that many previous models and systems have already been rejected?

The answers to these questions lie, I believe, in human nature itself; that is, in that specific human drive that makes most, if not all, people want to create order out of chaos. In the first place, as long as critics think they have finally found the right scientific "key" to the problem of critical pluralism, they might be expected to try, against all odds, to solve the puzzle, to furnish the "definitive" reading of any and all literary texts. As long as scientific literary critics consider their approach, like those found in other natural sciences, to belong to a "hard," as opposed to "soft," discipline, they will import models from equally "hard" disciplines (especially modern linguistic theory) in order to obtain supposedly irrefutable results.

But what should not escape our attention is that a primary belief subtending all scientific models of nature, as well as of literature, is a belief in progress. Progress is that without which scientific criticism is inconceivable. As Thomas Kuhn has suggested, the presuppositions and findings of all sciences, not just such literary criticism, are considered "facts" until such time as whole new facts or readings are presented to the otherwise homogeneous community of scientists/critics who agreed on the earlier "facts."[18] The new interpretation or reading is thus assumed, *by the wider community in question*, to have helped it "progress" or somehow improve with respect to its predecessors. To borrow one of Wayne Booth's many pluralistic voices:

> Let the voices multiply; the more voices we have, the more truth will finally emerge [...] Surely the more vigorous the conflict, the healthier the body critical. Instead of combatting conflict as a sign of confusion or giving up the whole enterprise of criticism in disgust, we might happily join in the melee ....[19]

In this respect, one realizes that a communal or societal presumption of critical progress is one of the pragmatic results of the co-existence of plural readings.

So, when one interpretation wins out over another, progress is supposed to have occurred within the scientifically-oriented community of literary scholars. Despite statements to the contrary any particular modern *anti*-scientific critics may make, the wider interpretive audience to which they belong and address themselves seems incapable of acting otherwise than to consider their gestures as progressive. This, moreover, is as it should be, for most intellectual and artistic thought of modern Western society derives from the fundamentally progressive nineteenth-century ideology subtending important historical phenomena like positivism and industrialization. (This point will be developed further in chapters three and four.)

For many modern students of the literary phenomenon the scientific model thereby becomes irresistible. Whenever "scientific" literary research discovers new readings or new textual facts, the latter simply *replace* previous readings, just as new scientific theories and data replace old ones. But, significantly, one should not fail to note that whether it "wants" to or not, so-called anti-scientific criticism usually functions *the same way*. Powerful anti-scientific readings end up replacing earlier readings regardless of what their authors might wish to say about them. It is empirically true, therefore, that most modern literary criticism is progressive. Its very success or influence in the profession signifies an implied societal accordance of its *progressiveness*.

Now, one might object that readers outside of an academic or professional context have only to read in a manner in which they feel like reading. In other words, if one does not purport to be a "scientist" (of literature), one is not obliged to accept or reject the present or past conclusions, results, or systems of scientific critics. This is no doubt true. However, as Kuhn points out, if among professional critics, teachers, and students (our real subjects here) a "paradigm shift" suddenly occurs in the accepted general model of literature, or even in earlier authoritative readings of particular texts, anyone coming from that same interpretive community who presumes to:

> resist after his whole profession has been converted [to the new
> model, or, more specifically, to the new reading of a given text] has
> *ipso facto* ceased to be a scientist (Kuhn, 158).

S/he must, therefore, conform to it or risk being excluded from the
group. To function as a critic in the Western world of literary studies
today (as always), one must as a consequence change one's
approach, reading, and interpretation whenever the whole profession
deems such changes emblematic of its own progress.

Logically then, since there are two major approaches to the
problem of literary pluralism—looking at the "text itself" or at
readers and writers of texts—modern students and critics of literature
must choose. Either they summarily reject the possibility of any and
all scientific criticism, and admit that any *non*-scientific approach to
texts they might wish to propose should also, in good faith, eschew
the scientific procedures of the former type of analysis. Or else, they
must simply accept the co-existence of different kinds of competing
scientific models, along with the concomitant need to judge which,
at any given time, is the "best" among them. In other terms, either
one believes in progress, as the self-appointed scientific critic does
shamelessly, so to speak; or else, one denies the possibility of
literary and aesthetic progress, giving away thereby the right to claim
any kind of "valid" or "verifiable" methodology. If one disclaims
any semblance of validity to one's method, however, it should not
be forgotten that such a disclaimer is tantamount to committing
critical suicide. By right, precluding the (perforce scientific) validity
of one's model should prevent others from ever taking it seriously.

Critically "valid" therefore means whatever a significant part of
the professional community thinks is valid at a given time and place.
It involves choosing between various methodological possibilities
afforded the "simple" reader. In Todorov's words,

> As a critic, I am in fact obligated to choose between one orientation
> and another [...]: the reason is not in their essential incompatability,
> but in the brevity of life .... But, as a reader, I have no good reason
> to make an exclusive choice: why should I deprive myself [of each
> approach's benefits]? (186).

This is why one can state with a good deal of certainty that all influential critical approaches are necessarily "scientific" to some degree or other. Were this not the case, we would hardly have anything to discuss vis-à-vis literature and its study. One reader's opinion and practice would always be just as good as another's, precisely because the *scientific* criteria of distinguishing one truth from another would no longer apply. Not even so consciously anti-scientific, anti-interpretive a critical method as that of Gilles Deleuze and Felix Guattari in their 1972 study, *Anti-Oedipus*,[20] can escape this dilemma. For, as Jameson has written, this *anti*-interpretive method can be, and often *is*, grasped "as a new hermeneutic in its own right" (*Unconscious* 23, note 7). One need only consider the number of applications to which this *non*-interpretive method has been adapted over the last twenty years to realize how frequently *anti*-logic or anti-science simply becomes co-opted as a new form of criticism applied to different textual criteria. It can therefore be asserted that every analytic method, "scientific" or not, ends with a single hermeneutic mode of its own, one which, in Wayne Booth's words,

> uses an eclectic search-and-scan technique to obtain materials from
> ... predecessors. The resulting mode then inevitably becomes, *for
> everyone else*, just one more monism to be either refuted or dissected
> in the search for useful parts.[21]

The thorny problem that remains, however, is to determine which is the "best" scientific model for a specific literary phenomenon. Clearly, the answer to this question can no longer have to do merely with metaphysical concepts, as eighteenth- and nineteenth-century aestheticians like Kant, Sainte-Beuve, or Renan would have had us believe. We can no longer look only to platonic ideas like Truth, Beauty, and Goodness when ascertaining the relative worth of a work of art. This is not because such entities do not still *exist*, but rather because we in the modern world never seem able to agree on just what they *are*. In spite of this though, certain important continental thinkers persist in proposing such models for literary texts. In France, for instance, Jean Cohen, whose *Structure du langage*

poétique (1966) established a vogue of statistical, scientific analyses
of literature, recently advanced the rather traditional idea that poetic
language ("le haut langage") is special because of the peculiar
aesthetic impact it has the reader:

> The sole purpose of all poetry is to produce, through art, a specific
> structural effect, which we can call the "dream effect," whereby
> each being and each thing, delivered from its negation, is returned
> to its own feeling-generating ["pathétique"] identity.[22]

Hoping to find poetry's particularity in the subjective area of dreams
and feelings, Cohen essentially repeats the traditional model
according to which the uniqueness of a text's formal structures
accounts for its privileged position among readers. It does not seem
to occur to him that what constitutes a dream to him might not
induce a dream-like state in others.

A second example of such a "scientific" impasse comes from the
work done by the Belgian research team, le groupe μ, originally
published in 1970 under the title *Rhétorique générale*, and translated
into English in 1981. For this group of rhetoricians, the theoretical
point of departure of their research depends on a thesis that looks
much different from Cohen's mentioned above. For them, the words-
on-the-page of a literary text are such that they actually

> end up disqualifying poetry as language. It is, certainly, the clear
> statement of these particularities [the specific words and word order]
> that reveals the nonlinguistic essence of literature.[23]

Instead of making the language of poetry "special" or "high," in
Cohen's words, the groupe μ begins with the startling assumption
that literature does not even qualify as bona fide "language," since
it is nonlinguistic. Yet, having said this, they then go on to furnish
us with page after page of formal tropes and other linguistic
"metaboles," as they call them, which would appear to characterize
the literary text. In the end, we are left with the statement that any
change in the linguistic code (a metabole) is "therefore, the necessary
condition of an ethos."[24] This ethos, moreover, turns out to be a set

of feelings generated by literature similar to the dream-like one we just saw in Cohen's formulation.

As if this were not bad enough, the groupe μ then qualifies their last statement by adding that although the metabole is the necessary condition of a special ethos, it is not a sufficient one. The said "ethos" is defined as an

> affective state raised in the receiver by a particular message ... whose *specific quality varies as a function of a certain number of parameters* (my emphasis 154)

We still do not know, however, how to define and delineate it, any more than we did Cohen's "dream effect." We are still left with, and in, the realm of the *je ne sais quoi*, the realm of the text's uniqueness, or essential *difference* that gives rise to a plurality of readings. In both instances, we thus seem merely to have learned that what makes a text special is the feeling generated by the specificity of its structures, as if we did not already realize this. To make matters worse, this whole argument becomes a study in circularity when we realize that it was this very feeling of difference that prompted the close examination of particular texts in the first place. If the text's *je ne sais quoi* caused each and every new critical reading, it hardly seems adequate to say that an analogous sentiment is also the *effect* of such analyses. We still have no idea why any other text, literary or non-literary, "great" or "trashy," should not, or could not, be used to prove the same points. So, if changes in "normal" linguistic codes are necessary, but not sufficient, to explain literature, then using and studying them in relation to certain texts only (and not all texts) are exceedingly problematic acts. It does not suffice to state this without recognizing the concomitant limitations of one's own scientific method.

Besides these Continental theorists, many Anglo-American critics have of course also dealt with the issue of interpretation. Studying the relationship between ordinary language-processing and the reading of literature, they have sought to understand these differences by first locating the common points of a text that most people can agree are in fact "there." As with their Continental scientific counterparts,[25] their preliminary goal has been to locate specific linguistic traits that most people can find. They begin to part ways with the former critics, however, when they consider the important role *difference* plays in all interpretations of the same works. I.A. Richards, for instance, accepts the co-existence of readerly disagreements, but adds this significant caveat:

> When two readers differ, they can discover and locate and describe their differences of interpretation only thanks to their consent together on other points.[26]

Richards acknowledges the appearance of differences of opinion, but implies that they pose no great theoretical problem in and of themselves. This is because, for Richards, consent, or what we might call "interpretive identity," saves the day for all otherwise unsettled and disagreeing critics. Another theorist with a similar view is Michael Riffaterre, who does not so much deny difference as he does simply relegate it to a secondary place of importance within the context of literary interpretation. For him, one of the toughest questions in criticism is this:

> Why, despite diversity of cultures, changing times, evolving ideologies—why do readers so often agree upon the interpretation of a literary work of art?[27]

Riffaterre's rhetorical question seems to fly in the face of years of evidence to the contrary. Instead of recognizing the plurality of readings generated over the years by any and all of the classic texts on which he himself works, Riffaterre dismisses them all in one fell swoop with the suggestion that when it comes down to brass tacks, as it were, we all tend to agree on the important points. In other words, disagreement exists for Riffaterre, but clearly this fact is not, in his mind, important for critics doing particular textual analyses. Nor is it anything to worry about for the theorist who wishes to generalize about the literary phenomenon or "event" between reader and writer.

There can be little doubt that such scientific perspectives represent well-defined methodological positions as well as ideological stances which these two critics have chosen to adopt. To emphasize identity to the well-nigh exclusion of difference is, nevertheless, equivalent to missing the peculiarity of literary works, which rarely give specific instructions[28] for their "proper" decipherment or reading. In the absence of special markers for certain kinds of privileged texts, another "simpler" scientific approach available to students of literature is to read all texts as if they were nothing more than samples of "normal" language usage. In a 1978 study, for example, George Dillon states that the reading of literature has three levels or stages: perception, comprehension, and interpretation.[29] Interestingly, the largest part of his study aims to demonstrate how each and every one of us perceives a given literary sentence. In perfectly scientific fashion, he insists that "readers process texts in the best proportional structure which renders a text grammatical"(182), something that was already known by Julia Kristéva and other members of the French *Tel Quel* group of the late sixties and seventies.

Yet, perhaps the most remarkable aspect of Dillon's book lies in its apparent inability to come to grips with his two other levels of a text's reading, i.e. its comprehension and, especially, its interpretation. Once he decides that perceiving a work's language in the above manner is the same as "processing" it, he then goes on to suggest that what makes literature great is how it requires "complex processing" on the part of readers. The last chapter of his study finally examines some of the "values," aesthetic or otherwise, that he attributes to such complex processing (170-181). The best value he can find reminds us, ineluctably, of the kind of vague affective experience with which one has now become all too familiar. For what Dillon concludes is that performing complex processing is an act that leads us to experience a special kind of consciousness. As if that were not already vague enough, he then adds to our general confusion by supplying the following truism: the intrinsic value of such an experience is simply "the value one places on that experience" (181)! In other words, in spite of potential widespread agreement on the *perceptual* level of a text, we are invited to entertain the notion that his other two levels, *comprehensive* and *interpretive*, are literally up for grabs. Thus, what he ultimately appears to be asserting is that we as individual readers can comprehend a work and interpret it in any way whatsoever, provided that these different ways lead to some type of change in the consciousness of each of us. Furthermore, each experience of this different consciousness will be of varied intensity and nature, since it depends on the worth we as individuals wish to place on it.

In this manner, we see how yet another (Anglo-American) scientific approach fails to live up to its maker's wish when confronted with the question of variant or plural readings. Though Dillon sets out to study the common practices found in the processing of any language use in order to discover the specific processes involved in reading literature, he ends up realizing that a reader's *subjectivity* is what really differentiates the latter from the former. This is why his initial examination of the objectivity of literature's language, of literature's specificity, leads him to a dead end. The dead end in question turns out to be found outside of the text, in readers. To be even more precise, Dillon's articulation of the critical process suggests that literature's specificity lies somewhere *between these two poles*, making the whole question still more complex than one might expect from a simple either/or-type situation. This is one more good reason for thinking that in changing our approach to the "problem" of literary pluralism, one needs to move "from texts to readers (and back)," as our chapter's title indicates.

A third recent scientific model[30] of this sort limits itself to poetry alone, rather than to all "literary" language. In the stylistic theory proposed by Timothy Austin, the author sets out to explicate

> the relationship between readers' shared syntactic competence and their similarly shared "experience" of a given text ... [For] at least some aspects of the literary experience of that text *will* be shared by all its readers. [Thus] the stylist merely seeks to discover the means by which language's role in shaping that experience is exercised"
> (11).

In many ways, Austin's ideas begin where Dillon's leave off. For him, too, there are three phases or levels through which the (scientific) stylistic critic needs to pass: the technical, perceptual or aesthetic, and interpretive. To his credit, Austin explains and illustrates his three levels far more completely than does Dillon. In his discussion of poems by Dryden and Byron, for instance, he points out how both poets succeed in creating an aesthetic effect by delaying, syntactically, certain parts of their verses. This stylistic trait, scientifically described by the analytical Austin, is said to be shared by the two writers. His subsequent observation of recurrent "syntactic patterns within poetic segments of the same arbitrary length ... rather than their mere presence in the text" (88) then allows him to characterize Augustan verse in contra-distinction to Romantic verse.

But, once again, the closer Austin gets actually to *interpreting* his data, the more our familiar problem of limitations begins to rear its ugly head within his stated, scientific literary model:

> stylistics will disregard at its peril the completely independent (and independently complex) role of aesthetics in the functioning of syntax as a medium for poetic expression (94).

One gets the impression from this kind of warning that the practice of locating commonly agreed-upon traits is fine as long as one does not have to *say* what exactly it is that one has found. Austin admits as much himself a little later on in his book when he confesses that

> the stylist may quite easily find himself with a great deal to say at one level of analysis [usually technical] ... yet be unable to take even the most preliminary steps toward an interpretive generalization (107).

Like the other scientific critics already examined, Austin thus cannot get beyond a purely descriptive kind of literary commentary. Instead, he contents himself with noting that:

> To the extent that stylistics rests [...] on linguistic bedrock [...] the
> interpretive stylist enjoys as good a chance as anyone of promoting [...]
> his critical insights into a given work (131).

As one can see, all of these theorists deal scientifically with the relationship between the plurality of readings that a given literary text generates, and the text's undisturbed, pure *difference*. They accomplish this by examining the various segmentations and reconstructions performed on texts by individual readers. Like most other objects in the world, texts have, after all, their own identities as marks on a page, whether or not people know how to read these marks "properly" or not.[31] On the other hand, the anti-scientific mode currently fashionable in some sectors of literary studies today would have us believe that certain texts are so radically different that they are not subject to the same type of analytic scrutiny to which most of us have become accustomed in other instances. A case in point is provided by a recent study of the works of T.S. Eliot and Wallace Stevens.[32] The author of this study, Michael Beehler, suggests that certain discourses cannot be reduced, segmented, or re-formulated in any idiom other than the ones they themselves embody.

Instead of singling out particular authors whose works function this way, however, one needs to ask why such modern beliefs seem to have to be limited to certain works and authors alone, and not others. Why can we not assume that, in theory anyway, *all* works deserve this special (non)treatment? Should we simply stop reducing works to a few notable or "key" passages and words, and thereby leave them alone so that they might signify "differently" ad infinitum? My own view is that we have an alternative here about which a decision must be made. The alternative is that we either leave all texts alone to exist as "pure differences" in the world (leaving aside the messy ontological question of what "pure difference" could really mean before symbolic articulation); or else we choose to talk about, or otherwise, analyze them. To choose the first option, as Beehler does, is to insist that

> if the repetition of insistent difference [particularly in Eliot and
> Stevens] suggests, on the one hand, a homogenizing uniformity, it
> at the same time affirms difference as pure difference, as an
> incessently heterogeneous and differentiating process without
> cognitive core or essential immanence (4).

In choosing to read literature in this manner, one precludes any
possibility of translatable or interpretable meaning above and beyond
that which inheres in the original words used by a given writer. In
essence, this choice leads one (Beehler) to the following position:

> The reiteration of difference ... prohibits a reductive thematization
> or conceptualization of difference; rather, it underscores the
> fundamental irreducibility of difference by allowing it to resonate
> with identity as the doubled voice of a problem, one ceaselessly
> redeployed rather than finally reduced (4).

Yet, what Beehler and critics similar to him seem to ignore in
making statements like this, is that the largest part of his and other
similar studies nonetheless lies beyond these ideologically-laden
preliminaries. It is all fine and good to *think* that one has avoided
"thematization or conceptualization of difference" simply by saying
one has. But to proceed then to thematize and conceptualize, by
means of hundreds of pages of examples and illustrations, the same
intrinsic, irreducible, pure "difference" supposedly found in the
works of Eliot and Stevens (or anyone else) is to contradict the thrust
of the initial theoretical stance. All one really has the right to do in
this respect is either to say that the works are radically *different*, and
to leave them alone to their own un-appropriated inner voices; or
else, one must admit that any further commentary, analysis, or
examination constitutes the very formalistic thematization which
appeared, at first, to be anathema to the anti-scientific critic. In other
words, it is not really a question of being a scientific critic or not,
for everyone who reads literature for a living, or for some purpose
other than mere pleasure and edification, *is* scientific to some extent,
as we see in the present case. Everyone who reads *critically* perforce
reads analytically and, *a forteriori*, scientifically. This is because
everyone who reads with a critical eye needs pragmatic limits to

his/her own discourse, as well as to the scrutinized text's discourse. Without these limits, the articulation of any argument (or *non-argument*) whatsoever becomes unimaginable. One, therefore, has to wonder whether the simple wish to be somehow anti-scientific is sufficient for this to be so.

Remembering the consequences of Pirandello's theatrical dictum, "It is so, if you think so," I should like to insist that we not accept this wish as sufficient. I want to argue that it is time for literary theorists and critics to reject such rhetorical sleight-of-hand. Beehler himself seems to reject it unconsciously when he recognizes the *pragmatic* double bind in which he finds himself right from the start. No sooner does he insist on the "pure difference" of the poems of Eliot and Stevens than he proceeds to quote from Henri Bergson's *Creative Evolution*:

> it is most often "expedient to disregard this uninterrupted change"
> [the text's pure difference] and imagine that which is "indifferent
> and unchangeable"— an immanent "ego," for example, whose
> uniform identity can be said to be repeated in difference and change
> (2).

Further on, he refers to William James' *A Pluralistic Universe*, saying:

> From any point of view, from any provisional, conceptual center,
> "something always escapes" resolution, "something else is self-
> governed and absent and unreduced to unity," and it is this
> insistently irreducible difference that James' universe suggests (15).

To my mind, very little about these philosophic statements can be contested. But the real issue for our purposes here is to ascertain how anyone so concerned as Beehler with the "irreducible difference" of a work still manages to find so much to say about it! If one prefers it expressed another way, the problem with the anti-scientific approach to literature as I see it is this: how can one *say* so much about what a work does *not* say? Proportionally speaking, what a text actually says should account, logically, for the largest part of any commentary made about it, even by advocates of its "pure difference." Failing that, the theorist is at a loss to know at any given point of a reading of a literary reading why it bothers to focus on any particular text at all, to the exclusion of others. Are we really prepared to say that talking about text X gives one the right to talk about any *other* single text as much as, or perhaps even more than, text X? I think not. The reason I think not is, once again, pragmatic. Most often in the profession,[33] whenever a reading deals more with *The Color Purple* than with *The Tin Drum* (when, let's say, the German novel was in fact chosen as the primary text for critical analysis), such a reading is simply qualified as one that has gone off on a tangent, as having not stuck "to the point."

Still, there are those who might argue that no such "point" exists, and that to move away from "it" is theoretically justifiable. Indeed, the whole subject of comparative literary studies seems grounded on this very issue. Theoretically speaking, I cannot deny that this objection has much weight. From a primarily deconstructive perspective, it can be argued that one does not write *about* a text or texts, but rather *from* ("à partir de") them. Yet, what I should like to underscore here is that if this is what really happens in most critical acts, we are forced to admit that much recent literary criticism and theory have been produced in remarkably bad faith. For most criticism and theory purport to concern themselves with specific works like *Madame Bovary* or *Bleak House*, and not just about what other texts and discourses those texts give rise to. Consider in this regard the titles of most articles, books, reviews, and professional papers. It does not take much searching among such titles before one discovers a very large number of specific allusions to particular works by particular authors.

What this means then is that if deconstruction and other supposedly *anti*-scientific approaches[34] were always what they claimed to be, one should expect them to avoid all of the essentially linguistic trappings of more scientific criticism. Such is not the case, however. The kind of linguistic selection and segmentation of the textual fabric found in "older" or less contemporary approaches appears to be unavoidable, even for the most astute anti-scientific critic. Saying there is no particular "point" or focus because, as often happens, one cares primarily about writing *derivatively* (that is, writing criticism that appropriates and "grafts" whatever other ideas and/or texts one thinks of on to others discovered in the course of a reading), does not always jibe with what most of these critics actually *do*. Invoking Cynthia Chase's deconstruction of *Daniel Deronda*, for example, two recent linguistic theorists, Ellen Schauber and Ellen Spolsky, object to this presumably anti-scientific analysis by noting that while Chase insists on the theoretically unjustified nature of all textual "criteria" or "features," she herself nevertheless finds enough such criteria to afford her the methodological luxury of doing her own "reading." To escape this critique, it is not enough, they argue, nor is it legitimate, for Chase to refer to the structuralist notion of *bricolage*, because to do so is to hold to a scientific notion which, conceptually, runs counter to the very deconstructionist (anti)model the critic herself espouses. "Bricolage," one recalls, refers to the structuralist's tendency to grab useful methodological and conceptual tools wherever they might be found in order to justify and bolster the "scientifically" sound analysis undertaken. In the words of Schauber and Spolsky:

> Since relevant units [in *Daniel Deronda*] must be determined somehow for any pattern, including [Chase's] deconstruction, to emerge, and since deconstructionist philosophy cannot give a rationale for the discovery of any units, even while recognizing their necessity, the blanket permission for bricolage may be invoked.[35]

But, from the perspective of these two theorists, such blanket permission cannot be properly granted to Chase. One cannot, or at least should not, according to Schauber & Spolsky, invoke an anti-scientific model, e.g., deconstruction, while at the same time utilizing a completely, or even partially, scientific approach. The partially scientific approach in question consists of locating "patterns" of identity, or more usually for this kind of critic, patterns of *pure difference*, through the observation of repeated phenomena. Theoretically, one does not have the right to have it both ways. That is, one cannot have Science, and consume it, too.

Instead, people in the literary profession must face up to the fact that they live in a pragmatic world in which the notion of a "best" reading or approach can only mean something like the "most useful," "most influential," or "most persuasive." Everyone knows that what is "best" for me is not necessarily best for someone else. It, therefore, behooves us to approach the issue in the way Spolsky & Schauber have in their call for a "preference model" of literature. Their model, which subtly informs the one the present essay seeks to advance, avoids the problem of differentiating between scientific and anti-scientific models, and helps us to come to better grips with the existence of different readings of the same literary texts thanks to "its ability to accommodate new, variable, contradictory and endemically insufficient data"(7) observed by different readers and critics. In this model, readings are neither right nor wrong, but are "only assessed as relatively stronger or weaker" (8). One thus has one more reason to shift the onus of textual *difference* away from the text "itself" to its reader, and then back again, because inasmuch as *non*-linguistic factors affect readings, "readers and communities of readers weigh different [textual] factors differently" (13). This, in turn, produces many of the most significant differences found in various readings of the same texts.

What all of these methods and approaches, scientific or otherwise, have in common, consequently, is their emphasis of form over content, of function over meaning. By disregarding what a literary text "means" in order to concentrate on *how* it means, all of these methods strive to define the essential meaning-producing linguistic operations occurring between the text and readers. These operations allow readers to gather any information whatsoever from the marks on the page in front of them. The problem with these kinds of approachs is that instead of anything so sticky or problematic as an author's *intended meaning* à la E. D. Hirsch, what the critic or theorist ends up obtaining from a work is his or her *own* (intended) meaning. The content or meaning continues thereby to be present, but has changed faces, so to speak. In Wayne Booth's words, a strange kind of contra-cogito has arisen in modern literary studies whereby instead of emphasizing either the text or the author of the text, we now have critic/readers aggrandizing themselves, suggesting that

> I [the critic] invent new readings, therefore, you, the author *are not*.[36]

We have no good reason, therefore, to believe in what Michel Foucault referred to as the fixity of a supposed "author." Calling this historically shifting function, as Hirsch has, the text's "significance" instead of its "meaning" does not solve the basic problem. For still other more serious theoretical difficulties await theorists who rely more on form than on content when attempting to answer questions about the nature of modern literature and its study. These difficulties must be faced by critics who either implicitly or explicitly refer to the concept of literariness. In other words, they must be resolved by *most* modern critics.

To confront these final difficulties, we shall now examine one of the more problematic literary genres, the prose poem. By studying this type of marginal text, which bridges the ontological gap between literature and non-literature, I hope to finalize my case not only for a shift from texts to readers, but also for a readjustment of our theoretical attention to the area between these two supposedly "fixed" poles of the literary phenomenon. A close reading of certain exemplary prose poems, serving as the last section of this chapter, will further a collective appreciation of the relationship between critical pluralism and textual difference. Its purpose is to underscore some final points and connections that link modern pluralistic readers and writers to the texts they either analyze or produce.

The Prose Poem's Deconstruction of Literariness

> ... objects approach zero
> as their theory approaches infinity.
> — Arthur Danto, "The Death of Art"

As if the problem of the prose poem's generic status had not already been difficult enough to resolve, a number of literary critics of the last ten years or so have sought increasingly to make of this kind of writing a test case for even more elaborate methodological and epistemological hypotheses. The prose poem has slowly become in this way a pretext for many wide-ranging theoretical discussions concerning literature itself. Michel Beaujour expresses this situation quite well when he states:

> the question of the prose poem allows one to catch a glimpse of all the contradictions which tear modern aesthetics asunder.[37]

While explorations into the formal and semantic characteristics of many other types of texts have continued at a steady pace, few other examples of "literary writing" have generated as much discussion about the boundaries between poetry and prose, or even between literature and "non"-literature as this one has.[38]

For these reasons, the complications involved in discovering just what it is that makes a New Novel "new" or a Modernist poem "modern" appear insignificant, even pedantic, when compared to those that arise whenever one tries to attribute a literary heritage to the "bastard" texts of Aloysius Bertrand and Charles Baudelaire. The prose poem has thereby unleashed an inherent subversiveness of its own into the heretofore relatively stable domain of literary genres. In other words, through its shaking up of certain fundamental, albeit insufficiently examined distinctions, the prose poem has gradually been turned into an exemplary case that most anyone can cite whenever he or she needs theoretical support for the inadequacies or insufficiencies of a given generic definition.

This should not be taken to mean that prior to the appearance of such works everyone agreed on the specifics of other genres.

Nevertheless, from the late nineteenth-century positivist essays of Brunetière on the evolution of literary genres to those of his twentieth-century structuralist avatars, like Todorov and Genette, one does get the strong impression that the boundaries between them can be pure and simple. Through a reduction of heterogeneous traits of particular genres to dominant common functions, one of the favorite pastimes of many aficionados of prose poems has consisted of finding an all-inclusive definition for them. In this manner, they have sought to articulate a convincing description of the prose poem's specificity. So just when it looked safe to go out of accepted critical practice, and to admit that perhaps, when all was said and done, one did not *really* know, after all, where to draw the line between this type of literature and "non-literature," along comes Suzanne Bernard and her long cortege of contemporary critical descendants with a vengeance for locating what we might call the "right stuff" of literary art in the dissected body of the prose poem.[39]

It would seem, therefore, that this textual species now constitutes a distinct, singular object of legitimate inquiry in the world of modern literary studies. Empirically speaking, one can, after all, find collections of prose poems, articles and books on the subject, even special sessions at serious conferences devoted to them. But if, in the present serious[40] context we choose to question this belief, it is not for the sole purpose of creating a critical ruckus, of "breaking glass," as Baudelaire does in "Le Mauvais Vitrier" when he narratively expands a common French phrase figuratively meaning a scandal (*casser les vitres*) into a literal illustration of disturbing proportions. My main goal here is merely to emphasize a point that needs further making. I refer to the idea, earlier suggested by Jameson, that literature "itself" does not "itself" exist. In other words, a text's pure difference cannot be comprehended or otherwise appreciated except when it is "broken," so to speak, until its totality is segmented and articulated.

Lest one misunderstand this point, I do not wish to suggest that academicians have stopped *acting* as if "literary" texts existed. I do not mean to imply that some people in the profession are not anxious, in a certain pragmatic sense, anyway, to see the *problem* of "la chose littéraire"[41] just go away. What we have to realize, though, is that since the common emphasis in the last twenty years of criticism has shifted from the text "itself" to the reader, our conception of literature in general, and of the prose poem in particular, has to change radically. Such an idea, which is probably no longer as iconoclastic as I make it out to be, must not have us think that the field of literary studies has to be scrapped. It simply reiterates the need to re-orient our critical priorities and practices.

My contention, therefore, is that in studying the various ways the terms "prose poem" and "literariness" have been defined by contemporary theorists in the final part of this chapter, we shall find ourselves in a better position from which to reject both the belief in some common stylistic features peculiar to this so-called genre, and especially our faith in the adequacy of the concept of literariness for all literary texts. The prose poem's history will thus allow us to complete this chapter's rejection of one of the principal, albeit sometimes unstated and unrecognized, conceptual supports of modern criticism. This rejection of literariness is crucial to a proper understanding of the rest of my study of both types of literary pluralism, critical and aesthetic. The main reason why it is crucial is that it destroys one of the most durable theoretical illusions which effectively mask the *historical* (not just epistemological) roots of pluralism.

The particular form my rejection will take here can best be described as "the prose poem's deconstruction of literariness." What I like about this phrase is that it has the advantage of underlining the inevitability of this rejection for the enlightened student of literary pluralism. Using such a formula does, however, leave me open to the potential charge of having succumbed to the temptation to theorize, both here and earlier in this book. I am aware that one of the current fashions in American scholarly circles is precisely to speak out "against theory."[42] Having said that, I shall nonetheless minimize henceforth any direct references to Derridean practice, first because I am not in total agreement with it, and second, because my use of the term "deconstruction" here is more or less synonymous with the idea of a kind of semantic "self-destruction."

The prose poem, perhaps more than any other type of writing, undermines the theoretical notion of literariness for one major reason. Simply stated, the reason is that it illustrates how, outside of the manifest and latent contents of a reader's own self or selves, there is *no-thing* to which this kind of text necessarily draws his or her attention. The use here of Freudian terminology reiterates my belief that all readers of literature, at least to a large extent, read DEFTly, to borrow Norman Holland's ingenious adverb. That is, whenever we read, we continually perceive words through our personal *d*efenses, *e*xpectations, *f*antasies, and *t*ransformations. We do so in such a way that we end up reproducing *ourselves* in the formal and semantic particulars we claim to find within the fabric of the texts under scrutiny.[43] The text's "unity," or lack thereof, derives in this sense from our own canonical, conventional notions of what makes any literary work either a unified whole or an anarchic linguistic event.

Now, if we recall that the notion of literariness consists of those very semantic and formal aspects of a work that, it is said, make most, if not all, readers take note of them, the legitimate counter-argument can be made that these same aspects of prose poems *exist* only insofar as someone in particular notices them. In choosing to bring these textual features out of what Barthes calls their otherwise "silent existence,"[44] the reader/critic symbolically articulates a different ontic status for them as bona fide "forms" within the confines of a text's margins. Significant forms thus magically appear on a prose poem's textual surface, a surface that is not immediately perceived as being significant, the way in which a sonnet, for instance, would be more readily perceived by most critical readers. Unlike other "non-aesthetic" objects, the majority of whose formal representations in language do not inhibit most people from accepting them as *really* being-in-the-world, prose poems become what they are in direct proportion to one's willingness to make them literary. This is why Derrida's notion of *le devenir-littéraire du littéral*,[45] of the becoming-literary-of-the-literal, is probably nowhere more pressing an issue to confront than it is in the context of the prose poem.

Even so, one may object that all texts require readers to take an active role in producing their literariness or "poeticity." It seems to me reasonable, in fact, that at some point or other in the description of what makes "a verbal message a work of art"—to borrow Jakobson's classic formulation of the concept of literariness—one should accept this essentially phenomenological view of literature as a dynamic interaction between text and reader. Where the prose poem stands out over other kinds of writing, however, is in the precise and immediate manner in which, historically, it took its distance from earlier literary genres. When Baudelaire, for example, first set out to try something "analogous," as he says in the dedicatory note to *Le Spleen de Paris*, to what Aloysius Bertrand had done in *Gaspard de la Nuit*, he soon realized that he remained

> bien loin de [s]on mystérieux et brillant modèle/very far from his mysterious and brilliant model.[46]

For our purposes, it is unfortunate, though indubitably significant, that he did not then give any specific details which might have helped us articulate the specificity of Bertrand's model. If he had really wished us to understand exactly why he felt so far afield from the prototypical text provided by Bertrand, we could surely have expected something a little more substantial with which to make our own evaluation or comparison. As it happens, Baudelaire even goes on a few sentences later in this famous preface to his friend Arsène Houssaye to ask whether his prose poems are *any-thing* at all. Contemplating his final products, he notes simply that they are

> quelque chose (si cela peut s'appeler *quelque chose*) de singulièrement différent/something (if that can be called *something*) singularly different.

Hence, what Baudelaire seems interested in is not so much those exact features of his generic model which he succeeds in copying, as it is in the supposed singular quality of his own creation. The questions of what he copied, and of how well he succeeded or failed in copying "it," seem of little import to him.

Already then, after examining just one historic relationship between two undisputed "prose poets," we must confront the dilemma of someone who claims to write within a certain generic tradition, but who is nonetheless unable to define formally this genre in the least. In his 1916 preface to *Le Cornet à Dés*, Max Jacob adds to our confusion when he insists that for a prose poem to exist:

> [il] doit se soumettre aux lois de tout art, qui sont le style ou volonté et la situation ou émotion/it must submit itself to the laws of all art, which are style or will, and situation or emotion.[47]

While Jacob remains satisfied with such a pat non-definition, one cannot help but notice that in invoking these vague general laws of art, he, too, neatly avoids the entire issue of the prose poem's generic specificity. Yet, curiously, he, too, maintains, just as Baudelaire does, that whatever this "something" called a prose poem is, it is assuredly *not* something already known, a previous model. As he contends later in the same paragraph,

> une page en prose n'est pas un poème en prose/a page of prose is not a prose poem.

Nowhere in Jacob's preface, however, does one find the slightest justification for this statement. In the light of André Breton's very liberal conception of a poem, defined in his more or less contemporary *Manifeste du Surréalisme* as

> ce qu'on obtient par l'assemblage aussi gratuit que possible [...] de titres et de fragments découpés dans les journaux/"that which is obtained by the most gratuitous asssembly possible of headlines and fragments cut out of newspapers,"[48]

Jacob's statement strikes me as utterly baseless. Whether he had any more precise idea of what made for a valid "page of prose" than Baudelaire had of what constituted the "brilliant and mysterious model" that he tried to emulate remains open to question. Saying that such and such a writer "situated" his works better than others, without giving at the same time some very specific examples of what he means is tantamount to saying not much at all. When it comes to the formal description of what one is doing as a "prose poet," the consequent rule seems to be this: for lack of a better critical lexicon and framework, one can always depend on the infamous *je ne sais quoi* of earlier aesthetic theory and criticism to rescue him or her from the necessity to be more specific.

From its very inception, therefore, the prose poem, though continually thought to be an original and distinct artistic object of critical scrutiny, is cut off from specific generic affiliation. As Hermine Riffaterre argues, "[it] is an entire genre born of [an] elimination principle."[49] Neither poets themselves nor commentators seem capable of successfully rejoining them to any particular scriptural practice. What is perhaps most significant though, is that these same individuals always *try*. At all costs, modern readers and writers alike are committed to saving these hybrids, as if the survival of larger, "fitter" literary genres, perhaps Literature itself, depended on it. Because no one can say for sure what it must, or must not be, the prose poem thereby obliges us to examine more carefully its idiolectic shape. In this sense, it would appear to manifest Jakobson's twin concepts of "literariness" and the "poetic function" in exemplary fashion.

Moreover, since this function draws a reader's attention to the specific form of a message, ironically enough, prose poems are more "poetic" to most critics than standard verse. Lacking well-defined models to duplicate, they make it incumbent on the reader to synthesize poeticity (not to receive it ready-made, as it were) from his or her appraisal of the words on the page. This appraisal invariably involves comparison with the stock devices of other "monumental" examples of verbal art, i.e. unquestioned examples of *true* literature. So the less a text appears at first to be literary in terms of stylistic conventions, paradoxically, the more it induces readers to read in such a way as to compensate for its missing links with literary tradition.

Small wonder then that Michael Benedikt, to cite but one case, sees the prose poem as merely a "different" version of poetry:

it is a genre of poetry, self-consciously written in prose, and
characterized by the intense use of devices of verse ....[50]

Eminently aware of the Tradition, as T.S. Eliot would call it,
Benedikt and others make the prose poem into a new "genre" where
there was none before. Of course, this type of text does repeat
certain stylistic aspects encountered elsewhere in literature. But it is
equally true that part of its nature consists in its rejection of earlier
devices. In Suzanne Bernard's words:

> il y a *à la fois* dans le poème en prose une force anarchique,
> destructrice, qui porte à nier les formes existantes, et une force
> organisatrice, qui tend à construire un "tout" poétique; et le terme
> même de *poème en prose* souligne cette dualité/there is *at the same
> time* in the prose poem an anarchic, destructive force [the text
> itself?] which leads it to deny existing forms, and an organizing
> force [the reader/critic?], who tends to construct a poetic 'whole' (p.
> 444).

From this angle, reading these desciptions of that pure textual
difference known as the "prose poem" should remind us of
statements by Bergson and James quoted earlier concerning the
understanding of any object in the world. All objects, all texts, can
either come "alive" or "die," according to when and how the
observer/critic behaves in regard to them. Yet, the prose poem, as
it evolved historically, must also be regarded as the limit of the
notion of "literature itself." One can define it as any short text
which, by dint of transgressing the canons of accepted literary
discourses, borders on a non-literary or "para-literary" discourse.

As with another literary cannon/canon rolling furiously out of
control on a ship in Victor Hugo's novel *Quatre-Vingt Treize*, the
prose poem, however, appears not only to transgress, but actually to
batter down the critical walls that separate different generic
categories into neat little packages of specific stylistic traits.[51] To
this extent, it makes the reader's burden heavier than it is when one
is faced with an instance of a genre antedating that instance. It also
thereby appears perfectly suited, as the marginally-literary text that
it is, to the theorist who seeks further answers to the question of

plural modern readings of literature. The prose poem projects the reader "downward" so to speak, from the generic level of textuality to a work's less extensive features; that is, to its particular syntactic structures and component lexemes. The reader must descend into its perforce *non*-generic parameters in search of other stylistic features needed to produce commentary or criticism. Were readers to remain at the level of genre, they would quickly realize—as the above examination of Baudelaire and Jacob already indicates—that *practically* nothing exists that could be used as a measure or standard with which to determine a given prose poem's specificity. Again, the operative function pertinent to our discussion here is that of the modern reader's needs or desires, his volition to make *literary* that which would otherwise remain *literal*, as Derrida formulated it.

Characterized then less by an absence of poetic devices than by a conspicuously antagonistic relationship with them, the prose poem simply subverts the domain of the literary, and shows it to be so many moments in the history of prescriptive aesthetics. This relationship is antagonistic because most of these poetic features are repeated only in order to be negated, or otherwise distorted. One thinks in this respect of Rimbaud's prose passage titled (paradoxically) "Sonnet," which forms the second section of the prose poem "Jeunesse" in his *Illuminations*. The title inevitably forces readers to fight with the text, as it were, for the purpose of turning the prose into something—a sonnet—which it clearly is *not*. Yet, no matter how hard one tries to twist or turn the prosody of the text in order to make it conform to a more standardized poetic mold one never really succeeds in any convincing fashion.[52]

Likewise, in Jacob's collection *Cornet à Dés*, the numerous prose poems called simply "Poème" defy readers' expectations and induce them into seeking out something about those texts that justifies the otherwise paradoxical label they are given. (We shall have much more to say about the first of these "poems" shortly.) So, to borrow Barbara Johnson's neat formula, we can state that,

> le poème en prose est une répétition de la poésie, à travers laquelle
> la poésie se différencie rétrospectivement d'elle-même/the prose

poem is a repetition of poetry, through which poetry differentiates itself from itself.[53]

This peculiar type of text deflates earlier attempts to describe and classify other examples of "literature" by exposing the transitoriness, even arbitrariness of the concept of genre. It calls into question the belief that other genres are universally agreed-upon sign-posts by which a work enters into a communion with the world of Literature. It forces us to ask whether there can be one, and only one, definition of a given genre. Yet, at the same time, the prose poem appears as a marvelous illustration of the permanence of literari*ness*. Although texts worthy of aesthetic privilege vary according to the time and place in which they are written, their capacity to call attention to their form is, once again (according to Jakobson, at least), what ultimately ties them all together into an ostensibly homogeneous category. From this point of view, the various literary *points de repères*, or always-already-valorized models they bring into relief, constitute the actual foundation for the qualifier "literary," or lack thereof. These models are the actual artistic monuments which assure a "proper" literary status for prose poems. Insofar as they are *like* literature then, we do not hesitate to assume that they, too, exhibit literariness.

Let us reflect a bit longer, however, on this deceptively simple, indeed, tautological nature of the prose poem's literariness. In two remarkable passages from his *Introduction du Poème en Prose*,[54] Maurice Chapelan unknowingly reveals the reasons why the student of literary pluralism must question the text's intrinsic power to call attention to itself. Chapelan's words also represent additional reasons to think that the specific problem of *critical* pluralism cannot be properly addressed without first accepting the general methodological shift from texts to readers sketched out so far. I have selected these passages both because they are derived from the very first full-length collection and critical assessment of French prose poems (published in 1946), and also because they indicate extraordinarily well why we must stop trying to situate poeticity in texts themselves.

Having "established" that what makes a prose poem literature is the way it resembles other literary texts (poems), and having done so

just as tautologically as the other critical sources cited earlier in this
chapter did, Chapelan suddenly admits the following:

> Que le poème en prose soit véritablement un poème, l'acquiescement
> de la sensibilité de chacun peut seul en apporter la preuve: sa vertu
> poétique [pourtant], *ce n'est pas en lui, c'est en nous*, au coeur des
> ondes qu'il y propage, qu'il convient en dernier ressort de *l'aller
> chercher/*That the prose poem is truly a poem, the acquiescence of
> everyone's sensitivity alone can prove this fact: its poetic virtue
> [however], *does not lie in it, but in us*, in the heart of the waves it
> emits is where we should *seek it* in the final analysis (emphasis mine
> p. xvi).

In other words, for Chapelan, the prose poem's essential difference,
its poeticity, does not so much lie within the fabric of the text itself,
but within the reader who reads it. In addition, when he attempts to
justify his grouping of texts on the basis of some non-existent
stylistic or generic commonality, Chapelan confesses that he will
only admit within the ranks of the prose poem those

> oeuvres dont les auteurs ont reconnu, de quelque façon, qu'elles *le
> voulaient être/*whose authors recognized, in one way or other, that
> they *wanted them to be admitted* (p. xvii, emphasis mine).

What we gather from the circularity of the prose poem's critical
history, therefore, is a fact of great importance to anyone interested
in understanding why the belief in modern literary pluralism
continues to grow unchecked. The fact is this: Whenever we read a
text, we are less in the presence of what I shall call "stories *for*
reading" than of what Jonathan Culler refers to as "stories *of*
reading."[55] That is, a prose poem cannot be defined in terms of
what it says, nor of how it says it, nor even of how it draws
attention to "itself." The only necessary, though assuredly not
sufficient, reason for thinking a prose poem special is that someone
has either needed or wanted to read into it something always-already
special. For lack of better textual evidence provided by less
problematic genres, modern critics thus tend to fall back onto the
prose poem in order to collect what may well be all too convenient

data for their personal, pluralistic reading theories, i.e. their stories of how they read literature.

Of course, one does not have to look far to discover a potentially serious problem with such an hermeneutic *modus operandi*. The critics who proceed in this manner never really ask themselves whether there is anything that "special" about the always-already-valorized monuments or, what we could call "intertextual supports" they find retrieved, re-articulated, or otherwise repeated partially or *in toto* by the prose poem under scrutiny. Sometimes, for instance, the scriptural "monument" lending its intertextual support is a different established genre, like the sonnet in the aforementioned example of Rimbaud's "Sonnet." In reality, however, the poet who chooses such a title does more to deny the importance of sonnets than he does to underscore it. After all, Rimbaud's "Sonnet," we saw, is *not* a real sonnet.

To choose that word as a title, consequently, suggests that Rimbaud, as reader of his own text, prefers to see (prose) poetry move beyond or away from this no longer acceptable generic option, as if that earlier stylistic model were not worth much of anything to someone interested in being an "absolutely modern" poet like him. In this sense, Rimbaud's prose poem draws attention to itself by first re-invoking what is not *itself* (a sonnet), and then assumes a more modern form whose very peculiarity suggests that the earlier form was, in fact, dismissible all along. Somewhere along the line, the concept of a *truly* legitimate literary form thereby disappears, never to be heard from again. Thus, one's attention is hardly being drawn to something in particular—be it a sonnet or a prose poem—since it is instead left suspended in a kind of limbo between two different discursive forms.

Seeing these forms in this way makes clear that the concepts of formal superiority or privileged position are little more than utopian chimeras, reinforced by *and* reinforcing, certain ideological and historical presuppositions and prejudices. For sometimes a common phrase (not some specifically "literary" monument) serves as an adequate linguistic grounding or support for the writing of a prose poem. Let us consider, for example, the oft-quoted French phrase,

Après moi, le Déluge!/"After me, let the Flood come!" This phrase subtends the entire text of Rimbaud's first *Illumination*, appropriately titled "Après le déluge." In the latter poem, images of renewed life-activity combine to create a newly cleansed world whose exact spatio-temporal situation is open to speculation. With small animals coming back out from their safe hiding places, beavers again building, mazagrans again steaming in the watering-holes, and stands re-opened for business, nature or Life itself seems to return to its normal state; normal, that is, until the poet orders the waters to inundate once again this mysterious realm whose location and significance are apparently known only to an enigmatic Queen, the Witch.

Yet, regardless of what the prose poem *means*, it is incontestable that in large part it functions as an act of understandable communication *at very least* because it recalls the aforementioned phrase. The title, composed of a truncated saying that would normally express the speaker's total indifference to events that might occur after one's death, signifies in at least two different ways that any reader can ascertain. First, it invokes the idea of *the* (Biblical) Flood. Second, it quite literally eliminates the subject ("I" or "We") who figures into the original quotation. Because of the dual signification of the title, the narrator who tells the waters, "... montez et *relevez les* Déluges"/"Rise up and regenerate the Floods [my emphasis]" actually undermines the significance of the historical Flood as a singular cataclysmic event. This finally forces us to ask just to whom this new voice belongs. In other words, the reader cannot help but wonder at some point about the nature of a mind that would question the validity of the Biblical Flood in this way.

One can thus easily understand how some readers might want to interpret the presuppositions of this command addressed to the waters as textual "proof" of Rimbaud's revolutionary character or ideology.[56] No longer certain of the number of times this Flood is presumed to have occurred, the reader knows only that the poetic universe invoked by Rimbaud comes into being *afterwards*. It matters little what came before. The poem reads as if what was really important to the narrator can in no way be construed to be the creator of this "illumination" himself, nor this imagined world in and of itself. It seems instead to imply that the scenes depicted, like those in any other real or imagined cosmos, should or even must be continually destroyed or left behind, i.e. *surpassed* by others, in the manner of a quasi-permanent revolution. In this respect, Rimbaud can be seen as a kind of prefiguration of one of Mao's Red Guards. To be sure, no explanation or justification for this idea of a continuous upheaval is given by Rimbaud, although he does refer to "l'idée du Déluge," and not the Flood itself. Thanks to his title, the notion of an eternally-recurring aftermath is nonetheless implicit in what he has written.

Whatever the case, the reading I have done of this prose poem hardly makes the common phrase "Après moi, le déluge" an exemplary reference-point from which one can judge the aesthetic power or value of Rimbaud's text itself. All one can say is that the poet has played with a well-known phrase that can be read underneath, as it were, the body of the present text. Such a statement does not in the least explain how the common has become uncommon, nor how the literal has become literary, to conjure up anew the ghost of Derrida. We have only spun our hermeneutic circle around one half-time more, like some kind of defective Wheel of Fortune, seeing "literature" suddenly rear its beautiful head in a place where merely "common" discourse had first appeared. As a result, we must resign ourselves to the knowledge that we still have not come any closer to solving the puzzle of the prose poem. Thinking one has isolated a portion of the literariness of this "Illumination," one has merely called into question the epistemological status of the very support one relied on heavily to explain it in the first place. For one must ask oneself whether the saying "Après moi ... " constitutes a sufficiently *special* building block with which the reader constructs a "literary monument," to use Michael Riffaterre's term for the semiotic construct that results from the production and proper analysis of a literary text.[57] If it does (which I myself believe), then we are forced to accept the idea that "ordinary" language can draw attention to itself just as readily as "literary" language can.

This realization, however, still does not entirely solve the more germane problems for us here, the problems of how or why a given text necessarily draws attention to itself, and of why the same textual entity, theoretically understood as pure undifferentiated difference, gives rise nowadays to an ever-greater plurality of readings. To be sure, the Rimbaldian example just discussed underscores the centrality of our previous general *linguistic* knowledge in establishing a text's so-called "literariness." But such cognitive re-creation just as often involves a specific *literary* competence as well. In many cases, for example, earlier literary conventions or themes provide readers with the intertextual backdrop or support they require to articulate the literariness of a given prose poem, as in Baudelaire's "Les Projets" ("Plans"). On at least one level of its functioning as a semiotic entity, the latter text plays off the whole Romantic obsession with travel (best exemplified perhaps by Gautier, Nerval, and, of course, Baudelaire himself), as well as off the dissatisfaction and radical disabuse experienced by those poets upon reaching any of their respective destinations, be it the Parthenon in Greece, Roman ruins in Italy, or the pyramids in Egypt. At some point in our differing responses to the work, Baudelaire's prose poem functions as an act of communication precisely because its narrator ends up *rejecting* the need to find a perfect (literary) place where, as he says, he may "possess the dear life of his beloved" (*posséder sa chère vie*). The narrator decides instead to travel mentally, as it were, while he remains at home, believing that "the plan in and of itself is an adequate joy."

Therefore, the usual choice of certain privileged travel destinations or locations (in the case of Baudelaire's fantasizing here, a beautiful palace, an exquisite tropical setting, a lovely cabin by the sea, and a clean and inviting inn) provides the primary motivation and, one might even say, "literary" interest of this text. Yet, *in the very process of writing about these places*, the poet has actually undermined their absolute value as special places reserved for poetic or otherwise highly romanticized treatment. After all, he has chosen *not* to go to any of these places, preferring instead to stay home without having to "constrain [his] body to change its position." In this sense, the significance of these places is *extrinsic* to them, and *intrinsic* to readers who have previously valorized them through a kind of cultural hypostasis. Readers with the "proper" literary background will, of course, transform tropical islands and beautiful palaces into conventional, and consequently, significant literary places. In so doing, they make these and other places into *topoi*, in the strictest sense of that term. But, the reader unaware of the unquestioned importance of earlier literary places can hardly be expected to recognize the "literariness" of any present texts that play with such previous models. To say that prose poems illustrate more than other genres the relevance of literariness thus, once again, merely defers the prose poem problem rather than answers it.

There have also been at least two attempts to make prose poems literary by seeking out pictorial structures within them that resemble paintings or other icons, to borrow Charles Sanders Peirce's term. Such readings transform prose poems into concrete or visual works that inevitably recall Apollinaire's more deliberate, conscious scriptural experiments in his *Calligrammes*.[58] Graphemic shapes found in the body of a specific text are shown to re-invoke other visual signs that have already been valorized elsewhere: either "outside" of the text, as examples of historically recognized art shapes and forms; or "inside" the same prose poem, as iconic reminders of various narrative aspects already developed by the text.[59] Since they are not "literary," therefore, in any apparent way (i.e. in any traditional way through a primarily *lexical* concatenation), these prose poems find themselves suddenly transfigured by the reader's own extra-literary, artistic competence, as if any artistic form whatsoever were intrinsically pertinent to the study of literature per se. Given the dubious relevance of these extra-literary supports[60] to the study of literary texts, we begin to see why some of the other more conventional ones already mentioned may be equally defective in their capacity to ground the literariness of prose poems. The more one tries to determine what constitutes the conventionality of such literary conven-tions, the more one is led away from actual texts to other factors. One soon realizes that in talking about literary conventions, one is concerned less with discursive than with historical phenomena. Upon closer inspection literary "facts" reveal themselves to be situated very specifically in time and place within particular aesthetic systems, and are in no obvious way transhistorical in nature.

Moreover, aesthetic criteria or subject-matter hitherto considered *non*-literary are often applied and promoted to a higher "literary" status in a newer work, as we saw in "Après le Déluge." This means that any attempt to define a given text's literariness in terms of anything other than that text itself would be doomed to fail inasmuch as the other texts used to "prove" its literary affiliations would only serve to defer the question of what made any or all of those other texts literary as well. Indeed, two of the same Russian Formalists who most exploited the notion of literariness, Chlovsky and Tynianov, allude precisely to the debt newer literature has to a so-called non-literary realm made up of texts like diaries, travel logs, and letters.[61] In Tynianov's words:

> il n'est pas un genre constant, mais variable, et son matériau linguistique, *extra-littéraire*, aussi bien que la manière d'introduire ce matériau en littérature, changent d'un système à l'autre. Les traits mêmes du genre évoluent./there is no constant genre, but a variable one, and its linguistic matter, *extra-literary*, as well as the manner of introducing this matter into literature, change from one system to another. Even the traits of a genre evolve (my emphasis 126).

In other words, one can only evaluate a text within a system, a system which, when further examined, turns out to be *sui generis*, unique in its own genre. It cannot be understood only in terms of opposition to some supposed privileged tradition or hypostasized monument. The critic or student of literature must instead consider the individual work, as Tzvetan Todorov suggests, primarily in "its relation to other forms of discourse [...] as exchange and transformation."[62] Todorov refers here to one of the major ideas advanced in Tynianov's essay "De l'évolution littéraire," when the latter states:

> Ce qui est "fait littéraire" pour une époque, sera un phénomène linguistique relevant de lr vie sociale pour une autre et inversement,

> selon le système littèraire par rapport auquel ce fait se situe./That
> which is a "literary fact" for one epoch, will be a linguistic
> phenomenon depending on the social life for another and inversely,
> according to the literary system by relation to which this fact is
> situated (*Théorie de la littérature*, p. 125).

From this point of view, literature is nothing more than just one of
the many forms of discourse which exchange and transform their
common attributes. No one form is superior to any other. A prose
poem proclaims itself "literary" by making us use other "literature"
as solid evidence for an essentially circular pronouncement. Yet, this
other, sociolectic body of literary intertexts, is an ever-changing
body of equally interdependent works whose specificity could not be
maintained outside of an historically and socially determined system
of established literature, i.e. a canon. The canon is the *type* of which
the prose poem is said to be a *token*, a slippery notion indeed when
one considers how the canon itself constantly changes.

   Victor Erlich comments on this apparent dilemma of Russian
Formalist thought in these words:

> Literary evolution brings about shifts in the hierarchy of literary
> genres as well as in the relationship between literature and other
> contiguous cultural spheres, e.g. science, philosophy, politics. Thus,
> the dominant quality of imaginative literature or of a literary species
> is subject to change. What remains constant is the very *feeling* [my
> emphasis] of divergence from non-literature.[63]

With that, we are back to the reliance on the *je ne sais quoi* feeling
noted earlier in our chapter among other critical statements,
statements which, admittedly, pertained not so much to the
specificity of prose poems as to that of literature in general.

   An instructive way to illustrate the many theoretical points just
raised is to look carefully at one of Max Jacob's own ostensible
"examples" of prose poetry, the first of his so-called "Poèmes" in
Le Cornet à Dés. Entitled simply "Poème," the text reads as follows:

"Que veux-tu de moi, dit Mercure.
—Ton sourire et tes dents, dit Vénus.
—Elles sont fausses. Que veux-tu de moi?
—Ton caducée.
—Je ne m'en sépare point.
—Viens l'apporter ici, divin facteur."
Il faut lire cela dans le texte grec: cela s'appelle Idylle. Au collège,
un ami, souvent refusé aux examens, me dit: "Si on traduisait en
grec un roman de Daudet, on serait assez fort après pour l'examen!
mais je ne peux pas travailler la nuit. Ça fait pleurer ma mère!" Il
faut lire aussi cela dans le texte grec, messieurs; c'est une idylle,
eidullos, petit tableau./

"What do you want of me, says Mercury.
—Your smile and your teeth, says Venus.
—They are false. What do you want of me?
—Your caduceus.
—I'm never away from it.
—Come bring it here, divine messenger."
One must read this in the (original) Greek text: that is called an
Idyll. In boarding school, a friend, who often failed exams, told me:
"If one were to translate a novel by Daudet, afterwards, one would
be well enough prepared for the exam! but I cannot work at night.
It makes my mother cry!" One must also read that in the Greek text,
gentlemen; it is an idyll, petit tableau.

What is there about this text that makes it into a work of art? The
reader who relies on the notion of literariness for an answer to this
question will immediately notice how this "Poème" is composed of
fourteen uncannily well-balanced lines. I purposely use the notion of
the uncanny because, as Freud demonstrated, the familiar seems
uncanny when, after first being occulted, it is then re-cognized by an
observer. This being the very first text in a series of so-called
"poèmes," the reader in possession of a modicum of literary
competence cannot help but make out the raw structure of that most
poetic of poems, the sonnet, within the fabric of the present poem.
In this game of now-you-see-it-now-you-don't, Jacob's *prose* poem
initially takes its distance, as do all the other texts in the collection,
from a traditional collection of "real" poems, i.e. *versified poems*,
only then to dare readers, as it were, to take the title literally and to

find something within the body of the work that justifies the strictly poetic appurtenance or affiliation the title implies.

This is not hard to accomplish. For, once one has agreed that the text is manifestly *not* a sonnet, one can go quite far in describing, analyzing, and interpreting it by temporarily repressing this fact, by admitting that a text which calls itself "Poème" must nevertheless somehow be a poem. Let us consider, for instance, the order of its pseudo-strophes, which can be read as an inversion of the conventional sonnet structure with the two tercets (literally, a six-line dialogue) preceding the two quatrains (eight lines). Or the repetition of the phrases "Que veux-tu de moi" and "il faut lire cela dans le texte grec," which, in the context of what we could now call an *anti-*sonnet, function as familiar kinds of refrains or codas often constitutive of traditional sonnets.

This formal skeleton of an established poetic form becomes all the more significant when it then reenacts thematically the whole literary process of reading and writing, reversing many of its most salient features. In the first place, the messenger god Mercury does not deliver anything at all, but rather receives a visit by Venus, as one might expect of the usual relation between, say, a Romantic poet like Alfred de Musset and his Muse. Yet, Mercury seems genuinely annoyed, not enchanted with this divine visitor, and eschews any type of intercourse with her whatsoever. By keeping everything to himself—his scepter, his smile, and his teeth, which are false—he rejects her repeated ouvertures to him.

In the same gesture, the reader comes to realize that in alle-gorical, or, as the narrator will shortly say, *idyllic* terms, Jacob has refused the entire notion of inspired poetry. Unlike a Musset or Hugo (or even a Surrealist like Breton), who in a certain way hoped to hear a message whispered to him, so as to have something "poetic" to communicate to his reader, this *prose-poem* character neither has, nor apparently wants, to deliver anything to anyone.[64] His unwillingness to act as the "divin facteur" he is supposed to be seems especially perverse here inasmuch as his would-be addressee, Venus—that most conventional symbol of (poetic) charm and beauty—clearly wants something from him.

In order to grasp the significance of this text even better, however, the narrator advises us to read it in the original Greek. If we did so, of course, the name we would come up with, "Hermes," would merely intensify our suspicion that what is really at stake in this work is the entire *herme*neutic enterprise itself, the process of interpreting a text so as to make it give up something it is "holding on to."[65] In other words, what is at stake is the whole procedure one follows in reading literature "properly," just as in our earlier example with Borges' tale of Pierre Menard. We might describe the procedure in the following manner: the reader of "Poème" inevitably comes to it with other poetic baggage, i.e. with a certain amount of what Culler and a host of others call "literary competence." In so doing, s/he begins interpreting it by asking it *for something,* just as Venus (or Aphrodite?) herself does of Mercury/Hermes. And, in its turn, the text (*the* parcel or message metaphorically delivered by Hermes in this exchange between reader and writer) resists giving itself, or even a part of itself (the synecdochic teeth and smile) up. As Mercury says, "Je ne m'en sépare point."

Yet, the problem of reading this prose poem is exacerbated in still another, more fundamental, fashion when the translation of this curious exchange (which Jacob calls an "Idylle") is brought up in the second part of the text. Although "idylle" in French refers to a small form or poem with pastoral subject-matter, it is also true, as Sydney Lévy indicates quite correctly, that in Greek:

> through its association with [idylle] is a "form without substance," which no theme, rural or pastoral, supports. Eidullos is a mirror image [...]. It is nothing but a film, a surface, a disembodied specter. Without being translated into French, that is, into the meaning it is given in French, it is a form that leads nothing nowhere ...[66]

Therein we find a etymological justification both for the formal mirroring of quatrains and tercets we observed earlier in our discussion, and for the thematic *mise-en-scène* of the acts of reading and writing a literary text.[67] The poem has no "point," no original or originary story-line it tries to re-present. It is instead an empty linguistic form whose sense is lost to the reader along a line of translations, a purely specular effect whose subject(matter), i.e. the dialogue, and mirrored object, i.e. the second-part commentary, are interchangeable.

Thus, "Poème" presents us with an exemplary allegory that utterly destroys any last illusions we may be harboring concerning the critical efficacy of the concepts of the words-on-the-page, the "text itself," and finally, of literariness, as tools with which to deal adequately with the general phenomenon of literary pluralism, especially its critical dimension. It does this by drawing our attention to itself as a peculiar linguistic form (an imagined dialogue between two gods), only then to keep deferring the message or content that we might otherwise be seeking to obtain from it. The second part of the poem never tells us what to make of the first part, except to insist that we need to read "it" ("cela," a twice-repeated *indefinite* pronoun replacing no particular noun, nor specific idea we can put our finger on in the dialogue) in the original Greek.

Interestingly, at the very beginning of one of the prototypical prose poem collections, Baudelaire's *Spleen de Paris*, the famous text "L'Etranger" has a extraordinarily similar dialogic form to that found in Jacob's "Poème." This bit of information is relevant here because, as Suzanne Bernard has already demonstrated, many of pieces in Baudelaire's collection did indeed serve as the models for some of Jacob's best pastiches.[68] In any event, it is a fact that in "L'Etranger," too, we have someone asking a similar simple question ("Qui aimes-tu le mieux?") of an unusual personage who never seems willing to answer in a normal, i.e. predictable way. Here is how the text begins:

> Qui aimes-tu le mieux, homme énigmatique, dis?
> Ton père, ta mère, ta soeur ou ton frère?
> -Je n'ai ni père, ni mère, ni soeur, ni frère.
> -Tes amis? .../
> "Whom do you love most, enigmatic man, pray tell?
> Your father, your mother, your sister or your brother?
> -I have neither father, nor mother, nor sister, nor brother.
> -Your friends? ..."

The syllabic structure of Baudelaire's first three lines suggests that he, too, like Jacob, was consciously or unconsciously playing with the fixed form of the sonnet; at the very least, with one of the most standard features of his *own* sonnets. Thanks to the ostensibly prosaic function-word "dis," that is, one can read those lines as attempts at legitimate alexandrine verses, the verse form so common in *Les Fleurs du Mal*. When placed at the end of the first line, "dis" forces us to pronounce the otherwise silent final syllable in "énigmati*que*," which, unfortunately, then gives 13 feet to the line when one counts that of "dis?"

But because of its tenuous place there, or, as it sometimes appears in other editions of the prose poems, at the beginning of line two (thereby successfully making the *second* line a twelve-foot verse),[69] one can hypothesize that it should be read at both places at the same time. Here we have another case of now-you-see-it-now-you-don't. For "dis?" must be read as a syllable in search of its "proper" position, an *enjambement* waiting to happen. Why else would different readers, e.g. editors, place it in different spots? This, I believe, is one of the major questions concerning proper typographical setting that editors of prose poems may never be able to answer. In large part, this is due to their not knowing what "proper" means in the case of an ill-defined, unsystematic genre like the prose poem. Baudelaire himself does not appear to have known what to do with the problem. In one of his earlier variants, in fact, he wrote "tes parents" instead of "ton père, ta mère," a phrase whose only perceivable significant difference with his final choice is that it does not contain enough syllables to induce us to read it as a proper alexandrine.[70]

But it also points to the much greater and more general problem of plural interpretations of all works. Depending on how one segments them, or re-articulates them, one effectively makes a text something other than just the "text itself." One thereby creates a continuum of *different* readings that, in practice, renders the very possibility of an ontologically "whole" text nil. One could, therefore, advance the idea that the two texts (by Baudelaire and Jacob) exploit the question and answer format in part, at least, because of their positions at the start[71] of non-verse poetry collections, where the questions act like meta-linguistic phenomena in the mind of readers trying to figure out what these "poems" *want*, what they are trying to accomplish qua literature. In this sense, Baudelaire's "Stranger" must be understood formally as a modern stylistic "alien" to the entire history of verse poetry. When asked, for example, whom he loves best among his mother, father, sister, brother, or friends, the stranger responds simply that he has no such relatives or acquaintances. When asked instead *what* he likes, his answers are similarly unsatisfying, while saying provocative things like, "Gold? I hate it as you hate God." Our collective difficulty in understanding what he wants, likes, etc. comes from our inability as readers to read him properly, from his foiling our every personal and societal expectation. This transgression of reading conventions bespeaks of a quintessentially modern character-type. Baudelaire's stranger will later find his counter-parts both in the inhabitants of Jacob's poetic universe, as well as in a character like Plume in Henri Michaux's, among many others we could cite.

   To conclude this close reading of prose poems then, one must admit that, at first glance, the prose poem does seem to be a marvellous illustration of the concept of literariness. For one to read it at all as "literature," and not just as a page of everyday prose, one's attention must indeed be drawn to each and every minuscule aspect of it. But the more one does this, the more one realizes that in the act of reading prose poems, and by extension, all texts, we merely re-produce, re-define, and re-formulate all our previous notions of what "true" literature is, whether we wish to or not. Such symbolic action or praxis is not necessarily *wrong*, nor unethical. Yet, surely, it is limited. Its limitations become obvious when one realize that the critical reading of even so marginal or minimal a "literary" text as a prose poem hardly helps one in the least visualize, or otherwise grasp, the literariness of any single text. In the final analysis, the prose poem's greatest value to students of literary pluralism lies in its intrinsic capacity to proclaim more boldly perhaps than any other type of literary text does the following: If you want "literature," here it is! Unfortunately though, after reading prose poems closely, we still do not really know what it is we have.

* * *

My second chapter has shown why the theoretical problem of plural readings of the same texts, i.e. modern critical pluralism, cannot be resolved merely by formal means. Whether one *deliberately* adopts a scientific approach to literature or not, the fact remains that any type of close examination of texts involves individual linguistic choices and decisions that always affect the notion of what is really on the pages read by critics. In this sense, theorists striving to understand why the same canonical works seem nowadays to generate more and more readings find themselves obliged to accept a more complex picture of the literary phenomenon. Given the relationship between a piece of literature and an individual reader, a literary text is above all a *phenomenon*. It is, in other words, an object which we first know through our senses, and which we then further describe through thought and analytic development. Paradoxical as it might seem, critical pluralism actually derives from the pragmatic undermining of a text's fundamental difference. It is the result of an individual act of *translation*, of carrying-over a piece of writing from its initial state of silence (or, if one prefers, its uninterrupted symbolic plenitude distinct from that of any other previously written text), to an *other* discourse. This second discourse, the critic's metalanguage, is inevitably caught somewhere between the symbolic system of the "text itself" and whatever language, or parts thereof, the critic shares with his or her professional audience. Were this not the case, it is hard to imagine what any critic whatsoever would have to say to anyone else about a given piece of writing. By disturbing, as it were, the uninterrupted flow of a text's own words, critics thus usurp the latter, and force theorists of literary pluralism to focus their energy instead on both sides of the phenomenon, the reader and the text, as well as on the conceptual space between them. Only by thus changing approaches to the source(s) of literary pluralism can one hope to understand better its contemporary manifestations.

Having now seen how and why the search for the origins of literary pluralism needs to be re-thought in terms of a more complex "source," the reader/text dynamic, we shall move once more in the next chapter to a new entity, the author as reader of him/herself. My third chapter examines the historical factors that have lead authors in the last two hundred years or so to produce texts that differ increasingly from those written before. It shall be argued that through a deliberate production of ever more *different* themes, styles, and genres, writers have, unwittingly perhaps, provided a literary model that modern critics have been hard pressed not to follow. Since modern authors as a group have striven to be original or somehow different from their predecessors, it will be suggested that their actions have tended to reinforce the contemporary critical shift from texts to readers that our second chapter has attempted to justify. At the same time, I shall aim to clarify why, given this assiduous *literary* search for originality and difference over the last two hundred years, one might similarly have expected modern critical readers to wish to find "more" difference in certain texts than these texts "themselves" already had. In studying the history of these related quests, we shall finally be dealing directly with the second, more properly "aesthetic" part of the story behind the rise of literary pluralism.

NOTES

[1] Frederic Jameson, *The Political Unconscious* (Ithaca: Cornell University Press, 1981), p. 9.

[2] See my *Repetition and Semiotics: Interpreting Prose Poems* (Birmingham, AL: Summa Publications, 1986), especially chapter four.

[3] One of the main goals of the present book is to examine more closely the history of some of these very conventions.

[4] I discuss some of the particulars of this hermeneutic coincidence in *Repetition and Semiotics*, pp. 111-112.

[5] This statement is made by Michael Riffaterre apropos, once again, of the reading of "Les Chats" done by Claude Lévi-Strauss and Roman Jakobson. It appears in his response titled, "Describing Poetic Structures: Two Approaches to Baudelaire's 'Les Chats'" in *Structuralism* (Garden City: Anchor Books, 1970), p. 202.

[6] In Jorge Luis Borges, *Labyrinths*, eds. James Irby & Donald A. Yates (New York: New Directions, 1962), pp. 36-44. All quotations are to this edition and appear in the text, along with page number.

[7] In William James, *Essays in Radical Empiricism & A Pluralistic Universe* (New York & London: Longmans, Green & Co., 1943). Further references to this edition are included in the text.

[8] I am aware of the limitations of this graphic metaphor in this age of video and computer screens. Reading any literary sign is still, however, a question of coming to grips, at some point or other, with *inscriptions* of some type.

[9] As is evident from his famous dictum, *credo quae absurdum*.

[10] This same point has been made quite convincingly, I think, in at least three other important, modern theoretical works: Stanley Fish, *Is There a Text in this Class?* (Cambridge: Harvard University Press, 1980); Daniel Delas and Jacques Filliolet, *Linguistique et Poétique* (Paris: Larousse, 1973), esp. pp. 168-169; and Eagleton's *Literary Theory*, esp. pp. 6-11.

[11] Fish, *Is There a Text?*, pp. 322-337.

[12] This has already been done to a large extent by Mircea Margescou in *Le concept de littérarité* (The Hague: Mouton, 1974) and by the various contributors to *Russian Formalism: A Retrospective Glance: A Festschrift in Honor of Victor Erlich*, ed. Robert Louis Jackson & Stephen Rudy (New Haven: Yale Russian & Slavic Publications, 1985), no. 6.

[13] See Roger Seamon, "Poetics Against Itself: On the Self-Destruction of Modern Scientific Criticism," *PMLA*, 104, 3 (May 1989), 294-305, especially 303.

[14] Shortly, we shall see how the reading of prose poems in particular underscores this weakness of formalist criticism.

[15] Jacqueline Henkel, "Linguistic Models and Recent Criticism: Transformational-Generative Grammar as Literary Metaphor," *PMLA*, 105, 3 (May 1990), 448-463.

[16] Tzvetan Todorov, *Critique de la Critique* (Paris: Seuil, 1984).

[17] Naomi Schor, *Breaking the Chain* (New York: Columbia University Press, 1985).

[18] See Thomas Kuhn, *The Structure of Scientific Revolutions* (Chicago & London: University of Chicago Press, 1962), especially pp. 158-171.

[19] Wayne Booth, *Critical Understanding: The Powers and Limits of Pluralism* (Chicago: University of Chicago Press, 1979), p. 4.

[20] Gilles Deleuze & Félix Guattari, *L'Anti-Oedipe: Capitalisme et Schizophrénie* (Paris: Editions de Minuit, 1972).

[21] *Critical Understanding*, p. 25.

[22] Jean Cohen, *Le Haut Langage: Théorie de la Poéticité* (Paris: Flammarion, 1979), p. 275.

[23] Group μ, *A General Rhetoric*, trans. Paul B. Burrell & Edgar M. Slotkin (Baltimore: Johns Hopkins University Press, 1981), p. 9.

[24] *Rhetoric*, p. 155.

[25] Remarkably, neither group seems to know much about, or acknowledge, the other in any of their footnotes. Personally, I take this mutual ignorance to be a sign of the sad state of cooperative research efforts between different countries, and perhaps also a measure of the hold the pluralist mentality has over all contemporary literary critics in the Western world. It appears to be less and less necessary for anyone to acknowledge one's intellectual debt to anyone else, no doubt in part for fear of seeming less "original."

[26] I. A. Richards, "Poetic Process and Literary Analysis" in Thomas A. Sebeok, ed. *Style in Language* (Cambridge: MIT Press, 1960), p. 9.

[27] "Hermeneutic Models," *Poetics Today*, 4, 1 (1983), 7.

[28] Certain critics, notably the two mentioned here, will argue that it is precisely in the nature of "true" literature to provide such instructional signs to each reader through the logical linguistic and/or semiotic processes it puts into play. In this scheme, the reader has only to respect the traditions and conventions of his language in order to see what everyone sees. Unfortunately, the empirical truth is that such agreement of points of view does not always occur.

[29] See his *Language Processing and the Reading of Literature: Toward a Model of Comprehension* (Bloomington: Indiana University Press, 1978), xvii. Further references to this book are included in the text.

[30] Timothy R. Austin, *Language Crafted: A Linguistic Theory of Poetic Syntax* (Bloomington: Indiana University Press, 1984). Further references to this work are included in the text.

[31] Rather than raise an ontological question, like the one about whether a tree falling in the forest *really* falls, if one does not hear or see it, I choose to ignore this kind of potential objection here. My own professional existence, as well as that of other literary critics, university literature departments, and the like, attests, it seems to me, to the relative *being-in-the-world* of literary texts, irrespective of their specific phenomenal existence to individual observers.

[32] Michael Beehler, *T.S. Eliot, Wallace Stevens, and the Discourses of Difference* (Baton Rouge: Louisiana State University Press, 1987).

[33] I am thinking here of situations like those found in most classrooms, in the meetings of editorial boards, and in lecture halls.

[34] From its beginnings, Derrida himself always claimed that deconstruction, or more specifically, grammatology, was *not* a science. It seems appropriate to remind all those students and critics who have made this non-science into a veritable industry over the last twenty years of this fact.

[35] Ellen Schauber and Ellen Spolsky, *The Bounds of Interpretation: Linguistic Theory and the Literary Text* (Palo Alto: Stanford University Press, 1986), p. 172. Further references to this work appear in the text.

[36] In his "'Preserving the Exemplar': or, How Not to Dig Our Own Graves" in *Dictionary of Literary Biography*, vol. 67, ed. Gregory S. Jay, *Modern American Critics Since 1955*, p. 313. This article is reprinted from *Critical Inquiry*, 3 (Spring 1977), 407-23.

[37] "Short Epiphanies: Two Contextual Approaches to the French Prose Poem" in *The Prose Poem in France: Theory and Practice*, eds. Mary Ann Caws and Hermine Riffaterre (New York: Columbia University Press, 1983), p. 57.

[38] Some of the more recent critical studies which treat prose poems as quintessentially "literary" texts include two books by Barbara Johnson, *The Critical Difference: Essays in the Contemporary Rhetoric of Reading* (Baltimore and London: The Johns Hopkins University Press, 1980), and *Défigurations du Langage Poétique* (Paris: Flammarion, 1979); Richard Terdiman, *Discourse/Counter-Discourse: the Theory and Practice of Symbolic Resistance in 19th-Century France* (Ithaca: Cornell University Press, 1985); Michael Riffaterre, *Semiotics of Poetry* (Bloomington and London: Indiana University Press, 1979); and my own *Repetition and Semiotics: Interpreting Prose Poems* (Birmingham, Alabama: Summa Publications, 1986).

[39] I refer here, of course, to Madame Bernard's seminal study, *Le Poème en prose de Baudelaire jusqu'à nos jours* (Paris: Nizet, 1959), which remains *the* starting point for any serious study of these texts.

[40] The question of how *seriously* one takes any particular usage of language recalls the extensive theoretical debate Derrida takes up with Austin in the former's "Signature Event Context" in *Glyph*, 1 (1977), 172-97. Obviously, regardless of the context, much depends on the decision to take an utterance seriously, as Jonathan Culler indicates nicely in his *On Deconstruction: Theory and Criticism after Structuralism* (Ithaca: Cornell University Press, 1982), pp. 115-119.

[41] I take this phrase from Shoshana Felman's book, *La Folie et la chose littéraire* (Paris: Seuil, 1978).

[42] After all, a recent collection of essays, *Against Theory: Literary Studies and the New Pragmatism*, ed. W.J.T. Mitchell (Chicago: University of Chicago Press, 1985) is entirely devoted to this controversial anti-theoretical stance, and has become very popular in many American critical circles.

[43] For more on Holland's theories, especially this notion of DEFT reading, see "The New Paradigm: Subjective or Transactive?", *New Literary History*, 7, No. 2 (1976), 335-346.

[44] *Mythologies* (Paris: Seuil, 1957), p. 194.

[45] *L'Ecriture et la différence* (Paris: Seuil, 1967), p. 339.

[46] *Oeuvres Complètes*, I, ed. Claude Pichois (Paris: Gallimard, 1975), p. 276. All other references to Baudelaire are to this edition, including page and volume.

[47] Max Jacob, *Le Cornet à Dés* (Paris: Gallimard, 1945), p. 17.

[48] In *Manifestes du surréalisme* (Paris: Jean-Jacques Pauvert, 1972), p. 49.

[49] Hermine Riffaterre, "Reading Constants: The Practice of the Prose Poem" in *The Prose Poem in France: Theory and Practice* (New York: Columbia University Press, 1983), p. 98.

[50] Michael Benedikt, *The Prose Poem* (New York: Dell, 1976), p. 47.

[51] In her article, "Exorbitant Geometry in Hugo's *Quatrevingt-treize*" *MLN*, Vol. 96 (1981), 856-876, Suzanne Guerlac argues that the unchained cannon on board ship in the chapter "Tormentum Belli" of Hugo's novel serves to disrupt, allegorically, the entire (generic) world of the novel. From our perspective, this chapter, (as well as many others from the Hugolian corpus that we cannot discuss here), must be seen as an example either of "poetic prose" or of long prose poems. These are the alternatives Suzanne Bernard herself proposes to describe analogous prose passages found in the works of Lautréamont, Chateaubriand, and several other writers.

[52] For more on this, see Roger Little, "Rimbaud's 'Sonnet'," *Modern Language Review*, 75, Part 3 (July 1980), 528-533. Little shows how the organization of this so-called sonnet is discreetly and, it would seem, purposely "aimed at disturbing self-satisfied response patterns ..." (533).

[53] Barbara Johnson, "Quelques conséquences de la différence anatomique des textes" *Poétique*, 28 (1976), 465.

[54] Maurice Chapelan, *Introduction du Poème en Prose* (Paris: René Julliard, 1946). Our two quotations derive from this edition, and are included parenthetically in the body of our text.

[55] *On Deconstruction*, pp. 64-83.

[56] I am thinking here of some of the Marxist readings of Rimbaud done by early collaborators in the Tel Quel group in France, specifically one by Jean-Louis Baudry, "Le Texte de Rimbaud (fin)" *Tel Quel*, 36 (1969), 33-53.

[57] If I choose to borrow this critic's terminology here, it is mainly because Riffaterre seems to me to be perhaps the most important literary theorist to date still relying heavily on the concept of literariness for support of his otherwise remarkably cogent and impressive textual analyses. See especially his *Text Production*, tr. Terese Lyons (New York: Columbia University Press, 1983) for countless examples and definitions of literariness and "monumentality."

[58] Cf. David Scott, "La structure spatiale du poème en prose: D'Aloysius Bertrand à Rimbaud," *Poétique*, 59 (1984), 295-308. In my book *Repetition and Semiotics*, I, too, devote several pages to analyses of what I call such "iconic paragrammatic features" in the prose poems of Baudelaire, Rimbaud, and Breton. See pp. 97-104.

[59] See my "Semiotic Analysis of Iconic Features in Literature" in *Semiotics 1985* (Lanham, MD: University Press of America, 1986), pp. 336-345, as well as my "Graphemic Gymnastics in Surrealist Literature," *Romanic Review*, 81, 2 (January 1990), 211-224.

[60] My isolation of these particular intertextual models, pictorialist, should not be seen as a condemnation of this kind of reading alone. Rather, it hints at how any and all intertextual models are equally susceptible to doubt, depending on the implicit beliefs, wishes, epistemological and methodological obsessions of any given reader or critic.

[61] See the former's "De l'évolution littéraire" (pp. 120-137) and the latter's "L'Art comme procédé" (pp. 76-97) reprinted in *Théorie de la littérature*, trans. Tzvetan Todorov (Paris: Seuil, 1965. Further references to their essays are from Todorov's translation.

[62] In his "Three Conceptions of Poetic Language" (pp. 130-147) in *Russian Formalism: A Retrospective Glance: A Festschrift in Honor of Victor Erlich*, eds. Robert Louis Jackson and Stephen Rudy (New Haven, Yale Russian and East European Publications, No. 6, 1985), p. 144.

[63] In his *Russian Formalism: History/Doctrine* (The Hague: Mouton, 1965), p. 200.

[64] In all fairness, it is important to recall that the poet in Musset's famous "Nuit de mai" acts a lot like Mercury here. He, too, has no real desire to deliver, give up, or "sing" anything either. The suffering and pain the muse tells him to express constitute a somewhat similar "content" to that requested by Jacob's Venus. But, contrary to "Poème," Musset's poem acts like an extended version of the classical trope of *preteritio*, in which the image of the pelican nevertheless succeeds in evoking all that which the poet insists he is, in fact, *not* going to express. In the process, therefore, he cannot help but deliver or surrender *something*, unlike Mercury in Jacob's text.

[65] Heidegger was the thinker who insisted on the etymological linking of Hermes with hermeneutics.

[66] *The Play of the Text: Max Jacob's 'Cornet à Dés'* (Madison: University of Wisconsin Press, 1981), p. 105.

[67] Lévy locates two other interesting mirror effects in that: 1) the first part of "Poème" supposedly represents a translation from Greek into French, whereas the second part goes from French into Greek, and 2) the word "Idylle" appears in French within the Greek context, and in Greek in the French part. See p. 106.

[68] *Le poème en prose*, pp. 629-30.

[69] At the end of line one in Claude Pichois's edition of Baudelaire's *Oeuvres complètes* (Paris: Bibliothèque de la Pléiade, 1975) and at the beginning of line two in Marcel Ruff's edition of *Petits poèmes en prose (le Spleen de Paris)* (Paris: Garnier-Flammarion, 1967).

[70] Barbara Johnson was the first to note how this slight re-writing or re-arrangement of words between the verse and prose poem versions of a particular line from "La Chevelure," for instance, could be understood in terms of metric syllabification. See her article "Quelques conséquences."

[71] The text by Jacob we have just discussed is the *first* in a series of similarly titled "Poèmes."

Chapter III
MODERN LITERARY QUESTS FOR ORIGINAL

Largely because of pluralism's influence in contemporary Western culture, most people assume nowadays that poets and artists of all kinds have tried to be "different" from their predecessors in some significant way or other ever since the beginning of time. This modern emphasis on, or idealization of, difference is often translated into the common belief that every different genre, style, image, theme, or even reading represents a more or less "original" production within the domain of literature. The present chapter deals with the real meaning of this belief, its history and limits, and its precise ramifications for the rise of literary pluralism.

From the point of view of critics, as well as of writers themselves, it is important to ask whether originality has always been desirable. For, when we read literary history with an eye towards the notion of originality, we discover instead that the primary modus operandi of Western writers throughout the ages has mostly consisted of imitating models provided by the Ancients. Their fundamental task has been to perfect, and then to go at least one step beyond, models created by certain powerful precursors, to borrow Harold Bloom's phrase. While most unquestioning, pluralistic, modern readers assume that writers who pick up their respective pens automatically embark on a particular original literary path (that, in some cases, is barely off the beaten trail blazed by others), what has guided most writers, in reality, has been the example set by earlier writers.

The paradoxical goal of most poets has, in this way, been to derive their own "original" voices, as it were, from the practice of excelling in their imitation of others. In very few instances before the modern period could one even conceive of originality without the necessary, albeit paradoxical pre-existence of literary models.[1] All of this changed, however, when in the course of different searchs for a new national identity—I am thinking here particularly of those of Germany, France, and the United States, as they can be observed in the latter half of the eigthteenth and beginning of the nineteenth centuries—people working in the literary domain frequently began to think of writing and reading in more *deliberately* original ways. They went about their literary business with the idea that they were producing something important *because* it was original, not just because it was something they either wanted to write, or felt they needed to write. In essence, those involved in the production and interpretation of literature strove to become fathers (or mothers) of themselves, to become their own origins. They wanted to break so definitively with their literary forebears, with tradition, that their scriptural praxis became, in their minds anyway, the literary parallel of various social revolutions taking place simultaneously in their own countries.

In France, for example, Victor Hugo refers precisely to this revolutionary dimension of the Romantic project in his famous "Réponse à un acte d'accusation" from *Les Contemplations*, where he says,

> Je mis un bonnet rouge au vieux dictionnaire [...] J'ai pris et démoli (sic) la bastille des rimes/I put a citizen's cap on the old dictionary [...] I took possession of and demolished the Bastille of rhymes.

Yet, one does not have to limit oneself to this or some other isolated passage, for the entire French (and American) Revolution, and their nineteenth-century aftermaths, could be understood as an immense longing for the freedom to be, or to do, whatever one wanted, regardless of the past. This essentially pluralistic longing for individuality or originality represented a iconoclastic wish on the part of poets to be "absolutely modern," as Rimbaud would put it later in the century.

What makes this wish and its concomitant discourse so important with the advent of Romanticism is that for the first time in literary history the desire for, and realization of, originality turn into bona fide criteria of aesthetic value. Originality, as a separate and distinct conceptual category, becomes the principle force behind artistic creation, and especially, behind various judgments of artistic worth. As a recent critic, Roland Mortier, has expressed it, the opposition between imitation and originality became acute

> only when the weight of tradition was felt to be a brake, and no longer a stimulus, when imitation was assimilated to a servile dependence which bridled genius instead of revealing it to itself.[2]

When this happened, as it did en masse with the English, German, and French Romantics, the social function, and even social status, of poets changed radically. As a result, they saw to it that in the course of the next two centuries the artist

> ended up distinguishing himself from the artisan: at times, the artist
> even signed his works, sometimes even represented himself in one
> biographical form or other (Mortier, 18).

The artist had become something significantly different from a gifted copyist,[3] who turned out newer "versions" of past achievements in literature.

I shall argue that it has thus been for *only* the last two hundred years or so, that poets in particular, and artists in general, have tried assiduously to create forms and to express feelings and ideas which differ in some significant fashion from those of their predecessors.[4] In a recent essay concerning the role originality played in the twentieth-century phenomenon of Russian Formalism, Karen Rosenberg supports this argument by stating that

> to a certain extent, we are still in the Romantic era, for originality
> is still praised in, and often even demanded from, the poet, and not
> just from him alone. The relative longevity of this emphasis on
> originality may obscure the fact that not all literary theories place a
> premium on literary novelty.[5]

Her argument is based not only on a close reading of Formalist theories, but also on her analysis of the reading public in eighteenth-century Russia. Instead of expecting or demanding that authors produce radically original works, Russian readers at that time were both reassured and pleased by the familiar, repetitive nature of neo-classical Russian literature. The reason Rosenberg's argument is so persuasive is that the situation she describes corresponds exactly to what, in literary historical terms, one might have expected to see, in Russia as in the rest of the West. Since the time of Aristotle's *Rhetoric*, what was supposed to please and edify readers of literature was that with which they were already *familiar*: common themes, stories, and stereotypes from earlier Russia literature and folklore, i.e. familiar descriptive systems which the Greeks called *topoï*.

The wish to belong to a kind of "avant-garde," while already strong in certain specific movements and/or schools, e.g. the French Pléïade poets of the sixteenth century, nevertheless manifests itself across the board, so to speak, beginning with the Romantic period in Western literary history. To a large extent, this wish to be original in the aesthetic domain seems so obvious, so natural to us all now, especially in modern critical circles, that to doubt its feasibility or desirability constitues a major affront to contemporary sensibilities. Nearly everyone, that is, seems to think it reasonable, if not also "good," in some quasi-moral or transcendental way, that poets continually seek to be original in style, thought, and emotion whenever they set out to write their next work. It may therefore be asserted that the idealization of the ethico-moral functions of literature, begun by Romantic poets themselves, has continued until our time, largely thanks to critics.[6] In this sense, being in the "avant-garde" of poetry and criticism, or being original with respect to what has already been done in those fields, has slowly come to be not so much *an* option for the individuals concerned as it has become the preferred, if not only, option open to any self-respecting writer or critic. Like cultural pluralism itself, the literary quest for originality is now generally taken for granted as something good in and of itself. Its desirability has now taken the form of an unquestioned article of faith for both artist and critic.

As was indicated above, however, the truth is that such a positive view of originality's role did not always enjoy the same popularity with all groups of readers and writers. If we single out French poets, we cannot help but note how much of their practice—from various medieval borrowings of Latin rhetorical devices to the classical theatrical "law" of Three Unities to the general acceptance of generic conventions in the majority of eighteenth-century poetry—reflects a much different attitude vis-à-vis writers, and their traditional tasks qua writers. Specifically, what these practices make clear is that during a period of nearly a thousand years, poets in France and other Western countries had a kind of aesthetic and ethical debt to pay to certain all-important precursors. Their main responsibility was to maintain the quasi-imperial power and prestige of these "classical" models through a dutiful and respectful carrying-over or translation (*translatio*) of them. Without "carrying over" the great ideas of imperial power (*imperii*), major philosophical studies (*studii*), and stories of both Classical Greece and Rome as well as medieval legends about King Arthur, Tristan and Isolde, and the like, medieval writers sometimes seemed at a loss for thematic material from which to create their "own" works.

Indeed, the anonymity of many such texts suggests that the substance of the work did not exhibit a poet's originality so much as what Chrétien de Troyes called the poet's "molt bel conjointure," the juxtaposition of old material into a somehow more elegant narrative configuration. The very notions of *translatio studii* or of *translatio imperii* (critical inventions to be sure, but nevertheless extremely useful concepts) would be unthinkable without first recognizing the general *un*popularity of originality during many centuries of writerly activity. The traditional approach to writing was thus limited, more or less,[7] to a proper imitation of the great poets and poems of what T.S. Eliot, in a mainly Anglo-American context, called The Tradition.

This does not mean, of course, that prior to the nineteenth century, no one ever sought to write a "really" new or original poem, play, or novel. The whole quarrel in France during the latter half of the seventeenth century between the so-called Ancients and Moderns, for example, centered precisely on this question of choosing between conventional styles, traditional wisdom, and more up-to-date ideas and forms. The quarrel pitted writers like Desmarets de Saint Sorlin and Charles Perrault, who extolled the art and literature of Louis XIV's age, against defenders of Antiquity, like Boileau, Dacier, and Longepierre. In England, too, there was a serious, though perhaps not quite as important, Battle of the Ancients and Moderns which dealt with the same issues. That "battle" arose in the 1690's when Wotton and Bentley took Sir William Temple to task for his praise of ancient learning over more modern scholarship, a debate which eventually led to Jonathan Swift's defense of Temple in *The Battle of the Books*. Still earlier than that, the Pléiade poets, in their strong defense and illustration of the French language, were obviously committed to the idea of writing poetry that in some ways, at least, would go beyond the Italian, Greek, and Roman models they had used until then. Even Montaigne in his *Essais* (II, 8) says that "strangeness" and "novelty" (*l'étrangeté* and *nouveauté*) are what usually give value to things (*donner prix aux choses*) in society, although he admits elsewhere that he, himself, detests all novelty! He states:

> I am disgusted by novelty, whatever face she may have, and am correct insofar as I have seen the damaging effects it can have.

This strong ambivalence we find in Montaigne's *Essais* towards originality is emblematic of the dubious worth this quality was assumed to have in works prior to the modern period.

But, as Roland Mortier has demonstrated, these discontinuous, if long-standing, debates were resolved for all intents and purposes around the end of the eighteenth century, with a resounding victory for the Moderns. In essence, what we observe is that with the advent of Romantic literary theory and practice in England, Germany, and France, the concept of originality in and of itself became a distinct aesthetic category or criterion for both the creation *and* appreciation of literary works. Whereas the quest for a certain distinctiveness had, to be sure, always tempted poets—from Dante and Milton to Shakespeare and Cervantes—it rarely took the form of a deliberate, articulated, common project as it did, exceptionally, with the Pléiade poets in France. This search became a veritable obsession, however, at the end of the Enlightenment, especially with the Romantics.

What, then, happened to imitation? In Tzvetan Todorov's words:

> The principle of imitation reigns as uncontested master over the theory of art during the first three quarters of the eighteenth century [...] There is not a single aesthetic writing of the period which fails to refer to it. [However, artistic imitation] disappears at the very moment it attains perfection [...] If imitation were the only law of art, it would have to cause the disappearance of art: the latter would

no longer be different from "imitated" nature. [Thus] for art to survive, imitation could not be perfect.[8]

In other words, since servile imitation, in theory, fostered only aesthetic stasis, it was inevitable that writers who wished to distinguish themselves from other writers become aware of the need to dissociate their verbal art from mere "imitation" of classic art. Not surprisingly, therefore, innumerable instances of a gradual shift in both literary practice and aesthetic attitudes towards imitation are found throughout the eighteenth century. In 1759, for instance, Edward Young was already beginning to turn his back in England on what he called "imitators" because, as he says in his *Conjectures on Original Composition,*

> Imitators only give us a sort of Duplicate of what we had, possibly much better, before; increasing the mere Drug of books, while all that makes them valuable, *Knowledge and Genius*, are at a stand. The pen of an *Original* writer, like Armida's wand, out of a barren waste calls a blooming spring ... (in McFarland 5).

On the other hand, in Switzerland, Helvétius does not want to go quite as far as Young in that, for him,

> the new and the singular in the area of ideas do not suffice to warrant the title of genius (Mortier, 110).

From Helvétius remarks, we infer that the "new and singular" writer might nonetheless warrant the title of genius, provided that s/he add something else—no doubt a *je ne sais quoi*—to an otherwise respectable and respectful imitation.

So, too, with Goethe, who is not much more at ease when it comes to accepting originality as the be-all and end-all of literary creation. Such acceptance is, after all, where Young's idea would appear to lead us. Goethe explains:

> The most original authors of our time are not original because they produce something new, but only because they are capable of saying certain things *as if* they had never been said before.[9]

The assumption here is that everything worth saying has already been said, and that one's literary genius derives essentially from an imaginative rhetorical dissimulation of the earlier sources behind so-called "new" styles and ideas.[10] A French forerunner to the Romantics, André Chenier, is equally reticent to break with the dominant aesthetic theories of his time when, in his famous late eighteenth-century poem "L'Invention," he states:

> Mais inventer n'est pas en un brusque abandon,
> Blesser la vérité, le bon sens, la raison./
> But invention is not a sudden decision
> to wound truth, common sense, and reason.

In what appears to be little more than an updated homologue of Boileau's seventeenth-century classical aesthetics, Chénier insists on the obligatory and simultaneous presence of truth, reason, and common sense in the midst of any attempt at artistic originality.

But, Chénier does represent a step forward from Boileau in that he strongly takes up the cause of invention against the more subservient notion of imitation. His most quoted and memorable poetic statement is one that summarizes perfectly his key historical importance in this context:

> Sur des pensers nouveaux faisons des vers antiques/ "Out of new
> ideas let us make ancient verses."

Wanting to have his cake (Antiquity, Tradition) and to eat it, too, (by asserting his originality or modernity), Chénier signals an important moment in the general change of attitude vis-à-vis literary originality which takes place at the time. His imperative implies the existence of two different kinds of literary originality: one of ideas, that we could loosely call "thematic," and another, more "formal" type regarding poetic structures. From Chénier's perspective, the great poet must eschew formal originality. S/he is free, however, to pursue the other type of originality inasmuch it permits the expression of new ideas. In a curious way, this conservative, albeit literary, view of the importance of structural revolution might help us explain why Chénier was eventually executed by French revolutionaries. Citizens of 1789 were, after all, intent on changing radically the *structure* of their society. But that is a much longer story I will leave for others to tell, should they wish.

In spite of Chénier's powerful imperative, one must wait until Madame de Staël before one can see clearly on the continent the same kind of serious break with imitation signaled forty years earlier by Edward Young. She was the one who really seized upon the specific originality of German literature in her *De l'Allemagne* (1810). For her, the sentimentality and yearning for a national identity which characterized the German spirit were the only ones she believed could be called "original." Of course, this sentimentality and its idealization had already been exploited in France by the pre-Romantic Jean-Jacques Rousseau, and in England by Wordsworth in his 1800 Preface to his *Lyrical Ballades*. Both of these non-German writers had also helped make feelings fashionable in so much European literature. In any case, the absolute equation between feelings, sincerety, and poetic originality postulated by Germaine de Staël was especially significant to the historical trend we are attempting to describe here. This is because it contributed immensely to the adoption of what both M.H. Abrams, in his now classic *The Mirror and the Lamp*, and Hans Eichner,[11] in a highly influential *PMLA* piece, have called an "organic" model over the "mechanical," or scientific, model that dominated literary Europe from the time of Descartes on.

Essentially what happened around the turn of the century that should interest students of literary pluralism was this: Instead of believing in an unchanging human nature, writers and thinkers of the time took greater and greater interest in what Eichner calls "the temporal, the local, and the individual" (16). According to Eichner, as well as Abrams, a new organic model articulated by poets and philosophers of the late eighteenth and early nineteenth centuries began to accentuate the dynamic real-human-life concept of *becoming* over the more static notion of *being*.[12] Evident in countless works by Hegel, Novalis, Keats, Shelley, Schleiermacher, Kant, and Fichte, the new vision that came to influence literature profoundly

was perhaps best articulated by Friedrich Schlegel who believed that
the world was not

> created once and for all by a perfect, supreme being, but has grown
> or developed [like an organism]—and growing, "becoming," *Werden*
> is its very essence (in Eichner, 15).

Prior to this time, the world was thought to be a complex, stationary
machine whose transcendent essence was a Book to be read, not
written. The world of literature thus had more or less concrete
models, hypostasized models, if one prefers, like those provided by
Homer and Virgil, Sophocles and Aeschylus, Pindar and Horace, or
Aristophanes and Plautus. To practice one's verbal art "in" this older
literary world meant that one had no business seizing a fleeting,
local, momentary flash of inspiration or *enthusiasm* (literally,
possession). If one were serious about writing "proper" literature,
one had to imitate formal and, more often than not, thematic models
as well. These models were, for all intents and purposes, etched in
stone. As the seventeenth-century moralist La Bruyère said it at the
start of his collection of human character portraits, *Les Caractères*,
Tout est dit/"Everything has already been said."

From this angle, it was believed that while time might pass,
eternal truths about human life and experience, or about artistic value
live on. The primary aim of literature and art was to preserve these
same truths in unforgettable "masterpieces." To cite but one of
countless variations on this theme during a period of two thousand
years, consider the following well-known Latin dictum: *Horae
cedunt, opera manent/Time recedes, while works remain*. Given the
poetic quandary of remaining faithful to both thematic and stylistic
models, while *at the same time* producing a supposedly new piece of
literature, it is no wonder then that originality as an aesthetic concept
should have enjoyed so little popularity in most cases before the
modern period.

But about two hundred years ago or so, Western society as a
whole began to construe the world more and more as being a
growing, living organism. This "epistemic shift" from the Classical
to the Modern model—so carefully analyzed by Michel Foucault in

related areas like philology, biology, and political economy[13]—led many thinkers to assume that the best way to represent, analyze, and understand the world was to rely on one's own individual *becoming*. This individualistic *Werden* served as a microcosmic model of how the universe itself functioned, and of how it signified. In an important section of *The Mirror and the Lamp*, for instance, Abrams has little difficulty in isolating what he calls a veritable "aesthetics of organism" in Samuel Coleridge's poetry. Other examples of this *vital* equivalence between art and life, between people and their environment—the so-called "pathetic fallacy"—are found in such widely-read works as *Atala* and *René* by Chateaubriand, or in George Sand's *romans champêtres*, like *François le champi*. As is readily apparent to most any reader of Western literary history, the same can be said about the vast majority of poetry written at the time in England, France, and Germany as well.

Coleridge also provides Abrams with a poetic rationale for what he names the former's implicit "theory of cultural pluralism."[14] This theory, pertinent to the general argument concerning "literary pluralism" developed here, allows for, even encourages, the expression of individual values over more dominant, usually upper-class, ones. However, what I wish to stress is that society in general, and the art world in particular, were suddenly presumed to benefit from such individual flights of imagination and fancy. The new vision or model which was emerging at the time simultaneously equated a poet's individual feelings and experiences with the most appropriate literary practices. To write "proper" literature thus began to mean creating a fictive world which continually took into account the full vitality of its characters, their psyches as well as their actions. More and more, the goal of serious writing was to create a literary cosmos which reflected the manifold aspects of the world(s) inhabited both by its living producer, the writer, and by its eventual consumers, readers. The good, bad, and ugly aspects of human society, as well as of nature, were in this fashion assimilated into literary works, since all these aspects could be found in individual reckonings with the real world. The equation between individual experiences and feelings and "good" literature was perhaps best underscored by the very title of Coleridge's *Biographia Literaria* (1817), which established an intimate connection between the poet's own biography or life and the more general practice and category of literature. Significantly, then, in Coleridge's long-term philosophic endeavor to find a way of mediating between the Knowing subject and the object(s) Known, Wordsworth's friend makes the following assertion in Thesis X of his biography: "the act of self-consciousness is for *us* the source and principle of all of *our* possible knowledge."

Helping us go one step further in our depiction of the said historic transformation, Hans Eichner next relates this new conceptual model to the German philosopher Schleiermacher's notion of the godhead, a metaphysical abstraction constituting the divine essence of the universe. In Eichner's words, the world at this time was no longer seen as "a "Great Engine" resting in God's hand" (15), as it was thought to be from the time of Descartes' mechanistic model of the universe on. Instead, it was slowly taking on the aspect of a great organism, a "cosmic animal" (Eichner, 15). To understand this so-called "godhead," or living, growing spirit subtending the entire world, one needed to accept the fact that God himself had to be "changing and imperfect." Quoting from Schlegel, Eichner writes:

> The godhead can only emerge in its full splendor through the mutually supportive *multiplicity of such individual views* [provided by "original" writers?], and *individuality* is, therefore, not a defect, but a virtue (my emphasis 19).

In the same passage, Schlegel then immediately adds that "the real value, and indeed, virtue, of man [is] his *originality*" (my emphasis). In other words, to the extent that different writers and readers, taken together, provide a multiplicity of individual views, they are actually constitutive of the god-head. Since the god-head is, by definition, "good," all individuals, precisely because they are individuals, can thus take pride in their valuable, even sacred, individuality. Throughout the nineteenth century, such god-like writers who poured out their own souls, or who sometimes instead exposed the "dark" souls of others, were thought to exhibit a certain (by definition) "positive" originality in the very act of writing in a personal, intimate, introspective way. Since the static, transcendental "nature" of the universe, of God, and of people was now problematic, it was of far less interest than the "splendour" of their respective individual "becomings." As a consequence, writers and critics began to underscore the comprehensiveness, accuracy, and/or fidelity of a given work's rendition of life's tergiversations: the dreams, fantasies, anxieties, loves, deceptions, successes, and failures that constitute life's specificity itself, especially as it could be related to their own individuality. Without a doubt, therein lies a significant underlying feature common not only to Romanticism, but also to the other major literary movements and schools of the nineteenth century: Realism, Naturalism, and even Symbolism.

Kant's influential philosophic ideas concerning the individual's reason and ethics also contributed greatly to the growing societal belief in the importance of the individual. Such widespread belief was, of course, fundamentally *pluralistic*, since in its endowment of greater worth to the individual, it could not help but attribute much value to multiplicity, i.e. multiple points of view, and diverse experiences of individuals. With respect to the epistemic transformation taking place all around the writers of the time, the sudden aesthetic privileging of individual thoughts and feelings, real human lives, and Nature, thus provided much of the impetus behind countless works. Among them were such lyrical poetic works as Marceline Desbordes-Valmore's *Elégies et Romances* (1819), Lamartine's *Méditations poétiques* (1820), Byron's *Don Juan* (1819); novels like Goethe's paradigmatic *The Sorrows of Young Werther* (1774), Senancour's *Oberman* (1804), Constant's *Adolphe* (1816), and Stendhal's *Armance* (1827); and plays like Vigny's *Chatterton* (1835) and Musset's *Lorenzaccio* (1834).

But this historic accentuation of individuality also explains the fierce individuality of specifically American writers like Ralph Waldo Emerson, Henry David Thoreau, Emily Dickinson, Walt Whitman, even Mark Twain, who felt an almost religious zeal to express themselves *as* individuals. Needless to say, this intense *self-reliance* (Emerson's term) or radical quest for originality on the part of nineteenth-century American writers has been continually pursued until our time, exemplified by such poets as e.e. cummings, Wallace Stevens, Ezra Pound, William Carlos Williams, Adrienne Rich, Gwendolyn Brooks, Amiri Baraka, and the Beat poets. Not coincidentally, Emerson's dictum, "Never imitate" gives rise in our century to similar pieces of aesthetic advice given by Pound ("Make it New") and Stevens ("It Must Change").

Given the new philosophic vision provided by both poets and philosophers, the concept of originality, or what one might call the strong "will-to-do-something-different" from what was done before, was thereby elevated in critical importance somewhere around two hundred years ago. This occurred *not* because it represented, at first, the creation of something that gushed "forward" out of nothing or nowhere, *ex nihilo*, as some may think today. Ironically enough (for many modern pluralists), the reason why originality first became crucial to the artistic enterprise was that, in the later part of the eighteenth century, it was most often presumed to be generated from a movement "backwards" or "inwards" to the *living*, not *fixed*, source of all art, i.e. the artists themselves and their fellow human beings. In this manner, the aggrandizement of originality in things literary was made somewhat more palatable to certain ambivalent contemporaries (like Goethe and Helvétius) for whom, on the surface, this newly-privileged concept resembled the older principle of imitation.

It was not really the process of imitation that ceased, therefore, but rather the *source* of what was imitated. While the Western Tradition in and of itself was relatively unaffected, the poet's precise relation to it was. Romantic poets, in their tentative quests for originality, were all too conscious of having arrived on the literary scene "late." They knew deep down that they could not be *as* original as they would have liked others to think they were. As a result, they suffered from what Harold Bloom calls a "psychology of belatedness," a concept not unlike that of the more familiar "mal du siècle" in post-Napoleonic France. As the Romantic movement grew though, such psychological "anxieties of influence" led to the use of increasingly transgressive literary forms. For this reason Bloom can legitimately claim that, "the romance-of-trespass, of violating a sacred or daemonic ground is a central *form* in modern literature" (my emphasis).[15]

Yet, although Bloom is correct in identifying the propensity in High Romanticism to what I would call "forward-looking," formal transgressions, the earliest modern quests for originality involved, metaphorically, at least, movements back to the *origin* of one's own identity as an individual. By returning to tap this inner "natural" source of inspiration, the earliest Romantic and pre-Romantic poets felt they were effectively imitating God in their pluralistic creation of new and multiple fictive worlds, worlds that, at the same time, were manifestly imperfect and constantly changing. Sometimes, this initial literary quest for originality also involved the poet's return to his or her own *national* identity, as a member of a people, or of a specific society. To illustrate this, consider the important epic poem on the life and passion of Jesus Christ which first appeared in Germany in 1748, Klopstock's *Messiah!*. Klopstock's poem was considered by many to be one of the most "original" German literary texts of the time. Indeed, it acted as a kind of model of future literature for the nascent modern German state. Inspired by Milton's great epic poems, Klopstock tried to do for German Literature what Milton had done for English, or Dante for Italian: re-write the language, and institute a new kind of literature.

Yet, paradoxically, the supposed originality of Klopstock's work, by virtue of its subject-matter, as well as of its medieval epic tone recalling the old German style of writers like Wolfram von Eschenbach, represents a step backward, in fact. As if that were not paradoxical enough, Klopstock's major structural "innovation" consisted of adapting the dactylic hexameters of Homeric poems (!) to his own work. This prosodic adaptation would later be utilized in other presumably "original" ways by Goethe and others. At this point then, in our story of the rise of the aesthetic side of literary pluralism, to follow an original path into uncharted poetic territory appears largely to have been equivalent to plunging back into the nation's creative, folkloric "roots." At other times, it meant exploring the hidden parts of the fabric of one's society, its peculiar individuals, traits, and problems, as well as one's own individual psyche and life.

When we think of more or less contemporary manifestations of this same poetic tendency—the early and pre-Romantic tendency to be original by metaphorically moving backwards or inwards to the Nation, or to Nature—we find similar phenomena in Scottish literature. MacPherson's mysterious eighteenth-century bardic *Songs of Ossian*, and historical and pseudo-historical novels like Walter Scott's *Ivanhoe* or *Lady of the Lake* fit nicely into this pattern. Elsewhere, too, there are other influential writers seeking originality through a literary revival of what may be considered *ab*original national types, often crystallized in the figure of a child, e.g., Victor Hugo's Gavroche. Hugo, Alexandre Dumas, Théophile Gautier, and George Sand resuscitate both the contemporary idiom and peculiar characteristics of various regions in novels like *Les Misérables*, *Les trois mousqetaires*, *Le capitaine Fracasse*, and *La mare au diable*, respectively. In the United States, Mark Twain amusingly probes the individuality, and consequent originality, of his American contemporaries by writing about *A Connecticut Yankee in King Arthur's Court*. What better way to underscore the originality of "Yankees" than to watch how they act in their linguistic cradle? Part of the novelty of *Tom Sawyer* and *Huckleberry Finn* also resides in their representations of the American "Negro"'s authenticity, his language and mores. And Longfellow reaches back even further than Twain, exploring a more native, *non-English*, source of American originality in people we now correctly call "Native" Americans, when he composes *The Song of Hiawatha*. James Fenimore Cooper does the same with a novel like *The Last of the Mohicans*.

All these works suggest that a trans-Western phenomenon was taking place. What we see here are deliberate attempts to be "original," even though these very different attempts at originality might seem to us now retrograde in their reprise of older, often poorly-regarded (at the time) cultural material. Retrograde, however, is too pejorative a term. Instead, we should speak of a discriminating return, a return to things of value from the past. It is just such a return that explains why, during the time of this conceptual transformation of originality throughout Europe, Lessing did not hesitate to advance the unpopular idea that Shakespeare—considered so "poor" an example of a playwright on much of the Continent for the previous two hundred years—should actually be seen as a model to be followed. Hugo would eventually follow suit in France with his defense of the same writer in his *William Shakespeare* (1864), as well as with his apology for Rabelais, an author "enlightened" philosophers like Voltaire had thought monstrous. Stendhal defended a similar position in his *Racine et Shakespeare* (1823). And what novel was more revolutionary, modern, and Romantic at the time than Hugo's *Notre-Dame de Paris* (1831), a tale set in *medieval* France?

To be an "original" writer at that time, therefore, frequently meant to go backwards to one's cultural, sentimental, and psychic roots. The new poetic method consisted of imitating the models of *one's self* and of other *selves*, often with conventional writing practices and habits. Individual fantasies, desires, preferences, hesitations, and passions often intervened in this new type of imitation. For this reason, instead of singing of "arms and men," (as Virgil did in the *Aeneid*), so as to edify the society in which the writer lived, a modern poet like Whitman will sing about his own self in "Song of Myself":

> I celebrate myself, and sing myself,
> And what I assume you shall assume,
> For every atom belonging to me as good belongs to you.

The idea here is still to edify, but the type of modern edification implied by Whitman entails an unconventional, fundamentally pluralistic, recognition of the *multiplicity* of human experience, not just the singularity of certain elite or privileged segments of society. So, when Whitman commences another of his famous original songs, it is logical that he not to sing the virtues of the "body politic," i.e. a conceptually fixed or static entity. Instead, he sings the "body electric." The prototypical image of the "body politic," as well as the reality behind it, find themselves thereby re-*vitalized*. Whitman's neologistic phrase "body electric" is important because it converts an older, attested English phrase (significantly, used in early American documents like the *Federalist Papers*[16]) into a newer, more original, version. This allows the poet to provide us yet another way of appreciating the different, more life-like, *organic* model that began to prevail in literary circles at the time.

To clarify this point, let me make a slight digression. Within the collective mythology of the nineteenth century, electricity was thought to have a central connection to the force behind human life itself. In 1780, for example, Luigi Galvani found that a sparking electric machine caused muscular contraction in frog legs which were in no way connected to his machine. Seeking to know where this life-like energy originated, he took his machine outside to see whether electricity from lightning—discovered earlier by Benjamin Franklin—could produce the same effect. The result was, of course, that it did, even when he brought the legs inside and touched the brass hook the legs were suspended on outside with an iron plate from inside his laboratory. Galvani correctly surmised that since the electricity could not have come directly from the outside, it must therefore have come from the frog's nerves themselves. Once this connection between a living being's movements and electricity was made, it was hardly coincidental that a contemporary novelist like Mary Shelley let her imagination take this scientific discovery to its fantastic, literary end, in a English Romantic novel like *Frankenstein*. The monster of the good doctor, we recall, was brought to "life" during an electrical storm.

The belief in this electric life force is also what justifies a character like Thomas Edison in Villiers de l'Isle-Adam's late nineteenth-century decadent French novel, *L'Eve future*. For those readers unfamiliar with Villiers' text, I can summarize the plot in one sentence. The novel is about the real-life, American inventor Thomas Edison who, like Dr. Frankenstein, supposedly brings a futuristic, female robot to life. Anyone familiar with classical mythology recognizes in this narrative situation a parallel with a very old story, one which follows the "classical" model. The story to which I refer is, of course, the story of Pygmalion. According to the classical myth, a female statue named Galatea, carved by the male sculptor Pygmalion, is brought back to life by divine intervention. Life is "breathed" into her from the heavens, as it were. Thanks to Pygmalion's profound love for his otherwise *inanimate* statue, and the Gods' pity, Galatea is divinely revived.

Now, if one compares the two major aesthetic models defined above, one can hazard the following generalization. To produce classical, pre-modern works, artists need the artistic past. This need is often translated by a reliance on, and imitation of, great authors (*auctores*). Just as often though, divine intervention is what artists require to do their work, to animate their otherwise *uninspired* creations. Whether through secular intervention of classical models, or divine intervention of the Gods, the Muses, or techniques like Deus ex machina, pre-modern artists thus generally depend on something, or someone else, to accomplish their tasks. Modern artists, on the other hand, usually take matters into their own hands, so to speak. The most radical among them assume, mistakenly, that they can in fact dissociate themselves totally from the past. In their different quests for originality, they, therefore, try to *galvanize* what they often take to be inert themes, ideas, styles, and images from the past, just as Edison does to Eve in Villiers' novel, and Whitman does to the "body politic." At the same time, by "electrifying" these older myths, characters, and ideas from their artistic past, they metaphorically breathe new life into them. They pluralize them, in other words. They make the old into the new, letting the rest of us keep both for our artistic heritage. This is how they contribute to the rise of literary pluralism.

For these reasons, the images encountered in Whitman's many songs are not just about God, heroic deeds, high-class people, lofty sentiments, refined objects (urns, temples) or noble animals (nightingales, lions) as in many earlier "songs of." Instead, one also hears about many different types of folks and their travails. In other words, one learns more and more about real people, about all the people who make up the modern "body politic," a body more fully alive. Through an emphasis on the authenticity of human emotions and, more generally, of all human lives (expressed so well by Shakespeare, Rabelais, and others who had fallen out of favor of the more idealistic, Cartesian thinkers of the Enlightenment), a modern method to write "originally" thus consists of utilizing the full range of one's inner-most feelings, impulses, and experiences, or else one's representation of such things in others. To be a great modern writer means that one seeks to be *original* in this essentially "inward" or "back-to-the-self" sense.

But this type of originality is hardly like the one we think of today whenever we loosely sling the word around in discussions, articles, and reviews. Later in this chapter I discuss how many other modern works rely on a more contemporary, "forward-moving" kind of originality, one that I believe helps better define some of our most recent aesthetic theory and practice. At this earlier historical juncture, however, the term "originality" connoted mainly the importance of writing straight from the heart, about really personal, unexplored aspects of human life. In other instances, literature came straight from the *nation*'s heart, as it were. Eighteenth-century confessional and epistolary novels like Richardson's *Clarissa*, Laclos' *Liaisons Dangereuses*, or even much of the Marquis de Sade's work, already signal the beginning of more widespread privileging of the "backward" or "inward"-looking brand of originality in question here. This explains why, as Hugo suggests in his *Préface de Cromwell* (1827), the proper goal of a modern poetics was to "imiter la nature," a goal which we could perhaps best translate as imitating and drawing inspiration from either one's own individual nature, or from one's place within Nature, or even from one's collective nature as a member of a particular people, be they German, French, English, or American.

With respect to this last point, let us recall that influential historians like Tocqueville, and especially Jules Michelet, also drew a genuinely poetic inspiration from their studies of the cultural roots of the American and French peoples. In Michelet's novels like *La Sorcière* and *La Femme*, one discovers a curious intermingling of romantic imagery, tone, and style with a deep historical knowledge of ancient and medieval sources. So, too, with a historico-poetic treatise like Chateaubriand's *Le Génie du christianisme* (1802), which attempts to demonstrate how it is in the very *nature* of christianity (as practiced both before and during his time) to be the most free, most "poetic," and ultimately, most *pluralistic* of all the world's religions. By staying close then to the three different "natures" to which I just alluded, poets and critics alike began to believe that one could attain poetic greatness thanks to his or her quest for originality. In addition to artistic success, poets who "imitated nature" could also hope to come away from their works with a better general comprehension of the universe itself, the universe both within and outside of themselves. Both poets and readers were assumed to gain much from this new and better cosmic understanding of life in all its multifaceted, literary splendor.

In order to reduce the phenomena described so far to more manageable entities for a general discussion of the rise of literary pluralism, I should now like to advance the idea that this "backwards," "inward-looking" type of originality is in large measure synonymous with what, earlier, I called André Chénier's implied notion of "thematic" originality. Let us recall that Chénier, along with Klopstock, was averse to "formal" originality, preferring instead to rely on older, time-honored genres like odes and elegies, (or, in Klopstock's case, Homeric verses). But neither writer had any problem with poetic attempts to express original ideas, i.e. to exhibit "thematic" originality. Chénier, Klopstock, and, by extension, many other of their contemporaries in Europe, felt this way because of their firm conviction that classical forms were still adequate, indeed, ideal for transmitting "new" ideas. Their conviction was totally unlike that of, say, a Rimbaud, who later in the nineteenth century declared that "new ideas demand new forms."

In essence then, when I refer to the "inward-looking" tendency of much pre-Romantic and early Romantic literature, this is just another way of speaking about those writers' quests for a kind of "thematic" originality. The kind of originality they sought was born of the new ideas ("pensers nouveaux") they themselves put forth, as poets, novelists, or thinkers of their time. These ideas were part and parcel of their many different depictions of human life in general, the human soul, and the soul of their people, in all their respective multiplicities. Literature thus became more *pluralistic* by dealing with characters, ideas, themes, and issues which, previously, were thought to be either uninteresting, or more frequently, inappropriate to "serious" literature. It is hardly coincidental then that characters like bandits, criminals, suicidal lovers, prostitutes, gamblers, maids, starving artists, or themes like adultery, greed, religious and existential anguish, exploitation, boredom, melancholy, ambition, evil, lust are all treated with increased frequency, and continually growing detail throughout nineteenth century Western literature. The rosy worlds of Dukes and Duchesses, Kings and Queens, and legendary epic heros, fundamental to a static view of the world and life, could not help but be reduced thereby to just one option among many other narrative possibilities. In light of the newly-formed American and French Republics, this more inclusive aesthetic treatment of a larger range of all the *people*, of the *res publica*, in various Western countries was no doubt as it should have been.

This is not to say that "modern" topics were never before treated in literary texts. The fact is that one finds most every one of the literary items mentioned above in any number of artistic works throughout the ages, in Chaucer, Boccaccio, and of course the *fabliaux*, for example. But what makes their usage so special in the nineteenth century is their sheer preponderance, their systematic appearance and re-appearance in all the major genres: poetry, prose, and theater. An exemplary case in point is that of Balzac's massive *The Human Comedy*. In a world where authority, tradition, and religion are increasingly coming under social and political fire, what better way to assert the value of the individual, of pluralism's basic relevance to the writing of modern literature, than to remove the divine aspect of Dante's earlier comedy, and to replace it with a *human* one? What better way to underscore the vitality or "organicity" of the literature of the time than to devote as much attention as a Balzac or a Zola did to the ostensibly infinite panorama of human types, situations, and behaviors.

Yet, the more new ideas, themes, and characters came to the attention of writers and their audiences during the nineteenth century, the more the former began questioning the applicability of older forms to the ideas themselves, as I suggested above with respect to

Rimbaud. If we are correct in thinking, generally, that Chénier and his Western literary contemporaries made the first big step towards turning a "thematic" type of originality into a major aesthetic criterion, then it is equally true that later writers were responsable for elevating "formal" originality to a similar, if not higher, level of literary worth. For, when the expression of new, individual ideas began to require a mixing of genres and styles (as they so often did in Romantic poetry, theater, and novels), and when they subsequently gave rise to stylistic forms never before seen, the quest for *both* types of originality became a full-fledged literary enterprise of the highest order. Indeed, though this double quest began in earnest less than two hundred years ago, it has still not ceased, as one can readily see from a reading of twentieth-century literature. Most writers, after all, still *aspire* to be original in one of these two ways, and frequently both at the same time.

The difference nowadays, however, is that with the late nineteenth-century agony, and twentieth-century death in the West of fixed, mechanistic, essentialist notions like Truth, Beauty, Goodness, God, the Author, tradition, "human nature," and even meaning itself, it has become increasingly difficult for writers to act as if there were any *thing* or any *place* to, or into, which they could go "back." As a result, they are increasingly prone to seek out what I call a "forward-looking" originality, one that is more "formal" than "thematic." Many "original" modern novels, poems, plays, or films today thus do not pretend to provide answers, for instance, to age-old questions, in large part because it is assumed that there are no such fixed things for all people, at all times and places. Nor do such texts encourage readers, through imagery or narrative structures already familiar to them, to think that they all belong to a vast human collectivity, or to a particular "people" replete with common emotions, problems, joys, experiences, and meanings to which they all have equal access, or which they can all come to understand better through the "inward-looking" eyes and pen of a poet. Even the idea of *instructing*, which, from Horace's time on, complemented the act of *pleasing* in the classical aesthetic notion of a great work of art, has in many cases, maybe even most, fallen by the boards, so to speak. This modern demise of the strictly didactic function of literature has left less room for anything but the enjoyment and entertainment value of a work.

The Modern Promotion of Different Forms

Literary originality in the most modern sense is thereby often limited to a quest for *forms* without as much regard for *content* as pre-modern literature had. In fact, anyone seeking either to place or locate "content" *in* a piece of serious modern literature is sometimes dismissed as a fool, as someone who has really not grasped what "real" literature is. Why else do large numbers of modern artists and writers alike sneer whenever someone asks them what their art is "about"? Everyone knows (or should, at least), that a given artistic piece's originality is itself what it is "about;" that the piece demands the participation and activity of the reader or spectator in order that it be "completed." I would, therefore, contend that at some stage of their conceptualization or realization, many modern literary quests for originality have constituted assiduous searches for unfamiliar forms and styles.[17] Features most often sought in these quests include: 1) bizarre images, 2) unusual syntactical structures, 3) radically unconventional prosody, 4) striking typographic dispositions of words on the page, 5) highly complex, sometimes consciously playful, spatio-temporal narrative configurations, 6) "counter-reason" scenarios, 7) minimalism, and finally, 8) a number of different "minority" writing styles that I will call "as X"-styles (writing *as* a woman, as an African or African-American, etc.).

Before I describe these key features of many modern literary quests any further, I must insist on two things. First, it is exceedingly rare to find either type of originality, thematic or formal, in isolation. Most of the time, writers seek to find a certain measure of both in their works. Second, the originality of a text can almost never be totally defined or confined by a single one of these unfamiliar forms. As one might expect, the vast majority of modern writings assume more than one of these forms at any given time. This fact, combined with the historical idealization of originality by writers already studied, merely confirms the relevance of pluralism to the history of modern literature which we are now re-examining.

With these caveats in mind, let us consider the above list in more detail. Regarding the search for the first four of these unfamiliar forms, one has only to think of the writings of most any Symbolist, Dadaist, "Cubist," Surrealist, or Concrete poet. Known for their formal trangressions of traditional versification, perfection of blank verse and prose poems, semantic incompatibilities, syntactic manipulations, and visual experiments, late nineteenth- and early twentieth-century poets throughout the West reveled in their use of all four of these unfamiliar forms. One thinks also of the works of less "classifiable" poets like Sanguinetti, Huidobro, Paz, cummings, Char, Ponge, and Bonnefoy, poets who were influenced by the important movements of their time, but who do not really fit neatly into such critical categories. Another group that comes to mind is the collective of French writers known as OULIPO. This school includes several major literary figures 1950s, 60s, and 70s like Georges Perec, Jacques Roubaud, and Raymond Queneau, who advocated the creation of "potential literature." Queneau, in particular, fits perfectly this description of the modern writer who seems more concerned with formal originality than with any specific thematic originality.

In a work like *Exercices de style*, for example, Queneau re-writes the same meaning*less* episode in ninety-nine different ways. As if this were not serious enough an affront to the very notion of thematic originality, it was Queneau who also composed the extraordinary book called *Cent mille milliards de poèmes/One hundred thousand billion poems*. This book represents a potentially infinitely long sonnet, one whose meaning depends far more on the individual reader than on the writer. It is made up of a regular sonnet whose first fourteen verses disguise several other layers of similar verses underneath them. The presence of these other verses, however, drives home the (modern) point that a pre-set thematic originality endemic to the sonnet was undesirable, and ultimately, impossible to imagine. For each separate verse forms a page that can be turned by the reader at will. Readers can thus turn to the second page of "first verses," and the third page of "fifth verses" (to take just one example), and create a much different poem. The "one hundred thousand billion" virtual forms of this sonnet therefore cloud, even negate, any *particular* theme, meaning, or new idea which Queneau would supposedly have come to his typing paper to "express." Its formal originality thereby supercedes whatever thematic originality one might bestow on it *ex post facto*.

Two important points to remember in this respect are made by one of the foremost theorists of OULIPO, François le Lionnais. In the beginning of a well-known anthology of their work, he writes,

> The truth is that the Quarrel of the Ancients and the Moderns is permanent [...] Must humanity rest and content itself with making news ideas out of ancient verses [*sur des pensers nouveaux de faire des vers antiques* — an allusion to Chénier]? We don't believe so.[18]

In other words, one must never forget that the modern quest for both types of originality is an on-going one. This is why I am not suggesting that the search for formal originality is the only one available to writers anymore. Yet, as le Lionnais's second point makes clear, new ideas do not necessarily come before, or rely on, old forms for their expression. Rather, they are often the *result* of modern forms. Consequently, in the vast majority of "oulipien" works:

> the effort of creation has to do with all the formal aspects of literature: alphabetic, consonantal, vocalic, syllabic, phonetic, graphic, prosodic, rhythmic, numeric constraints, programs and structures [...]. On the other hand, [from the moment OULIPO writers began their project] *semantic* aspects were not broached, meaning having been subordinated to the pleasure of each author and remaining outside of any preoccupation with structure (23-4).

Let us now return to the fifth of my "unfamiliar forms" used by many writers, to wit, highly complex, oftentimes playful, spatio-temporal narrative configurations. This form may be the most extensively sought-out of them all. Consider the many novelistic innovations in narrative space and time advanced by so many modern writers, formal innovations like "mise-en-abîme," flashbacks, and sudden changes in locale, mood, and tone. Other traits associated with such complexity or playfulness include sentence fragments, chapters that can or should be read in different orders, excessive use of quotation, allusion, or foreign languages. I think here of people like Gide, Proust, Joyce, Céline, Grass, Cortázar, Borges, Pynchon, Pirsig, Vannegut, Eco, Calvino, Sollers, and Bradbury. One could also cite "new novelists" like Butor, Sarraute, Duras, and Robbe-Grillet. In fact, in the introductory note to his 1970 novel, *Projet pour une révolution à New York*,[19] Robbe-Grillet reveals the astonishing nature of this modern quest for formal originality in these terms:

> What is new is that such phantoms [i.e. characters], which used to surge forward out of abysmal depths, nowadays come to light in all their superficiality as "images d'Epinal" or cartoons. They no longer strike us as being anything other than the flat figures seen in a card game, devoid in and of themselves of any meaning or value, but to which each player [or reader] will give meaning, his meaning, placing the cards in his hand and then, putting them down on the table according to his own order, his own invention of the game being played [...] Love is a game, poetry is a game, life must become a game ....

What Robbe-Grillet suggests in this telling passage is that in a good deal of modern literature, original forms often produce and precede much of the text's "meaning," not the other way around. While the writer may indeed come to the work with something to *say*, s/he also leaves much that is *unsaid* for the reader to piece together, and ultimately, to determine.

No longer satisfied with any so-called content other than that which must be recovered retroactively, many modern writers have little reason in this sense to pursue Chénier's thematic type of originality, since his or her "new ideas" are now supposed to flow out of the phenomenological confrontation between the reader/spectator and the work. This type of writer comes to a work without a fully conceived, pre-packaged thematic content to be expressed, leaving much of that semantic recuperation (or critical re-creation?) up to the reader.

My sixth unfamiliar form, "counter-reason" scenarios, refers not only to works like those in the "theater of the absurd," but also to those that contain ostensibly absurd, non-sensical, or even *unreasonable* scenarios and plots. When I speak of reason in this context, I refer not to my own vision of what "reasonable" means, but rather what the dominant ideology's view is at a given place and time. Such texts often graphically depict scenes of excessive violence, drug-induced delusions, grotesque behaviors, convoluted sexual perversions, and psychoses. In the first case, we remember a plethora of post-1870 plays or theoretical writings on theater by people like Jarry, Pirandello, Ionesco, Beckett, Brecht, Büchner, Artaud, Anouilh, Genet, Albee, Peter Schaffer, and Peter Weiss in which this formal quest for "counter-reason" manifests itself clearly. But one also should recall the novels and short stories of Kafka, Bataille, Vian, Castenada, Hunter Thompson, Hesse, Burroughs, Anthony Burgess, Henry Miller, even Pauline Réage (*L'histoire d'O*). These other searches for an unfamiliar form so transgress traditional narrative that they begin to create their own type of original *content*. They are thus modern not because this multifaceted, "counter-reason" form was never experimented with before, but because they recur with such notable frequency in what we think of as "modern" literature.

The seventh original form, minimalism, is for all intents and purposes the opposite of the last one. The use of this form underlies many modern attempts at literary originality which aim to evoke a great deal of meaning with very few words, with very simple words, or minimal narrative time and space. It can also be used to condense narrative time and place. Ironically, part of the originality of Joyce's *Ulysses* also belongs under this rubric, since its eight hundred page-form(at) is devoted to a single day in the life of Leopold Bloom. This is yet another reason why my reader must not see these forms as anything other than useful heuristic tools with which to read modern literary theory and practice. However, a poet like Emily Dickinson, and Imagists like H.D. and the young Ezra Pound (who was heavily influenced by the Japanese poetic form of haiku) more readily exhibit this tendency towards formal simplicity or condensation. On many occasions, so do William Carlos Williams, Carl Sandburg, Wallace Stevens, Robert Frost, and Howard Nemerov in the United States, and Jules Supervielle and Jacques Prévert in France.

In the theater, Samuel Beckett is an obvious example of minimalist form, especially the older he grew. His one-minute play called *Birth*, and other recent short works, like *Catastrophe* and *Ohio Impromptu*, realize, in exemplary fashion, the modern dream of an absolutely content-less form. Had he lived any longer, one might have expected his aesthetic ideas to take forms so minimal that he would have literally said or written nothing. Perhaps they already did! Unfortunately, we will never know about such extreme formal originality. The thematic potential of simple, minimal prose though, like that found in works such as *Quelqu'un/Someone* by Robert Pinget, a work about trying to write a work, or, say, *L'Amant/The Lover* by Duras, or even certain naive or "quaint" stories written by Hemingway, Jack London, and Saint-Exupéry, also suggests the importance of this type of formal quest for originality in the general history of the rise of literary pluralism. Such simplicity and/or naïveté also manifests itself in many modernist paintings. Think of *fauvisme*, primitivism, and even certain examples of constructivism. In this ever-growing plurality of minimalist forms, we thus find another source of much of our modern aesthetic theory and practice.

The final "unfamiliar" form exploited by many modern writers is an entire style, the "as X"-style. I use this admittedly bizarre label to describe various deliberate acts of writing *as* a particular member of a so-called minority ("so-called" ideologically because in the case of modern American women, for example, they are actually the *majority* in this country today). The minority in question can be either artistic, social, racial, ethnic, or sexual in nature. Such minority groups are, by definition, assumed to have been suppressed by advocates of "good," i.e. ideologically-laden, canonical, literature. Writers who practice the "as X" style represent pluralistic voices that in most instances have to fight to be recognized within the specific spatio-temporal boundaries of canonical literature and criticism. The first texts which fall under this category are, of course, national or nationalist writings, beginning (as we have seen) with most Romantic literature. To write *originally* as a modern German, American, or French woman, for example, implied writing about important aspects of individuals within those societies, aspects that were unexamined and unappreciated at that particular time. It often implied delving into the nation's aboriginal, cultural roots (cf. Klopstock, Michelet, Longfellow). Since writing in this style sometimes also involves the use of a "common" idiom previously excluded from the ranks of acceptable literary practice, certain popular words, phrases, turns-of-phrase, character portraits, and everyday situations are suddenly privileged.

In other cases, the originality of such stylistic innovations leads to the acceptance of certain works in a society that had initially rejected them. The quest for this kind of style explains both the "battle" over Hugo's *Hernani* and its ultimate triumph within the canon of French literature. The play was, after all, poorly regarded by many powerful individuals and institutions when it was first staged. However, because Hugo's original style allowed for a fuller and freer expression of important issues, like politics, social classes, law and order, passion, and beauty, it eventually won over far more theater-goers than the young, iconoclastic Romantics could probably ever have imagined in 1830. Even more illustrative of this type of modern style are the autobiographical texts of Frederick Douglass, Richard Wright, James Baldwin, Malcolm X, and Toni Morrison. Unlike earlier autobiographies, like those of St. Augustine, Montaigne, or Rousseau, the style of these works reflects the different thoughts, feelings, and experiences of a *people*, a people quite distinct—in various ways, and for various reasons—from other people of their time. In these African-American texts, the writer does not depict his own life for the pre-modern purpose of assimilating his or her experiences into a larger, collective experience supposed to be that of all other readers. On the contrary, it is the profound *difference* of their experience from that of most of their society's readers that African-American writers seek to convey. The search for a specific black identity outside of the master-slave relationship, for instance, is what generates a quest for a new form of expression, one different from that of the White man. Such quests end with the creation of a new language, an original style, based in large measure on a kind of written transcription of oral tradition and spoken language.

So, too, with the particular styles of black Francophone poets like Senghor and Césaire, in their differing articulations of what the former called *la négritude*. To paraphrase Rimbaud, new ideas and (re)new(ed) identities therefore demand new forms, or at least, it so appears in much important literary theory and practice of the last two hundred years. Without original forms of writing, essential differences can be neither articulated, nor appreciated, nor acted on in political, social, economical, or artistic ways. The pluralistic voices of various nationalistic movements in Latin America also play a major role in the rise of the aesthetic side of literary pluralism. Striving to break away from European influences in general, and Spanish ones in particular, modern Latin American writers have perfected various styles, e.g., magic realism, *as* Latins. Likewise, by writing *as* women, a host of women like Colette, Virginia Woolf, Simone de Beauvoir, Alice Walker, and Marguerite Duras, have succeeded in disclosing many elements of women's insufficiently described historical identity, their largely unwritten specificity.[20] Their assiduous and diverse efforts to create original literary styles have led some contemporary French feminist theorists to posit the existence of an *écriture féminine*, potentially the most original of all these "unfamiliar" modern forms. As with the "counter-reason" form, the radicality of the "as X" style is such that it clouds the distinction between formal and thematic originality. For what (or whom) this style talks "about" oftentimes ends up appearing just as new or original as the manner in which it does so. In both cases, though, it only seems that way, since so-called minorities or abnormal behaviours have existed for a long time.

Finally, I must emphasize that the list of forms just presented is in no way exhaustive. Within my general scheme there are no doubt sub-categories as well as mixed categories of unfamiliar forms whose utilization constitutes still other modern literary quests for originality. Moreover, few, if any, writers seek only one of these forms to the exclusion of others. If I have chosen to expand on this list, therefore, this procedure must not be construed as meaning that the "forward-looking," "formal" type of originality—which Edward Said defines as "something formed *in the writing*"[21]—is, or was, the only means by which the modern poet expresses new ideas. Modern writers often come to their works with specific "new" ideas articulated in "older," less formally-threatening, ways. We have seen, in fact, how the earliest Romantics felt they were expressing "new" ideas, though they couched them, initially, in more or less traditional literary forms, or hybrids thereof. At that time, writing lyrically and/or dramatically about one's own personal difference(s), or about those of one's people, or about those of humanity itself, was thought to be already sufficiently "original" for it to qualify as expressing new ideas. The so-called organic, as opposed to mechanistic, model found in their works already constituted a "thematic" novelty in its juxtaposition of such concepts as individuality and vitality with the "splendor" of multiplicity.

But, as was suggested earlier, when poets first started to exhibit this *pluralistic* urge for the paradoxically "backwards" or "inward-looking" type of thematic originality, they firmly believed it could still be expressed with more conventional forms. This no doubt explains why a centuries-old fixed form like the sonnet could enjoy renewed popularity in the hands of Parnassian and Symbolist poets. As Baudelaire writes in his *Salon de 1859*:

> ... never did prosodies and rhetorics prevent the production of originality. The opposite, to wit that they helped originality blossom, would be infinitely more true.

From the moment writers started to search for originality, however, many of they seem to have realized how intimately linked such new ideas could, and even had to, be with new forms. The

Romantic mixture of genres, along with its mixture of the sublime and the grotesque, already hint at the modern need to break out of established literary molds and forms. Romanticism itself has often been defined simply as "freedom in literature" (see Hugo and Baudelaire). Since freedom in this context refers to the dual possibility of expressing what one wishes, and how one wishes, it is logical to think that both types of originality were present in the minds of writers from the very moment they began to take this concept seriously.

During the first one hundred years or so of the rise of aesthetic pluralism (approximately 1770-1870), it is thus not surprising to observe that most *formal* experimentation was, by our present standards anyway, rather tame. One might object to this generalization by citing important exceptions such as the trials of Flaubert and Baudelaire in 1857 caused by their scandalous re-writing of realist novels and "flower poetry," respectively. These two forms or genres were ones with which contemporary French society *thought* it was familiar. Yet, in none of these cases did the forms alone provoke the strong reactions of the reading public. Instead what most disturbed the conservative, usually bourgeois, opponents of such formal experimentation was the dangerous spirit or idea behind them. One therefore has to wait somewhat longer before a more "pure" quest for formal originality breaks off from its thematic counter-part. Only then does this type of modern literary quest develop a conceptual life of its own.

The exact time when this happened is difficult to pinpoint. But Julia Kristéva provides as good an indication as anyone in her seminal book, *The Revolution of Poetic Language.*[22] There she locates an overwhelming appeal for revolutionary forms around 1870, with writers like Mallarmé and Lautréamont (Isidore Ducasse) taking the lead. In essence, what these writers and later writers like Joyce and Céline did, according to Kristéva, was to effectuate a radical divorce between language and syntax, and between conventional structures and meanings. On a large scale, they tried to give to words an autonomy that words had never previously had. Taking seriously the unexpected meanings produced by the original lexical and syntactic configurations they created, these writers were engaged in an aesthetic project that culminated early Romantic efforts to inject more of what I have been calling thematic originality into their works.

Significantly, however, their project did not depend on the pre-existence of their own presumed new ideas and meaning as much as it did the reconstruction of ideas and meaning by readers. Instead of first having something new or different to write (as Chénier would have said), they chose simply to write differently. They did this because they became convinced that meaning could grow, as an *organism* does, out of the reader's encounter with their texts. Thus, we find Lautréamont extensively re-writing both Baudelaire and the much earlier writer Blaise Pascal, frequently perverting some of the latter's best-known *Pensées*. The idea was to be both thematically and formally original, even though Ducasse's quest for thematic originality depended in its initial stage on the paradoxical formal recovery of "old" ideas. In other words, to be new for Ducasse meant, in large measure, choosing new forms for old ideas. These new forms would themselves generate new ideas.

Mallarmé acted similarly when he wrote a sonnet using the outrageous syllable "-yx" as a rhyme. This unfamiliar form became the vehicle by which old poetic images like the "Styx" river or the stone "onyx" were given new meaning, new life, in a word. Baudelaire, on the other hand, perfected the modern form known as the prose poem while continuing to write sonnets, saying that his collection of prose poems, *Le Spleen de Paris*, was essentially the same as *Les Fleurs du Mal*, but with more "freedom." His own "old" ideas, couched in familiar poetic verses, were thereby assumed to metamorphose into "new" ones thanks to the original form he perfected. All these examples indicate well how complex a concept originality had come to be by the end of the nineteenth century.

Yet, we must not forget that both the "forward" and "backward" types of originality still play a powerful role in much twentieth-century literary practice. If the latter seems in many cases to have "won out" over the former, it is mainly because of the powerful *effect* many modern literary works have had on modern critical practice. Since critics, professors, and institutions decide for themselves which books and which poems are "worth" reading, and since we have come to believe less and less in the notion of a text's ultimate meaning, the (critical) privileging of form over content was in all likelihood inevitable. After all, to the extent that modern critics have tended to sidestep universalist questions of significance and value, what else is left for them to talk "about," at least in an initial stage of their different readings of texts? Chapter four will explore this and related questions more completely.

Just the same, it is incorrect to think that writers have completely lost sight of the first type of originality. It is misleading to imply that they have never had anything to "say" before producing their works. To appreciate how lasting an influence the "backwards," or "inward-looking," version of originality has had in the last two hundred years, and how constant an effect it has had on the rise of literary pluralism, it would be instructive to consider the case of the founder of the Surrealist movement in France, André Breton. To a great extent, Breton may very well have been one of the last modern inheritors of the early nineteenth-century aesthetic notion of thematic originality. For, after Surrealism, the critical links between Nature, the Universe, God (or godhead), one's self, and one's artistic originality, which were first made by, at least, two generations of late-eighteenth and early nineteenth-century poets and critics, seem to have slowly disappeared. As we shall discover later in the next chapter, they were eventually replaced by a truly contemporary aesthetic of "moving-" or "looking-forward," of originality for originality's sake.

Studying Breton's work in detail allows us to trace an exemplary transformation of the concept of originality from its earliest modern incarnation to more recent avatars. It will at the same time remind us of how closely linked the two types of originality have always been, even when one type seems to prevail over the other in a particular text. After examining the literary treatment of this dual concept in Breton, we will be in a position not only to grasp better its historical significance in and of itself, but also its relationship to the final notion indispensable to our examination of literary pluralism, *progress*.

Breton's Theory and Practice of Originality

As "unfamiliar" as images in Surrealist art, film, and literature may be, it would be a gross error to conclude that the artists who created them were any more concerned with originality— in the common contemporary sense that word has taken, i.e. something spectacularly new or different having no obvious connection to the past—than other modern artists have been. Unlike the more anarchistic[23] Dadaists who inspired them, the Surrealists were not interested in revolution for revolution's sake. Their gesture or project, at least as far as Breton was concerned, had a far more defined goal than the simple creation *ex nihilo* of something different. If we consider Surrealism then, to be the twentieth-century parallel to Romanticism, as have countless other critics before me, two pressing questions come to mind. First, how does Breton define his own poetic originality? And second, what do his personal ideas tell us about the role the Surrealist movement plays in the history of this important notion?

Let me begin by noting how from his earliest writings on, Breton wanted to take his distance from individuals he disdainfully called "poets." As he says in *Les Pas Perdus*, "Were it not for him [his friend Jacques Vaché], I probably would have been a poet."[24] This suggests that from Breton's perspective no true *esprit de son temps* ("spirit of his time") would ever deign to write in a manner that, over the years, his fellow men had come to assume was, in some shape or form, standard operating poetic procedure. According to Breton, no self-respecting artist who worked with, and in, the medium of written words could help "losing his neighbors" ("égarer ses voisins," *PP* 14). If one truly wanted to progress as a "bel esprit," one would be well advised, from this point of view, to cease thinking idealistically of the activity known as writing.

As a result, the sole progress possible in the literary domain could occur only upon first challenging what Breton refers to as "written poetry" ("la poésie écrite"); that is, a conventional type of composition dear to many earlier writers. Breton was convinced that most older approaches to poetic creation were inappropriate for his generation and society. He was committed to the idea that these approaches had to be replaced by an avant-garde practice that would no longer produce "mere" literature. One thinks here of Verlaine's earlier and analogous scorn for imperfect poetry, that ersatz literature to which he referred as *tout le reste* ("all the rest"). In any case, the practice as conceived by Breton had only begun to be exploited by certain writers in the second half of the nineteenth century. The most important of these in France were Lautréamont, Rimbaud, Saint-Pol Roux, and Germain Nouveau:

> Written poetry is losing its very reason-for-being day after day ... these [earlier] authors never made a profession out of writing (*PP* 115).

This wish of Breton's to eliminate conventional writing practice, i.e. the imitation of stylistic models provided by the Tradition, explains why he greatly admired Apollinaire's demand for a "reinvention of poetry." Apollinaire, of course, was the great proponent of "l'Esprit nouveau," which one might translate not only as the "New Spirit," but also more loosely as "The Spirit of (or for) the New."[25] In his celebrated poem "La Jolie Rousse," Breton's friend underscores the important choice all writers need to face when he writes:

> Je juge cette longue querelle de la tradition et de l'invention 'De l'Ordre et de l'Aventure'/I judge this long quarrel of tradition and invention 'Of Order and Adventure'

Needless to say, Apollinaire's own final judgement came down squarely on the side of "adventure." So has that of many of our most important and influential modern writers. As we saw earlier in this chapter, this is especially true with respect to "formalistic" adventures.

Yet, the progress Breton had in mind cannot be fully understood except in terms of a more general, human movement *backwards* towards a better condition, a more complete and satisfying existence. Instead of weighing the pros and cons of Apollinaire's version of the quarrel of the Ancients and Moderns, Breton combines both Order and Adventure. His own "adventurous" automatic writing technique aims to recover a salubrious primordial Order for what he believed was the sake of his entire society. This desire to fuse philosophy and poetry with life itself recalls similar Socratic and Platonic ideals, not to mention those of the nineteenth-century utopian thinker Charles Fourier, whom Breton admired. A generally idealistic underpinning was thus evident everywhere in the Surrealist's work.

What I wish to emphasize, consequently, is how intimately linked the values of poetic originality and human progress are in Breton's *oeuvre*. From his perspective, the most important artistic consideration for writers and critics alike lies in the catalytic power of images in Surrealist poetry to help society learn more about itself, about the many different selves who form it. If the products of his espoused automatic writing style do not lead him and/or his readers to the formulation of a "collective myth," their *originality* has served no real purpose.

Without a doubt, Breton's notion of a collective myth is analogous to the "modern mythology" which his friend and fellow heir to nineteenth-century aesthetics, Louis Aragon, sought to record in his Surrealist novel, *Le Paysan de Paris* (1924). I will have more to say about Aragon shortly. For the moment, let us just remember that Aragon's poetic practice, like that of his Romantic predecessors, consisted of seeking out that which was "local" and "fleeting" in life. This quest was made possible by collecting various poetic *trouvailles* ("finds") in the course of real and imagined "aleatory movements" (i.e. peregrinations controlled by a kind of deified Goddess of chance, "alea") which Aragon made around Paris, often in the company of his fellow Surrealists. Such movements allowed him to include in his modern mythology various "signs" of contemporary life in France. These signs included everything from shop facades to gasoline pumps to newspaper stands. What continually caught his eye in such signs was the mysterious connection they appeared to have with archetypal forms. Noticing them meant that society at large could discover, or better still, *re-*discover, re-produce, preserve, and admire the archetypal forms related to them. Thanks to this recuperation of what was in fact "old," Aragon and his Surrealist friends felt that their fellow citizens would foster among themselves a greater sense of community and cohesive social identity.

Not surprisingly perhaps, aleatory movements often lead these literary "adventurers" to several important and popular flea markets and pawn shops in and around Paris. These places are definable precisely on the basis of their new or "original" juxtaposition of more or less familiar, older objects. In this way, the objects and spaces which most attracted the Surrealists were themselves, frequently, concrete amalgams of Apollinaire's "Order and Adventure." Yet, the new poetry or lyricism promoted by Breton, as well as by Aragon, does differ formally from that of earlier "writers." Citing the well-known hypnotic trances of another Surrealist friend, Robert Desnos, Breton states:

> It seems to me certain ... that the new lyricism will find the means of *translating* itself without the help of books (*PP* 174).

In other words, the mere formal originality of certain new poems did not qualify as a bona fide aesthetic criterion unless it could be translated into practical action, into real social change. For the "pope of Surrealism," poetry was useful to men and women only when it avoided giving them false hope in the inherently positive value of any and all literary progress, as it pertains to mere formal innovation. He and others, as we shall see, felt this way because progress in literature does not follow the same trajectory as it does in science. Moreover, to Breton, science or any scientifically-based project, like new writing "methods" or "techniques," be they automatic or otherwise, were beneficial only when they brought humanity closer to nature, a process which he claimed true poetry could facilitate:

> The scientific study of nature has no value except on the condition that *contact* with nature through poetic and, I daresay, mythical channels be reestablished. It remains clear that any scientific progress accomplished within the framework of a defective social structure only works against Man, and serves to aggravate his condition. This was already the opinion shared by Fontenelle.[26]

Here Breton alludes to an earlier, Golden Age of Nature, a primordial state of bliss in which opposites, incarnated by the quintessential figure of the Androgyne, were fused. Recovering this anterior state of existential union became the single most significant purpose for his writing, since this recovery resulted from a so-called "state of grace" with which Surrealist poets were occasionally "blessed," in Breton's words. In the often-quoted beginning of his *Second Manifesto*, the mental place ("lieu mental") the poet comes to inhabit while in the trance-like state of automatic writing becomes the "culminating point" or "supreme point" of human existence itself. In this place, all opposites "cease to be perceived contradictorily," and reunite as one.

The emotional and cognitive rewards of this mystical reunion were so great in Breton's opinion that whatever poetic originality he may have exhibited has to be evaluated—within the context of his own thought—in direct proportion to his success or failure in restoring the "eidetic image" of this original state. For him, the discoveries of automatic writing help us better understand why the modern separation of direct perception of objects, and their subsequent re-presentation, are but unfortunate accidents. These accidents result from our having somehow forgotten an earlier, more unified mind-set. The main benefit of automatic writing (an example of *formal* originality) was thus, in theory,[27] that it let readers capture, almost effortlessly, traces of this primordial mind-set, as if the latter were a "new" idea (an example of *thematic* originality, as we described it earlier).

Due to the child-like nature of this antedeluvian world to which Breton, metaphorically, would have had us return (a world analogous to the newly-cleansed one found in Rimbaud's *Illumination*, "Après le Déluge," which he greatly admired), he also believed that we could discover much about this earlier state by studying vestiges of it in specific, privileged individuals:

> All of the experimentation now undertaken would be of a nature to demonstrate that perception and representation—which seem to the ordinary adult to be so radically opposed to one another—must be considered merely as the products of dissociations from a unique, original faculty [...] of which traces can be found in primitive people and children.[28]

Throughout his works we find this idea of a perceptual and emotional re-union which Surrealism aspired to bring about, one that would result "from the conciliation *into one lone being* [...] of everything that can be expected *from the outside and the inside*."[29]

The crucial point for Breton, however, is that this universe has always been there, well before modern art and science came along to fragment it into separate domains. Though it was not created *ex nihilo*, it has remained hidden nevertheless to most people since the beginning of History. One of the most original goals of Surrealist poetry was precisely to learn how to read the present world as if it were a "cryptogram"; in other words, "to recover the secret of a language whose elements ceased to behave [merely] like ship-wrecks on the surface of a dead sea."[30] To accomplish this, it was necessary to avoid putting words to what he calls a "strictly utilitarian" usage. Only in that manner would one be able to emanicipate them, to give back to them the power they supposedly had in an earlier era. When I talk about originality in Breton's scheme of things, I am not talking, therefore, about the merits of individual poets who create, control, or manipulate something new. Rather I refer to the intrinsic value of any and all deliberate formal attempts to let loose this same thematic *something* to which, failing a better term, Breton gave the name "poetry."

The desired transcendence is thus a dynamic entity which the local, ostensibly fortuitous, and original insights of automatic writing are supposed to make available to both writer and reader. Like his Romantic and Symbolist forebearers, Breton's writing models almost never come from an external stylistic tradition, but rather from within himself, from within his own individual vision and experience of life. Louis Aragon makes a similar point in his *Traité du style* (1928) with respect to Surrealist poetics itself. In that text, the latter is defined as,

> recognized, accepted, and practiced inspiration. Not as an inexplicable visitation, but as a faculty that is practiced.[31]

What Aragon shares with Breton—and, I might add, Mallarmé as well—is the belief that words have so much inherent beauty and force that, ultimately, they reduce the poet's role to a most mechanical one indeed. Writers who lack genuine talent will, of course, continue to hope that their poems exhibit a certain novelty when they are read by the public. The least talented writers will continue to think that the individual differences their works bring to the body of literature are, by definition, "original" traits that, for that very reason, are worthy of the reader's respect and admiration. In this regard, Breton breaks away from the Romantics' privileging of individual differences in their earlier quest for originality.

As Breton understood poetic originality, however, the concept really came into play only when one became adept at formally transcribing particularly powerful, albeit fortuitous lexical sequences. The original poet, to be sure, had a feel for the "emotive power" (Pierre Reverdy's term) of certain lexical encounters. But, he also had to act vigilantly in order to manipulate and arrange them formally in such a way as to bring about a kind of poetic explosion of meaning and form. In the end, these sequences of words alone were the entities which "made love" to each other in the text, to borrow Breton's famous dictum, "Les mots font l'amour."

The discovery of original images thus constitutes the most important task of the poet who sits down in a comfortable place, as Breton advises in the "Secrets de l'Art Magique Surréaliste" section of his *Manifeste*, and begins to write rapidly, without preconceptions. It is no doubt significant that the word "origin" reappears in this same section, where Breton advises the poet to reject any word "whose *origin* [my emphasis] seems suspect." What he suggests here is that "true" originality, or what I have been calling "thematic originality," has much to do with a specific, i.e. correct, *origin*. This suggestion is one to which I shall return presently. In any case, the problem of differentiating between "valuable" and worthless transcriptions of what thought dictates remained a serious one for Breton. For him and his compatriots it remained a kind of theoretical thorn in their critical side. To see how annoying a problem this was, consider a very telling remark in the same passage from Aragon's *Traité du style* quoted above. While stressing the need for energy in the exercise of what Breton called one's "original faculty," Aragon admits that the results of automatic writing are "of an unequal interest." In other words, while all surrealist images are created equal in principle, practically speaking, they are not all equal.

Here again, Breton's particular conception of poetic originality, reminiscent of the Romantic prototypes, helps to resolve another apparent enigma. Let us recall the reason why he chose not to publish many of the poems he and his friends wrote. In Breton's *Second Manifesto*, he reveals a major objection to these texts when he states that they kept the poet, and presumably, the reader,

> as uninformed as always about the *origin* of that *voice* that it behooves everyone to hear (my emphasis).[32]

I have underlined the word "origin" in the last quotation in order to re-emphasize the peculiar nature of the Surrealist's quest. In this example, and others we have already seen, one is confronted with an extraordinary situation in which the ultimate index of a poem's originality, in Breton's perspective, lies in its capacity to return both writer and reader to a particular mental place or *origin*.

It would appear, then, that the supreme or culminating point of the mind alluded to earlier is simultaneously the point of departure *and* of destination for surrealist poetry. Insofar as the former point is the location where, precisely, opposites are no longer supposed to be perceived as such, there is a certain consistency in our fusing these apparently different points. What makes one automatic poem "better" than another, therefore, is that the first exhibits more *origin*ality than the second; it comes closer to conjuring up the common mental place from which a sacred, quasi-redemptive inner voice *origin*ates in us all. In Breton's opinion, formal originality is positive only when it generates thematic originality, which is precisely why he appears to be so faithful an heir to Romanticism's aesthetic legacy.

As unsatisfying as Breton's actual argument may seem, it is surely much less so than Aragon's, as set forth in the above-mentioned paragraph of *Traité du Style*. Reminiscent of Reverdy's classic 1918 formulation of the poetic image (which combined "emotive power and poetic reality"), it, too, stresses the idea that a "good" poem exhibits both "strength and novelty." In addition to these rather vague, intangible qualities, Aragon cites still another aspect of the so-called "valuable" automatic text which he describes in even more problematic fashion. He says simply that such poems are "well written," and that "writing well is like walking straight." In the wake of Formalism, New Criticism, and Structuralism, it is practically impossible to over-emphasize the uselessness of this comparison. Whereas it pretends to explicate a phenomenon by means of a "common-sense" reference to the ordinary action of walking, it merely exacerbates our confusion by calling into question the notion of doing anything whatsoever *well*.[33] Exactly how does writing resemble walking? Better yet, in which precise ways can we presume to say even figuratively that one writes as if he or she were stumbling instead of walking *straight*?

Clearly then, what results from this extended interrogation is that *no* definitive, formal guiding principle exists for differentiating among good, bad, and ugly automatic poems. The final "judge" of quality in this, and so many other matters involving surrealist practice, had to be Breton himself, much to the ultimate chagrin of most of his earliest collaborators. I do not mean to suggest that his fellow poets did not, or could not, determine better than he which poems were somehow superior to others. I am merely trying to stress that, given his unshakeable faith in the inherent value of the mental origin of the surrealist voice, he could accept as truly original only those contemporary poems which best manifested his *personal* vision of this psychic point, or of what we might call the original image-reservoir of all thought and writing.

Indeed, on one of the rare occasions when we find the term "originality" in its nominal form, it appears in the following telling remark at the beginning of his first *Manifesto*: "I do not believe in originality for originality's sake." This statement confirms fully what I am trying to say about Breton's hesitant, "backwards-looking" version of originality, which he inherited from its earliest Romantic proponents. To move forward without looking back, to appear original at all costs, as artists even closer to us seem to want to do, was thus *not* Breton's goal or ambition. Moving "forward" or ahead in the field of literature was inextricably bound in Breton's view to his respect for what lay behind, beneath, or inside of the present. Therefore, the word "originality" and its many derivatives function throughout his work much like the rhetorical trope of syllepsis.[34] That is, they often signify figuratively *and* literally in the same instance. On the one hand, "original" images are valorized for their formal specificity, because they have presumably never before appeared in the course of literary history. Their formal novelty breathes fresh life thereby into the tired static world of written poetry, a world of *being*. On the other hand, what really makes them original for Breton is their configurational and semantic propinquity to that unspeakable, unsayable origin of thought to which the Surrealist poets tried to remain attentive. This origin can never be articulated; it can merely be alluded to, for it is precisely that dynamic psychic source which gives rise to all other (poetic) utterances, the realm of *Werden*, i.e. of "becoming."

We should also note that Breton hesitated to qualify as "thought" the *thing* which derives from this inner source of inspiration. Consider, for example, the following sentence, which we read in one of his very last texts entitled *Le la* (1960):

> The 'dictation of thought' (or of something else?) to which Surrealism wanted to submit itself *originally* ["originellement", my

emphasis], and on which it wanted to rely through so-called
'automatic writing', to how very many risks in waking life have I
said its audition (active-passive) is exposed.[35]

In this passage, one can clearly appreciate the double function and
meaning of the word "originality" as I have attributed it to Breton.
While Surrealism's most striking stylistic or formal innovation was,
to be sure, its reliance on a new type of "automatic" writing, the
latter's most important feature lay in its capacity to return both
writer and reader to a (the?) utopia, or "supreme point," that is
forever *becoming*. As ambivalent towards the contemporary aesthetic
of "originality for originality's sake" as his Romantic predecessors
were, Breton shared with the latter, almost a century later, a
"backwards" or inward-looking model of the concept. His own break
with the stylistic models handed down to him, however, was even
more radical than that performed by the poets and critics who first
began the wide-sweeping privileging of the notion of originality. For
they "merely" violated, for the most part, conventional practices, as
when Hugo exploited the *anti*-classical "alexandrin trimètre," or
when Rimbaud wrote "false" sonnets. On the other hand, Breton and
company proposed a whole new writing *procedure*.

Before concluding, a final pertinent comment on Breton's text,
Le la, needs to be made. Breton admits that Victor Hugo's "Bouche
d'ombre" never spoke to him in the same way, nor even to the same
extent, as it did to the earlier major poet. Yet, the only thing that
appears essential for Breton in this regard is that this same
mouth/voice spoke to him *on occasion* ("parfois"). The words it
proffered, he insists, were addressed to him alone ("à moi seul"). He
knew this to be the case because he perceived a distinct similarity
between this other voice and his own. These remarks remind us how
the idea of originality in Breton's conceptual framework has two
different sides. For, as it turns out, a few words whispered to him
personally ended up forming the structure of a kind of "collective"
poem which he said was the one he cherished most throughout his
life. The title he chose for the poem, "Les Etats Généraux," evokes
perhaps the most *collective* act of creation in French history, the
making of the Republic itself.

The allusion to this quintessentially collective act, however, serves as the title to what Breton would have had us believe was a poem whispered to him alone. In reality, Breton first heard a simple one-sentence image, "There will always be a shovel in the sands of dreams," that he then segmented in such a way as to form a much longer poem, much in the same fashion as Mallarmé did with his *Coup de dés*. Thus, while he loved "Les Etats Généraux" because of the specific "personalized" phrase/image which inspired him to write it, he used the image as a pretext for a more elaborate poetic re-invocation of a longstanding wish. As we saw earlier, his wish was for a new "collective myth" in which everyone could partake and participate. The desire to be an original poet, therefore, never prevented Breton from keeping a common social sense about the goals he set forth for his artistic and political practice. In other words, he never wanted to be merely an original poet. His real ambition was to become an original *thinker*.

His texts then are not original because of their "mere" literary re-presentation of what Apollinaire first called "surreality." Their ultimate specificity consists instead in a singular *presentation* of a different reality, a more holistic, anterior existence. His revolution, his originality, was thus as much social, political, and "thematic" in nature as it was simply formal. This makes sense, of course, for the Romantics, in the name of contemporary social and political revolutions, had already proclaimed the start of a formal revolution with their sudden emphasis on originality. Between the start of the nineteenth century and the beginning of the twentieth, however, we find an important difference in the respective literary situations. Social revolution in the earlier time was happening *in spite of* poets and critics, instead of *as a result* of them, as the Surrealists, haughtily perhaps, felt was true for them.[36] Early Romantic writers worked for the most part from within, or alongside of, literature's norms and conventions, in order to affect their society as a whole. Later Romanticism, Symbolism, and Surrealism though, by virture of their growing commitment to *formally* revolutionary writing techniques, represent the real beginning of our contemporary obsession not only with thematic originality, but even more importantly, with the formal variety.

This is why, at the end of the first *Manifesto*, Breton can say that "Existence is elsewhere." By the early twentieth century, Chénier's "new ideas" could no longer be expressed in the old forms. As Rimbaud had declared in 1871, new ideas, and new perspectives on the world and human existence did indeed have to take on radically new forms in order to be expressed faithfully. But, significantly, Breton's radical break with the formal conventions he inherited did not undermine his *personal* adherence to older utopian ideals. His work thus forms an important historical nexus between the first kind of originality prized by so many Western writers from two hundred years ago, i.e. a thematically "backwards" or "inward-looking" variety, and the more modern tendency to seek otherness and difference through radical formal originality. To express this idea in another way, we might borrow a neat formula from an influential article on Surrealism and say that "the originality of [Breton's] textual organization is not a *sign* of surreality, it *is* its surreality itself."[37]

* * *

In terms borrowed from Thomas Kuhn's concept of a scientific revolution, I can now summarize the crucial, if gradual, shifts in aesthetic praxis that have occurred over the last two hundred years or so. For Kuhn, such shifts are changes in what he calls a given society's *paradigms*, which are: "accepted examples of scientific [or, in this case, literary] practice [that] provide models from which spring particular coherent traditions of scientific research" (Kuhn, 10). The change in the way both poets and critics alike viewed the notion of originality represents nothing less than a change in one of the West's fundamental literary paradigms: the deliberate imitation of earlier models. This essential paradigm change in literary history amounts to the artistic equivalent of a scientific revolution, since the textual practices (or Kuhn's "coherent traditions of scientific research") to which it gave rise in both creative and critical literary domains were radically transformed. Instead of having more homogeneous (in the case of France, *centralized*) literary institutions, with a few schools and individual writers here and there trying to express themselves differently from others, the period in question saw the creation of an artistic scene where more and more kinds of schools and movements multiplied at an unprecedented rate after Romanticism. One need only think in this regard of all the "-isms" that have appeared and disappeared since that time: realism, parnassianism, symbolism, decadentism, naturalism, cubism, dadaism, surrealism, existentialism, etc., etc.

The subsequent multiplicity and diversity in styles, genres, and forms which followed has, moreover, continued to increase up until our own time. Radical modifications in the prosodic conventions of fixed forms like the sonnet or classical alexandrine verses, which we find in Hugo, Baudelaire, Rimbaud, Verlaine, and Mallarmé all partake of this general explosion of poetic traditions. Prose poems, blank verse, "automatic" poems, concrete poetry, "stream of consciousness" novels, New Novels, theater of the Absurd, and Minimalist texts constitute still other radical innovations found in the wake of this massive shift towards individual styles, towards "literary pluralism," in a word. But what needs to be underscored is that all such movements and changes were fueled, so to speak, by the earlier impetus provided by Romanticism itself, which gave us our first glimpse of the new, modern emphasis on originality and individuality. When post-Romantic poets set out to practice their art, in the vast majority of cases, they proceeded from their suddenly unshakeable belief in the prestige and intrinsic worth of originality. In a few cases, like Breton's, a theoretical ambivalence towards originality still obtains, one that seems to belie the more general literary phenomenon taking place.

Yet, ever more radical formal *practices* in modern times (including Breton's itself) suggest the extent to which such theoretical objections often fall by the wayside, so to speak, when poets actually confront the white paper in front of them. Thomas McFarland expresses this paradigm shift in these words:

> Armoring himself in the concept of originality, the aspiring creator
> has simply "denied," in the Freudian sense of defense mechanism,
> the cultural reality around him [i.e. earlier literature produced
> largely by stylistic imitation] and thereby continued to produce. The
> innovations of the last hundred years or so, including many of those
> in Romanticism itself, culminating in Dadaism and Surrealism, are
> all attempts, by hyperemphasis on the concept of originality, to deny
> the relevance of the exponentially increasing deluge of culture. (8)

What McFarland implies by this last phrase is that modern writers
tend not to recognize their own debt towards previous and,
sometimes, contemporary artists or art forms. This is because of
their pluralistic "hyperemphasis" on originality.

Just because they do not always choose to recognize it, however,
does not mean that it does not exist. Moreover, although his
assessment of recent literary history is generally correct, I for one
would extend McFarland's historical limits by about sixty years.
After all, there is no need to stop at Surrealism when appreciating
the magnitude of this paradigm shift, which is correctly situated at
the turn of the eighteenth century. For one has to ask: Have writers,
artists, and even critics since 1930 really *stopped* thinking about
being original in some way, or about creating something new? If so,
why have we insisted on calling various twentieth-century textual
practices by names like *New* criticism or *New* novel,
*Post*structuralism and *Post*modernism? The answer, of course, is that
we have *not* stopped thinking of modern literary productions in this
manner. The fact is that most critics still insist on using terms such
as these because we live and work with a new paradigm, or more
precisely, with a paradigm of *newness*.

This new paradigm, whose birth was first evident with the advent
of Romantic thought and practice, thus represents the major historical
origin of what we have been calling "literary pluralism." The rise of
this phenomenon has coincided with our increased critical
valorization of synonyms for originality: new, different, novel,
cutting-edge, path-breaking, or in a more popular vein, mind-
blowing, far-out, and the like. Philological evidence confirms this
argument in a remarkable way. European dictionaries from the
eighteenth century, as well as Furetière's seventeenth-century French

version, contain short, meaningless entries under the term "originalité," summarily making of it either a stylistic weakness, or else, a pejorative personality trait, as in the expression, "C'est un vrai original"/he is a real *original* (read *bizarre character*). In the literature of Revolutionary America, too, we find analogous scorn for the word/concept "originality" in Thomas Paine's immensely popular *Common Sense* (1776). In reference to William the Conqueror's conquest of England, Paine writes:

> A French bastard landing with an armed Banditti and establishing himself king of England against the consent of the natives, is in plain terms a very paltry rascally *original*. It certainly hath no divinity in it (my emphasis).[38]

Beyond its obvious importance for my philological argument, this passage is significant for another reason as well. It indicates how, in 1776, the unquestioned links between, on the one hand, political freedoms and cultural pluralism—concepts which form the very foundation of American Democracy, as espoused by Paine and others at the time—and, originality, on the other, were *as yet* not being made. To justify "literary pluralism," as I have defined this two-sided phenomenon here, on the primary basis of an aesthetic and/or critical quest for *originality*, would thus have, in all likelihood, been unthinkable for many of our own "Founding Fathers."

However, the nineteenth-century encyclopedic Larousse (1874), suddenly (and, it may at first seem, inexplicably) devotes three very long columns to the definition and refinement of this term. Given its earlier inferior role and place in the social, as well as literary domain, one cannot help but be more than a little surprised by the very beginning of the said entry. According to this dictionary, "originalité" is now "la qualité maîtresse"/the *master* characteristic (my emphasis) that defines the great writer and great poet. The question we must therefore ask is this: What transpired in the hundred-year period between the time originality had a kind of secondary status, and the time when it began playing a central role in the literary domain? To answer succinctly, what happened is that this notion emerged gradually from its historical, conceptual darkness to shine like a powerful beacon to guide poets and critics who were looking for something to say.

Now, some might object that, at best, this philological evidence represents a set of isolated, albeit interesting, coincidences. To counter this objection, we would do well to consider a similar phenomenon which took place in England as well. Historical data available to us here come from a close reading of the introduction to the nineteenth-century English project originally known as the *New Oxford English Dictionary*. Undertaken in 1857 by the Philological Society, the OED (or, as it was first called, the NED, the *New English Dictionary*) contains a discussion of the adjective "new" which gives witness to an implicit ideological commitment to the concept of originality from the start of that massive project. A resolution passed by the Society states that its secretary, Mr. H. Coleridge,

> had clearly convinced the committee of the inadequacy of its [earlier] proposals [for upgrading the existing dictionary] and had shown that nothing short of a "completely new" work would suffice.[39]

According to the introduction to the OED, it was in this "natural way" that the epithet *New* arose, "which appeared on the title-page of the Dictionary when the time of publication arrived." Interestingly, the adjective was eventually dropped in 1895 when the designation become the more familiar OED we know today. Thirty-eight years after the project began was apparently too long a period during which one could expect the editors to continue using the then-anachronistic "new." The fact is that it would take another thirty-three years for the final version to appear in 1928.

Nevertheless, one has to wonder how any group of scholars really believed that a dictionary—of all things!—could ever be "completely new." Since the English language, then and now, contains many of the same words and meanings used before and after the appearance of the presumed new work, such collective pretense can only be explained by the historically-specific value placed on the notions of novelty and originality by that society as a whole, and, in particular, the English intellectual community. At all costs then, even that of simple logic, it seems to have been necessary by the end of the nineteenth century for serious scholars to claim that they were producing something completely new. And they claimed this, even though any type of lexicological tool, like a dictionary, depends, by definition, on a whole body of previous language and language uses. The absurdity of this "completely new" project thereby appears to have eluded some of the very people most closely involved in it. But such is the power of the myth of originality on the imagination of modern writers and critics who are not able (or willing?) to distinguish between degrees of originality. One is, therefore, compelled to recognize that an extraordinary transformation and elevation in stature of an abstract concept occurred somewhere between the two centuries. Both aesthetic practice and critical pronouncements point unmistakenly to an historic shift towards a more pluralistic model of language, literature, and, a forteriori, their respective critical understanding.

But in what ways, one might ask, is this a "pluralistic" model? First, because writers were henceforth invited en masse to create works with an eye towards how their new works could assist in moving an entire field of so-called "literature" beyond the more or less stable thematic and formal models furnished by tradition. The more "new" works could be produced, the more pluralistic the literature. Inasmuch as political and cultural pluralism was growing in importance and influence, so, too, it was assumed, should its literary manifestations. Since deliberate attempts at expressing new ideas only went so far, the quest for thematic originality soon gave way to a more exclusive search for new forms. In the extreme, this formal quest generates its own kind of thematic novelty.

Second, insofar as originality had suddenly become privileged, various critics could set for themselves the task of isolating and describing what turned out to be many different versions of "originality" in creative writings they chose to analyze. If more than one version could be discovered (as was so often the case, and still is),[40] then critics had every reason to adopt, even to promote, a "pluralistic" approach to their own subject matter. This is exactly what they have done, thanks to the historical force of a second widespread belief of Western society, the un-ending belief in progress.

Since the present chapter has been devoted to the rise of the aesthetic side of literary pluralism, I shall now put aside the question of the critical appropriation of this notion of originality until I have discussed the related concept of "progress" in greater detail. My next chapter will examine more thoroughly the particular links that tie modern critical practice to the twin concepts of originality and progress. These links will ultimately help complete the study of what I have been calling "critical pluralism." In the light of originality's historical emergence as a dominant aesthetic criterion then, a final crucial question arises: What is the relationship between this new belief in originality's primacy in things literary, and the simultaneous popularity throughout European intellectual circles of the notion of progress? To answer this question, we shall first have to understand why we should be interested in the simultaneity of these two historical phenomena.

NOTES

[1] In an important book, Thomas McFarland has labelled this situation the "originality paradox." See the first chapter of his *Originality and Imagination* (Baltimore: Johns Hopkins University Press, 1985), pp. 1-30.

[2] Roland Mortier, *L'Originalité: Une Nouvelle Catégorie Esthétique au Siècle des Lumières* (Genève: Droz, 1982), p. 11. Further references to this work are included in the text.

[3] This is one more reason to think that Flaubert's late nineteenth-century novel about two bizarre copyists, *Bouvard et Pécuchet*, is so ironic, and so scathing a critique of contemporary aesthetic attitudes.

[4] To this group I might also add *critics*, whose ever-varying interpretations of the same canonical works make it clear that they, too, are anxious to be original somehow, and in their own fashion, regardless of the relative worth of their different hermeneutic methodologies or conclusions. More on this in chapter four.

[5] Karen Rosenberg, "The Concept of Originality in Formalist Theory," in *Russian Formalism: A Retrospective Glance*, p. 166.

[6] This point will be developed in much greater detail in chapter four.

[7] In his *Theory of the Avant-Garde* trans. Michael Shaw, 4th ed. 1987 (Minneapolis: University of Minnesota Press, 1984), Peter Bürger comments on Adorno's views of "newness" and claims that the latter's aesthetic theory does allow for a certain originality among more traditional poets, but only on the condition that the *more or less* "new" be created within the confines of three major generic constraints. Burger accepts this idea in general, but challenges Adorno's claim that modern literature differs radically from older literature because it negates "the entire tradition of art" (p. 60). In his opinion (and mine, as this essay will suggest), the modern form of "newness" is instead more a question of attitudes, appearances, and *packaging* (p.61) than of any "truly" radical break with tradition.

[8] Tzvetan Todorov, *Théories du symbole* (Paris: Seuil, 1977), p. 142. Just as Bürger does in his previously cited comments on Adorno, Todorov also posits three degrees of imperfection that help recuperate, in the discourses of several eighteenth-century theorists, the theory of imitation as the fundamental law of art. In both cases then, we find a historically significant resistance to change before the advent of Romanticism, as well as a strong allegiance to the aesthetic primacy of imitation.

[9] My emphasis, Mortier, p. 124. It is interesting to note the similarity between Goethe's point of view and that of a modern American advertising executive, who was recently quoted as saying, "Originality is the art of concealing your sources." In both cases, one gets the idea that although neither really believes in the concept, neither wants to speak as if the possibility of true originality were completely non-existant. See "The Director who started a Revolution," *New York Times* (Wednesday March 25, 1992) C6.

[10] See Harold Bloom's remark in *A Map of Misreading* (New York: Oxford University Press, 1975), p. 66: "At the center of the Romantic vision is the beautiful lie of the Imagination, the only god [...] but what is the Imagination unless it is the rhetorician's greatest triumph of self-deception?"

[11] In "The Rise of Modern Science and the Genesis of Romanticism" *PMLA*, 97, 1 (January 1982), 8-30.

[12] In the twentienth-century terminology of Jean-Paul Sartre, this distinction can perhaps be best understood as the difference between a *pour soi* consciousness reserved for thinking beings, and the *en soi* of things.

[13] In Michel Foucault, *The Order of Things* (New York: Vintage Books, 1973), especially the chapter devoted to "The Limits of Representation," pp. 217-249.

[14] M. H. Abrams, *The Mirror and the Lamp* (Oxford: Oxford University Press, 1953), pp. 218-225.

[15] *A Map of Misreading*, pp. 35-6.

[16] I thank Professor David Konig, a specialist of American History, and colleague of mine, for his verification of this.

[17] The notion of unfamiliarity is, of course, one of the major aspects of the Russian Formalist concept of literariness.

[18] See the collective work *OULIPO: la littérature potentielle* (Paris: Gallimard, 1973), pp. 19 & 21.

[19] Alain Robbe-Grillet, *Projet pour une révolution à New York* (Paris: Editions du Minuit, 1970)

[20] *As* heterosexual women or lesbians, as the case may be.

[21] Edward Said, *The World, The Text, The Critic* (Cambridge, MA: Harvard University Press, 1983), p. 135. Said insists that to discover a work's originality we need to turn our eyes to the *future* (cf. my "forward-looking" type of originality) in order to "de-Platonize our thought," as Foucault and Deleuze want us to do.

[22] Published originally under the title, *La Révolution du langage poétique* (Paris: Seuil, 1972), and recently translated by Margaret Waller as *The Revolution of Poetic Language* (New York: Columbia University Press, 1986).

[23] In this context, we might also call them more "formalistic," since they did not seem to care much about their "thematic" originality.

[24] *Les Pas Perdus* (Paris: Gallimard, 1969), p. 9. Further references to this collection of essays by Breton are incorporated in the text, followed by PP and the page number.

[25] The obvious parallel here in painting was "l'art nouveau."

[26] André Breton, *Entretiens* (Paris: Gallimard, 1973), pp. 251-2.

[27] Unfortunately, in practice this semantic recuperation by the public often failed because the formal innovation of automatic art was regarded as too radical, too arcane.

[28] *Point du Jour* (Paris: Gallimard, 1970), p. 188.

[29] *Arcane 17* (Paris: U.G.E., 1965), pp. 147-8.

[30] *Du surréalisme en ses oeuvres vives* (1953) in *Manifestes du Surréalisme* (Paris: Jean-Jacques Pauvert, 1962), p. 311. Compare this idealistic image to that of Robbe-Grillet's disillusioned cartoon-characters mentioned above.

[31] (Paris: Gallimard, 1980), pp. 187-9.

[32] In *Manifestes*, p. 163.

[33] In order to avoid any misunderstanding of my point here, I should indicate that in the original French Aragon uses the adverb "bien" in the context of both statements: 1) a poem "bien écrit", and 2) writing well "bien écrire."

[34] See Michael Riffaterre's extensive work on this trope, especially his article, "Syllepsis" *Critical Inquiry*, 6 (Summer 1980), 625-38.

[35] In *Signe Ascendant* (Paris: Gallimard, 1968), p. 174.

[36] Lest it be forgotten, the principal organ of the Surrealist movement was the periodical, *La Révolution surréaliste*.

[37] Laurent Jenny, "La surréalité et ses signes narratifs" *Poétique*, 4 (1973), 520.

[38] Quoted in Howard Zinn, *A People's History of the United States* (New York: Harper Perennial, 1980), p. 69.

[39] See the section "The History of the OED" in *Oxford English Dictionary*, 2nd. edition, ed. J.A. Simpson & E.S.C. Weiner, vol. 1 (Oxford: Clarendon Press, 1989), xxxv-lxi., esp. xxxv-xxxvi.

[40] I refer here to countless articles, books, and papers I have read over the years with titles like "The Originality of Poet X, Y, or Z."

Chapter IV
CRITICAL PROGRESS

> Critics, who are people in search of images for acts
> of *reading*, and not writing, have a different burden
> [from poets], and ought to cease emulating poets in
> the over-idealization of poetry.— H. Bloom[1]

I have now examined the historical rise of originality as a preeminent aesthetic concept among modern writers. Originality is the first of two major concepts that helps to explain the rise of literary pluralism. The second, *progress*, is closely related. What I now need to do is to reconsider how the contemporary over-idealization of originality by modern writers has affected the critical reading of literature, the critical side of literary pluralism. The reader will recall that in chapter two the particular part of the "problem" called critical pluralism was approached mainly from a theoretical point of view. In the light of several important epistemological and ontological issues, the principal idea advanced was this: the dialectical relation between texts and readers found in most acts of reading generates, in and of itself, a pluralistic attitude towards interpretation, at least as it is commonly practiced in the West. Since what a text "is" has come to be understood as involving both the words-on-the-page *and* the individual readers of such words, literary criticism cannot avoid becoming more and more pluralistic, irrespective of any efforts to the contrary.[2] The prevailing opinion is that because critics are different, so, too, must their readings be.

In order to complete this historicization of current hermeneutic practice, however, I need to investigate the topic of critical pluralism further. To appreciate fully its meaning and function, it is necessary to take into account particular texts, and particular historical events and shifts that have also contributed to its rise, just as I had to do in the preceding chapter with aesthetic pluralism. Appoaching the question of multiple readings, of critical pluralism, "merely" from a social or philosophic perspective, does not suffice, therefore, no more than it did in dealing with the dizzying plurality of modern *aesthetic* texts. Of course, the belief in such a neat slice of literary pluralism into two well-defined halves is admittedly utopian. The fact is that both the aesthetic and critical varieties of literary pluralism overlap with each other so much today that the expository strategy adopted here is increasingly difficult to justify. I shall argue presently that this overlapping has been caused precisely by a kind of historical fusion of a large number of poets *into* critics, of poets who often assume the role of critics and readers of themselves.

In spite of this, however, I can, and will, continue to examine two sides of literary pluralism, since they do clarify my view of the real "problem," i.e. its rise. While it has been extremely useful for critics like Wayne Booth and K. M. Newton to scrutinize the social and philosophic underpinnings of critical pluralism, the present chapter considers specific, historical factors as well. After examining in greater historical detail the rise of critical pluralism, I shall conclude by offering some additional epistemological, psychological, and sociological underpinnings—not always stressed by other students of literature and pluralism—to this part of our problem. In the process I will have finally laid bare most, if not all, of the key reasons why a large majority of present day *littérateurs* believe that 2001 different readings of the same work, as well as 2001 different creative texts, are not only desirable, but necessary.

Let me repeat a final time: examining these phenomena, as I have thus far, is not a moral issue of right or wrong. I do not mean to say that the rise of aesthetic and critical varieties of pluralism is "bad." I do not, moreover, wish to plead for a reactionary stance vis-à-vis these phenomena rather than for the liberal one currently espoused by myself and most of my colleagues in the profession. What I want to stress instead is that a study of this type represents nothing more than a *critically* indispensable search for answers to the questions of *why* and *how* these historically anomalous beliefs have arisen in our society. Although some may now think I have lost my focus by returning to the subject of critical (as opposed to aesthetic) pluralism, I must emphasize that the historical connection between progress and our main problem simply could not be fully understood before first appreciating originality as the quintessential modern aesthetic criterion. My last chapter provided just such an appreciation. The present one, on the other hand, speaks more to the links between originality, progress, and the critical side of literary pluralism. As such, it completes my analysis of both sides of the "problem" in question.

Progress and Modern Literature

Texts cannot escape History any more than other cultural artifacts can. To the extent that they are produced within a given society, it is reasonable to think that one of their reasons for being (produced) reflects some of the aspirations of that society as a whole. This does not imply that they will mirror the latter completely, nor that they will absolutely take their distance from them. But it does suggest that since the eighteenth century saw a tremendous increase both in the demand for individual rights and freedom, as well as in scientific and philosophic thought, one might expect to find various traces of this increase in some form or other in that society's literature. The increase in individual freedoms brought on by historical developments in the eighteenth-century simultaneously generated greater and widespread belief in the inherent values of individualism and originality, as was demonstrated in the last chapter.

It also led, however, to a societal belief in the possibility of various kinds of *progress*. The American and French revolutionary quests for more freedom can even be said to constitute what has been called "the very principle of progress" in the modern sense.[3] Without the freedom to question, experiment, and produce something different from what had already been produced, progress of any type would have been inconceivable. Without freedom, the writer's impact on, and critic's evalaution of, literature cannot increase. One might say, consequently, that the critical knowledge and aesthetic practice of literature, minus the freedom to discover different things and to write *differently*, respectively, are really not knowledge or creation at all. They are instead forms of critical and aesthetic stasis, a moribund mind set and an imitative practice. Their indefinite continuation eventually leads to what Tzvetan Todorov, quoted in the preceding chapter, claims is the "disappearance of art."

With scientific and philosophic advances on the rise, and with visible material progress evident for certain social classes, it seems logical that some of the greatest "literary" writers should, at the same time, have also been considered the best philosophers and/or scientists. If such writers were not always universally extolled for the accuracy or profundity of their philosophic or scientific views, at the very least they were often counted among the strongest believers in the notion of progress. In France, for instance, one thinks of *philosophes* like Rousseau, Diderot, D'Alembert, and Voltaire, who not only wrote some of the most respected novels and poems of the time, but also wrote a good deal of its most important "enlightened" philosophy. And much of the latter, was, of course, imbued with a belief in the possibility of progress. Voltaire, in particular, was widely regarded as the best French *poet* of his time (!), despite the fact that few people today are interested in his poetry. To say that such canonical pillars of our present notions of "great" French literature and philosophy were also among the principal architects of that most scientific of projects, the *Encyclopédie*, makes one suspect, therefore, that a curious admixture of conceptual fields was taking place during this period.

In addition, poets like Schiller in Germany and Wordsworth in England were at more or less the same time "reinvent[ing] the hope of progress" in the field of poetry, as Murray Krieger has pointed out.[4] In a study by Jerome Buckley, the powerful influence of progress in Victorian literature, too, has been duly recorded.[5] The concept, earlier confined primarily to philosophic and scientific domains, was thus slowly creeping in, as it were, to the verbal arts. In Krieger's words, progress in the arts could be affirmed precisely "because it [was] related to their role in fostering an open, egalitarian society."[6]

Now, although the case has already been made for thinking that the mechanical, scientific model subtending most Western literature was replaced by an organic one, with the coming of Romanticism, it is important to realize that in philosophy (specifically, criticism), the scientific model continued to dominate after the eighteenth century. Not only was science gaining prestige as a result of the Industrial Revolution—particularly, the sciences of physics and biology—but scientific *method* was also being incorporated into the influential doctrine of such mechanistic, logical philosophies as positivism. So extensive, in fact, was the influence throughout Europe of Auguste Comte's ideas, along with the prototypical modern notions of progress articulated by Fontenelle, Condorcet and, of course, Hegel, that some of the earliest and best nineteenth-century critics in France, like Taine and Sainte-Beuve, could hardly escape their influence. If Thomas Kuhn is right in thinking that "science is the only field in which the concept of progress is really marked" in a clear-cut fashion (161), we can, therefore, infer that the act of "making progress" was, right from the beginning of modern, *scientifically*-based literary criticism, one of its principal goals. This inference is justifiable insofar as the majority of critically-minded *littérateurs* of the time were as thrilled as most other intellectuals were by the obvious progress made by scientists in other fields. It is thus reasonable to think that they, too, would have wanted to make their own kind of progress in their own field, a "critical progress."[7]

By creating a formal "science of literature," Valéry and his structuralist and poststructuralist heirs in the twentieth century would, in this scheme, only have furthered the cause of progress begun in nineteenth-century criticism. Indeed, the path-breaking group of French structuralists and poststructuralists in the 1960s known as *Tel Quel* took its very name from Valéry's many critical journals, which contain several seeds of modern "scientific" literary criticism. Before this, however, the criticism written by a considerable number of major Romantic poets and novelists already manifested a certain longing for scientificity, specifically in regard to the scientific notion of progress. It included works like Coleridge's *Biographia Literaria* (1817), Shelley's *A Defense of Poetry* (1821), Poe's *The Poetic Principle* (1850), the preface to

Gautier's *Mademoiselle de Maupin* (1835), Stendhal's *Racine and Shakespeare* (1854), and, once again, Hugo's preface to *Cromwell* (1827). At the same time, the relative under-privileging of the scientific model in *creative* literature generated a rather uneasy and ambiguous relationship between the newly esteemed concepts of originality and progress. As was observed above, the initial version of this new aesthetic obsession with originality was actually *opposed* to the scientific notion of progress. To be original in literature when originality first began to be sought out, one was supposed to return, *not* to move forward, to one's own individual or national roots.

In this respect, progress per se, in the sense of "advancing towards something" would have been theoretically impossible in the arts. At least, it would not have been possible in the same way as in criticism. The objective scientificity demanded of criticism was simply incompatible with most of the literature of the time. As Victor Hugo expresses it is his *William Shakespeare*:

> There is neither rise nor fall in art. Genius is always at full strength.[8]

Two paragraphs later Hugo adds, "[True] Art cannot be perfected."

Nevertheless, the concept of progress is rarely absent from a large number of *critical* discussions found in the nineteenth century, many of which just happen to have been authored by several of the most celebrated poets and novelists of the time. In an exacting, if somewhat repetitive, study of the ideas of French Romantics concerning progress, Elwood Hartman surveys the vast range of opinions held by these writers.[9] For Hartman, an important ambiguity exists among French Romantic writers vis-à-vis two types of progress, which he calls *human* and *aesthetic*. He begins his study by stating that:

> Perhaps the greatest stumbling block to the acceptance of the concept of progress in the arts is the idea that progress implies a kind of annihilation, a relegation of past accomplishments to history. In science, for example, the latest knowledge replaces preceding information, proving it wrong or insufficient (5).

Although I agree with Hartman's opinion generally, what he fails to emphasize sufficiently is the historical co-incidence of many Romantic poets and novelists with the main art and literary critics of their time. To be sure, writers like Hugo, Shelley, Coleridge, Goethe, Nerval, Stendhal, Gautier, and Baudelaire did not always need to stress the possibility of artistic progress when they sat down to create their own fictional worlds. All they needed was some notion of taste, i.e. an opinion of what was "good" or "bad," in order to formulate their own aesthetic texts. Moreover, as they all admired some previous "great" literature, it is hardly surprising that they had to temper the purely scientific ideal of annihilating "past accomplishments" with the reality of art. For, contemporary "good" art did not, and still does not, *annihilate* earlier art.

Yet, several of these poet/critics did indeed believe at various points in their careers that society at large could benefit from their writings, and that as a result, their society could register a certain *human* progress in the extra-textual sense. When it came to the question of whether Art itself could actually be improved or perfected, of whether *aesthetic* progress was feasible, most of them vacillated, however. What Hartman's survey suggests, therefore, is that, on the whole, the notion of progress was less prominent and less manageable for French Romantics writing creative texts than was the notion of originality. Yet, when such writers sat down to write critical texts about literature, the criterion most used, even if implicitly, to evaluate particular works was that of progress. So, if you were a great writer, it was thought, more and more, that you were original. If you were a great reader, you (and we) were progressive, i.e. we made critical progress.

For these reasons, it is possible to make the following generalization: originality is to modern creative writers what progress is for modern critics. Any methodological or epistemological originality exhibited by critics themselves, and any originality discovered by critics in the literature they read, has to be linked, conceptually, to a perceived ability to make scientific "progress" through the various interpretations and analyses advanced. This situation is exactly what one might expect of people living in an industrial, scientific age. Just as with the larger field of science, to progress *critically* has, for the last two hundred years, meant that previous studies or "readings" have had to be discarded, or, at least, put aside indefinitely when judged deficient in some way or other. Opinions about "good" and "bad" readings are fine, but only on the condition that they be based on hard, scientific, objective considerations.

I shall assume then that poets and critics of the nineteenth century were the first to begin assimilating, as a group, the general societal belief in progress within the fabric of their poetics, even though they did not necessarily always couch it in these terms. While they were the first, they certainly were not the last. They did not, in other words, always claim that their *own* literary productions inevitably led to either human or aesthetic progress per se. Such a claim may well have seemed too presumptuous to most of them, and may have needed to be replaced by the more modest attribution of simple "originality." Their critical opinions of other writers did nevertheless usually entail the notion of progress whenever they made a positive assessment of a different writer's or movement's work.

The historic infusion into modern literary studies of the societal beliefs in science and progress was first, and perhaps best, articulated in one of Friedrich Schlegel's *Critical Fragments* of 1797, no. 115. According to him,

> The whole history of modern poetry is a running commentary on the following brief philosophic text: all art should become science, and all science art; poetry and philosophy should become one.[10]

Appearing one year before the journal *Atheneaum* was founded in Jena by the Schlegel brothers, Schleiermacher, Novalis, and Schelling, this fragment effectively encapsulates the conceptual revolution wrought by this small but influential group of German poet/critics.[11] For them, (literary) art had to reflect the contemporary societal faith in science and all its supporting concepts. To advocate the *scientificity* of literature was tantamount to advocating a scientific type of criticism, which, alone, could render properly the specificity of modern literature. As the first truly "avant-garde" artistic group in modern Western history, the Jena school initiated a scientific, progress-based, model for what would later become a whole series of working artist collectives throughout Europe: naturalists, symbolists, impressionists, dadaists, surrealists, etc. "Critical progress" is thus a term that includes both the scientific, critical articulation of a given artist's originality, and the critical perception of one's own progress within the interpretive field. Modern critics implicitly believe that some progress has been made in the arts when an artist has demonstrated originality. Likewise, critics think they have progressed *as critics* whenever they define or delineate "original" approachs to already-interpreted texts.

What was especially new among the writings in the six issues of the Jena group's *Atheneaum*, which appeared over a mere two-year period, was something that Germaine de Staël noticed first. Madame de Staël recognized that literature was not the only new and significant German contribution to Western culture. It was rather German literary *criticism*, or as she put it, "literary theory,"[12] that represented the major novelty produced by the Jena group. I wish to argue that modern literary theory was made possible precisely because of the general historical shift we saw earlier, on the part of artists, towards the notion of originality. Since the world around writers was suddenly construed as forever changing and unfinished, and since the artist was increasingly committed to the task of representing this universal flux, the literature that began to be produced reflected more and more upon itself, upon its own transitory ontological status. It was, as a result, more lyrical, open-ended, inclusive, and "organic" than the static, closed, "mechanical" literature that preceded it.

Yet, an even more striking feature of Romantic literature lay in its capacity to produce its *own* theory at the same time it was producing itself. In large part, Romantic literary theory came into existence in order to justify, complete, and complement Romantic literature. In the words of P. Lacoue-Labarthe and J.-L. Nancy, Romanticism is "theory itself as literature, or, in other words, literature producing itself as it produces its own theory" (12). This critical self-reflexion, characteristic of some of the nineteenth and twentieth century's best writers, spawned a new kind of discourse, a discourse we have come to accept, with Madame de Staël, as modern literary theory.

To develop these points further let me expand the meaning of progress as it applies to literature and literary studies. Robert Nisbet, one of the authoritative Western historians on the subject, effectively restates the two types of progress alluded to above. Like Elwood Hartman, Nesbit defines progress as advancement in not one, but two, possible ways. The first way in which society progresses, states Nisbet, involves the acquisition of new, material *knowledge*, a movement I call "objective" progress. The second type of progress consists of a more human or humanistic advancement on earth, one to which I shall attach the label "subjective."[13] Nisbet's reduction of these related trans-historical, trans-national beliefs allows us to understand better the historical connection between the aesthetic concept of originality, and the critical concept of progress. For, it appears that nineteenth-century Western writers and critics unwittingly fused their cherished belief in these two forms of progress with their sudden hyperemphasis on, and over-idealization of, originality.

This conceptual fusion was made possible, quite simply, because of the semantic closeness of both notions. If aesthetic originality has any value whatsoever, it is because within any example of original writing we find an aesthetic criterion, i.e. originality, for the attribution of progress. A second reason why these ideas influence each another is that both progress and originality possess, so to speak, two dimensions. These dimensions (subjective and objective, and thematic and formal, respectively) often overlap each other. Presently, I shall examine some examples of this overlap. In any event, thanks to certain unquestioned lexical slippages from the vocabulary of originality to that of progress (and back), and from the notion of subjectivity to objectivity (and back), critics appear to have frequently emulated poets in their quest for "stories" of their own, as Harold Bloom says. In taking to heart the originality of their approaches or readings, the collective acts of critics have in many cases been translated, at least by *their* readers (students, teachers, writers, and other critics), into gestures that signal progress. Some modern critical stories thereby rival, in certain instances, texts that are more visibly "aesthetic" in terms of literary creativity.

Now, whether or not one agrees with any specific assessment of progress at any given place or time, Nesbit demonstrates that such assessments have routinely taken place throughout Western history. It is therefore empirically true that both the subjective and objective dimensions of progress exist as bona fide conceptual frameworks for the determination of progress. These frameworks or standards have allowed various societies, or members thereof, to determine whether one kind of progress or the other has actually occurred. With respect to originality, however, the situation is somewhat different. In the last chapter, I argued for two types of originality: the first, historically speaking, was a backward-looking, thematic kind; the second, a forward-looking, formal variety. If one is correct in thinking that both types of originality have been to modern artists what progress has been to modern critics, then it may also be assumed that the more complex, two-sided notion of progress is equally pertinent. To justify this assumption, one need only recall a simple historical fact. With the advent of Romanticism, human society at large was believed to make significant gains, i.e. progress, through the artistic expression of new ideas, new selves, and new identities. In this case, the critical progress made is clearly *subjective*. That is, individual subjects within a particular society benefit from it.

Likewise, the quest for formal originality, when seen from the reader's perspective, leads critics to speak or write of a certain *objective* progress within the field of literature. The nineteenth-century encyclopedic Larousse dictionary (1874) sheds light on this point when, under the word "progrès," it states:

> Of all the branches of human activity, those that seem the least applicable to *progress* are belle-lettres, poetry, and the arts. One can say, nevertheless, that modern [literary] historians, by the exactitude of their narrative, and by the breadth of their views, are far superior to the best historians of antiquity. Moreover, our time has produced

new literary forms; Romantic drama, the modern novel, and has
made of the newspaper an admirable intellectual weapon [my
emphasis].

What one should note in this passage is how the raw concept
described in the dictionary entry mixes two different types of
progress. In the first place, the description implies that objective
progress has been made through the creation of "new literary
forms." In addition to that, though, critics themselves are said to
have advanced because of the "breadth" and "exactitude" of their
modern analyses.

When, however, the author of this entry quotes the Chénier verse
already commented on here several times ("Sur des pensers
nouveaux faisons des vers antiques"), he brilliantly succeeds in
recouping the otherwise lost idea of a second type of progress,
subjective. Immediately after his Chénier quotation, he writes:

> That poetic verses cannot be more beautiful than they have already
> been, so be it; [but] if, to the merit of equally beautiful verses, one
> added the further merit of new, *more noble, more profound, and
> more vast thoughts, thoughts worthy of a superior man*, isn't that also
> a kind of "progress?" [...] We are so much better than our fathers in
> every respect that we must keep as a veritable *article of faith* this
> faith in progress that supports our march forward [my emphasis].

This dictionary definition illustrates clearly that many intelligent
people at the time were eager to apply the idea of progress to art, but
just could not seem to find the right way to do so. Yet, when we
split our conceptualization of the idea of progress into two parts, we,
in fact, indicate just such a way.

The privileging of modern thoughts and modern forms over older
ones, explicit in these two passages, must therefore be taken quite
seriously. Combined with the unquestioned, quasi-religious zeal for
progress present in the same definition, the idealization of new
thoughts and new forms over old ones embodies the very historic
fusion of originality and progress advanced above. Furthermore, to
the extent that this dictionary is a critical text, not an aesthetic one,
it is important to notice how it opts for a vocabulary of *progress*

when dealing with the *originality* of contemporary literature. In reference to French literary history, this is what makes Charles Baudelaire (and his Symbolist legacy) such an important piece in the conceptual puzzle I am trying to sketch out here.

To begin with, Baudelaire did not think much of objective or material progress. He basically disdained the idea because it was so integral a part of contemporary bourgeois ideology. As the quintessential dandy, Baudelaire could hardy avoid rejecting such a retrograde idea. In his celebrated poem "Le Cygne"/*The Swan*, for instance, he describes a hideous scene of multiple construction sites. These sites are, to his way of thinking, the sign of a pre-meditated destruction of the older Parisian landscape. His scornful attitude about the objective, physical "improvements" made to the city by Baron Haussmann is reflected in the ironic, albeit lyrical, tone of lamentation he adopts:

> Andromaque, je pense à vous! Ce petit fleuve,
> Pauvre et triste miroir où jadis resplendit
> L'immense majesté de vos douleurs de veuve,
> Ce Simoïs menteur qui par vos pleurs grandit,
>
> A fécondé soudain ma mémoire fertile
> Comme je traversais le nouveau Carousel.
> Le vieux Paris n'est plus (la forme d'une ville
> Change plus vite, hélas! que le coeur d'un mortel);
> [...] Paris change! mais rien dans ma mélancholie
> N'a bougé....

> Andromache, I think of you! This small river,
> Poor and sad mirror in which, years ago,
> The immense majesty of your widow pains would shimmer,
> This lying Simois through which your tears did grow,
>
> Suddenly gave birth to my fertile memory
> As I crossed the new Carousel.
> Old Paris is no more (the form of a city
> Changes faster, alas! than the heart of a mortal)
> [...] Paris changes! but nothing in my melancholy
> Has changed....

Yet, in his prose poem "Le Joueur Généreux"/*The Generous Gambler*, Baudelaire has a character say that one of the Devil's best ruses is in making people believe that "*Progress doesn't exist.*" Given the Baudelairean narrator's penchant for masks and role playing, it is hard to know exactly what to make of this last declaration. Are we to take it seriously, seeing that it is the Devil speaking? Or is this a sarcastic and somewhat sadistic play on words, like the classic philosophic dilemma of a Cretan who says that all Cretans are liars? It is well nigh impossible to decide with certainty from these aesthetic treatments of the subject where Baudelaire himself really stands on the matter of progress.

While the ambivalence of Baudelaire vis-à-vis progress resembles that of many other Romantic writers, though, it does deserve a closer examination. In his diary notes known as "Mon coeur mis à nu"/*My heart laid bare* Baudelaire writes,

> The belief in progress is a doctrine of lazy people, a doctrine of *Belgians*. The individual must count on his neighbors to do his tasks.

> There can be no progress (true, i.e. moral) except in the individual, and by the individual himself.
> But the world is made up of people who can only think in common, in groups. Hence, we have *Belgian Societies*.

Racism aside, Baudelaire makes it critically clear in this passage that the only type of progress possible, as far as he is concerned, is subjective, i.e. one pertaining to subjects (writers or readers) themselves. To the extent that our splitting of the idea of progress is correct, this statement is consistent with Baudelaire's long allegiance to traditional poetic forms, most notably the form of the sonnet. In spite of Rimbaud's eventual critique of him on this point, he obviously felt that most of his "new" ideas could be expressed with "old" forms.[14] This is just another way of saying that from a self-conscious, critical perspective, Baudelaire equated his own thematic originality with a subjective kind of critical progress. To him, *objective* progress in the arts had no real meaning anyway.

Yet, Baudelaire greatly admired a writer whose vision, and especially practice, of literature brought him closest to the scientific, progress-based ideal espoused by the Jena group in Germany and by Louis-Xavier de Ricard[15] in France. The Jena group's ideal concerned the very possibility of an objectively "best" art form. The writer Baudelaire admired was, of course, Edgar Allen Poe. Poe was a great critic and portrayer of the evils of cold-hearted calculation in the worldly affairs of men and women. Yet, Poe never expressed the view that this same calculated, pre-meditated, analytical approach to life (which, in *The Poetic Principle*, he claimed he used in composing *The Raven*) could ever be adapted by society in any positive way. He had no faith in society's global capacity to progress in one sense or other. For him, modern Industrial-age men and women, primarily in the ever-growing United States, possessed such important faults and weaknesses that they had no real ability to improve the lot of all people on earth. Most people were doomed to suffer, regardless of any efforts to the contrary. One cannot avoid thinking in this respect of Rousseau's earlier disdain for modern civilization, or of Vigny's contemporary mockery of the so-called progress of the Industrial age in his poem "La Maison du Berger," or of similar texts by Emerson and Thoreau written in the United States.

On the other hand, the tormented Poe, while accepting the neferious nature of his society's industrial and scientific predelections, felt that what I call "subjective progress in art" was possible on the condition of adopting the very formalistic, objective *machinery* he rejected outside of art. Paul Valéry expresses Poe's historical significance for us in these words:

> Poe was the first writer who thought to introduce into literary production, into the art of forming fictions, and even into poetry, the same kind of analytic spirit and calculated construction whose manifestations and failures, in other areas, he deplored.[16]

In other words, what I have called the subjective and objective modes of the general concept of progress became fused, at least in their *literary* incarnations, in the person of Poe. He accepted the possibility of objective and subjective progress in the arts because of his faith in the power of formal innovation. The thematically original fictions produced by Poe in his horror and detective stories, and haunting poetry, were thus formally contrived and calculated to provoke strong feelings in his reader. Their highly constructed nature led to what Poe, in a well-known passage from *The Poetic Principle*, called the "Rythmical Creation of Beauty." This modern type of beauty was free of many conventional depictions of beauty, and did not depend completely on stock images. It was thereby free to grow out of ugliness, horror, and evil, if that was where the poet's aesthetic pre-conceptions and predelections led him or her. In his mind, attainment of this new type of unconventional Beauty generated subjective progress in the poet and reader. As Poe wrote of Beauty,

> Its sole arbiter is Taste [obviously, a critical construct]. With the Intellect and with the Conscience, it has only collateral relations. Unless incidentally, it has no concern whatever either with Duty or Truth.

Though he felt this way about progress in literature, he does not appear to have believed that this could be applied to the masses outside of more or less elitist, artistic circles. This is due to the fact that, for him, the masses of his time were too concerned with bourgeois ideals like Duty and Truth. More often than not, they did not understand the true nature of aesthetic creation.

It was Poe, then, who inspired Baudelaire to perform the same kind of conceptual fusion of objective and subjective progress within himself. The important result was that Baudelaire became, as we know, an important *critic* of art and literature, as well as one of our most important modern poets. Indeed, much of what constitutes Baudelaire's (and Poe's) modernity lies precisely in this self-reflexive analytic propensity within the closed world of art, a world meant for the "happy few," to quote Stendhal. Using mostly traditional Christian and Renaissance imagery and forms, Baudelaire deliberately set out to stand many time-honored literary conventions on their head, in poems like "Bénédiction," "Le Reniement de Saint Pierre," "Un Voyage à Cythère," "La Béatrice," "A une Madone," "le Masque," "La Muse malade," "La Muse Vénale," and "Le mauvais moine," to mention only some of the more obvious examples. His pre-meditated, analytical approach to the deconstruction and trangression of conventional poetic themes and images, through the frequent use of a restrictive literary form like the sonnet, indicates the extent to which Baudelaire's own peculiar subjectivity ("There can be no progress except in the individual") fused with his artistic practice.

It also illustrates his fundamental lack of concern for contemporary obsessions like Duty, Truth, and Goodness, a lack which, as we know, got him in trouble with the censors of the Second Empire. This explains why, at the start of his essay, "L'Art philosophique," Baudelaire can say the following:

> What is pure art according to the modern conception? It is the creating of a suggestive magic containing both the *object* and the *subject*, the world exterior to the artist and the artist himself (my emphasis).

In this manner, Baudelaire, via Poe, succeeds in reconciling our two types of critical progress, while at the same time creating paradigmatic modern works. Objective aesthetic concerns were deliberately married for the first (but certainly not last) time in literature to subjective ones.

One cannot insist enough on the adverb "deliberately" in this regard. For other Romantics, like Hugo, Gautier, and others also wrote criticism along with their other more "literary" texts. Baudelaire was perhaps the first French writer, however, to wed the two scriptural practices in the same creative work. Literary progress would never again be possible without the prerequisite *critical* perception of originality. Poet/critics who delineated such originality were then be in a position to translate it into the meta-linguistic, scientific discourse of objective and subjective progress. It goes without saying that the fusion of these planes or dimensions continue to serve as veritable hallmarks of literary modernity.

We should therefore not be surprised when, in his essay "A quoi bon la critique?"/*What good is criticism?*, from his *Salon de 1846*, Baudelaire suggests that the best form that a modern critical analysis of art works can take is that of a sonnet or elegy. The formal precision of a sonnet, combined with its remarkable thematic potential provides the modern poet/critic a perfect linguistic vehicle for the expression of both kinds of progress, objective and subjective. A hundred years later, Harold Bloom will follow Baudelaire's lead (perhaps unawares) by suggesting in *The Anxiety of Influence* that the best critical essays are always, essentially, prose poems. And what does Roland Barthes in his *Fragments of a Lover's Discourse*, or Jacques Derrida in *Glas* propose if not this same overlapping of analysis and creativity, of objective and subjective discourses, discourses which are, in all cases, grounded on the belief in progress? In this fashion, the whole modern blurring of the line between "literature" and "criticism" must be conceived as an inevitable historical result of various late eighteenth- and nineteenth-century aesthetic concerns. While this blurring appears to be a very recent development to many modern readers, it seems instead to have two hundred year old roots which allow us to speak of the evolution of this belief.

Towards a "Fin de siècle" Criticism

At various moments in nineteenth-century France, a certain group of critics—among whom I include not only a "pure" theorist such as Madame de Staël, but also poets such as Hugo, Baudelaire, Verlaine, and Mallarmé—became conscious *en masse* of the revolutionary character of the movements in which they were involved. From Hugo's *Préface de Cromwell* to Mallarmé's "Crise de Vers," Romantic and Symbolist writers alike did not stop acting as if they were prophets, announcing both the agony of a presumed limited or limiting aesthetic, *and* the birth of a new, and fundamentally different, artistic idea or order. By studying some of the important texts of the above-named poets, I now propose to sketch out an early form of criticism which accounts for the critical attribution of literary progress mentioned above. I shall call the type of criticism in question "fin de siècle"[17] criticism. The reason it is important to insist on this label for a cross-literary genre (which Hugo had already baptized "une autre critique"/an *other* criticism) is that it cannot be restricted to Romantic literature alone.[18] Even though Hugo had originally envisioned this criticism in the exclusive terms of the movement of which he was one of the heralds, my use of the label "fin de siècle" is meant to characterize a pervasive style whose traces are found in other nineteenth- and twentieth-century movements as well. This is why I shall henceforth use the expression "fin de siècle" as if it were synonymous with the phrase "end of an aesthetic period," not just as a conventional label for the late nineteenth century.

Before I consider this critical genre, I first need to ask an ancillary historical question. I refer here to the historical causes which created this common will seemingly shared by so many nineteenth-century French writers. This will is one I have already called the *will-to-difference*. Thanks to it, many poets of the period purported to distinguish themselves aesthetically, and sometimes even morally, from many of their contemporaries. From the start I admit that I do not pretend to furnish all the answers to the question of the origin of this common will. Instead I hope to underscore only those specifically historical ones that seem most important to the evolution of this will. It seems to me essential, nevertheless, to look seriously at the number of poets who, for differing reasons, kept their distance from poetic ideas which they considered outmoded. Otherwise, it would be difficult to explain the apparent mania to be "absolutely modern" which existed among so many of them.

Was this critical over-idealization of individuality and originality merely the newest version of the age-old argument between the Ancients and the Moderns? Were these young rebels, or Jeune-France as Théophile Gautier called the most active Romantics, really defying the tenets of, and adherents to, a more traditional literature? Or was this avant-garde action performed instead primarily in the name of some unspoken principle of youth, in the name of a kind of Aristotelian topos that always pits the young against the old in a fight between the new and the old? It is tempting to answer all these questions in the affirmative, especially if one takes into account the disdain which separated the two sides in the infamous "battle" over Hugo's 1830 play, *Hernani*. This battle was at that time in France the most striking demonstration of a clearly wide-spread desire among a certain group of poets and other artists for an aesthetic alternative. What is more, the fact that the young Romantics, in particular, praised their time and century, making of them special moments in History, suggests that they were not, indeed, could not be, afraid to fight for such a just cause.

Yet, the same worry that people had to be, at any cost, *of their time*, if not in advance of it, by right should lead us to postulate something else about them. To the extent that they believed, rightly or wrongly, that they were suffering intellectually, and sometimes even physically, from their determined place in history—from the infamous "mal du siècle"—one might suppose the following: Rather than continue their "suffering," these writers more often than not wished to cure themselves of it. Their "cure" frequently took the form of a kind of confession, as one can see in cases like those of De Quincey, Musset, Baudelaire, Dostoievsky, and so many other contemporary literary penitents. The malaise which ate at them, and which had pushed them in their youth to oppose vehemently certain literary norms and conventions, in the long run, allowed them—or so it would appear—to produce within themselves a creative space. This space represented a sort of open imaginative wound, if you will, from whence their own works were released, as larvae.

To extend this admittedly unsavory, but eminently Romantic, metaphor, I might recall Hugo's aggrandizement of the grotesque, especially when juxtaposed to the sublime; or Baudelaire's accursed flowers, and his cadaver, "La charogne," whose decadence was, and remains today, exemplary in its horror; or Lautréamont's vicious *Chants de Maldoror*. In all these cases, something beautiful was supposed to emerge out of something ugly. Late nineteenth-century decadent literature from Wilde to Villiers de L'Isle-Adam reeks, as it were, of such a poetics. Provided this hypothesis is correct, then, one could say that the nineteenth-century poets who transformed themselves into "fin de siècle" critics, from the moment they began commenting on contemporary creative works, did not hesitate to take a continuing masochistic pleasure in suffering from their period in history. Instead of "wasting" their time debating past vs. present values, they abandoned their temporal orientation to worry only about a sort of permanent future, about what one recent critic has called the "anxiety of anticipation."[19] This perpetual future was close to the "state of grace" that Breton and the Surrealists later professed. It permitted them, or even, induced them, to create something that was always to be thought of as *new*.

Of course, it also tended to make them less appreciative, as time went on, of what the past and present actually had to offer them. One should remember in this regard what Baudelaire wrote in the last line of his poem, "Le Voyage." There he advises the poet/traveler to follow "Le Capitaine Mort"/Captain Death, and dive with him to the bottom of the Ocean in order to find newness: "Pour trouver *du nouveau*"/In order to find the *new*. Not coincidentally, this "newness" is italicized by Baudelaire, as if to imply the especial quality of this novel entity. It is this continual critical quest for novelty, which, as we saw in the last chapter, can either take the form of a look forward, or a kind of paradoxical nostalgic backwards glance (cf. "Le Cygne": "Andromache, I think of you") that relates to the rise of critical pluralism as I have been defining it throughout this book.

These "fin de siècle" poets/critics thus acted in such a way as to make their audience believe this: that what they were searching for in artistic creation beyond all else was simply *something else*, *something other*; that progress in poetry, as in anything, was possible. Their attitudes constituted, in this fashion, a crucial moment in the victorious battle of the Moderns over the Ancients in their century-old critical quarrel. This is the sense in which one should understand the musical poetry extolled by Verlaine in his "Art Poétique," which he compares to verses flying "towards *other* skies and *other* loves" ("Vers d'autres cieux à d'autres amours") (my emphasis). The metaphoric music demanded of late nineteenth-century poets was thereby explicitly associated with a longing for *otherness*, even though this longing had started much earlier in the century. Poets who had begun, in earnest, to seek originality in their creative works at the end of the eighteenth century, for the implicit purpose of "progressing" aesthetically, thus heavily influenced the evolution of modern literary criticism. By analyzing and critiquing their *own* works, along with those of their contemporaries, they, unconsciously perhaps, fused progress with originality. They as a group were thus among the first writers to have assimilated their belief in some kind of literary progress in texts where less critical readers found "mere" originality.

In order to appreciate better the direction or "bonne aventure" (Verlaine) that these poets/critics advocated, let us return to its historical point of departure. However one may wish to conceive of it, all progress involves a point more or less situated in time. In order that this point, or better yet, *given aesthetic state*, give rise to a movement deemed progressive, there must be something from which to flee. By definition, this previous point or state of departure will lose its value to the extent that one prefers to follow a metaphoric road to the art of tomorrow.

In what ways is this new orientation described by the pioneering writer/critics whom I take to be representative of "fin de siècle" criticism? Let me begin with the example of Madame de Staël. The profound influence of Madame de Staël over the tastes of the period, as well as over literary doctrine (in this case, Romantic), is beyond contestation. The historical import of her work in the present context lies in its being the primary source of a "fin de siècle" criticism concerned with the poet's *morale*. In her seminal work *De la Littérature* (1810), she defines the emotional state the great writer needs to overcome as "the painful feeling of the incompleteness of one's destiny." This feeling of emptiness, or lack, (which, later in the century, will prove to be more characteristic than anything else of post-Napoleonic "mal du siècle"), describes the morale of a large number of French writers of the period. According to Madame de Staël, an initial weak morale generates, in the best case, a progressive movement in the productivity of a poet. This movement contains artistic merits which the critic automatically assumes. The reason for this is that their weak morale obliges poets to become "mou"/soft, as she says.[20] From this point of view, poets who wish to make themselves gradually into "great" poets first have to move away from this weakness and, in the process, change their image as well as self-image. Failing such self-transformation, they can only remain great "melancholic" fools.

The only possible progress which Madame de Staël thus affords Romantic poets demands that they "fill" their emptiness, and that they be "crushed" should they fail to possess the requisite moral strength. In some places, she refers to this strength as "the heroism of morale," in others, "the enthusiasm of eloquence," and in still others "the ambition of glory." In every case, we continually discover in Madame de Staël's "fin de siècle" critique, portraits of artists who must first turn their back on their "moral failure" side (*raté moral*) before they can become truly inspired artists, beings "full of God's spirit/breath," (which is, after all, the etymological sense of the term "enthusiasm.") The originality of this gesture, then, signifies a kind of "critical progress" in the eyes of this earliest of modern critics.

Victor Hugo, on the other hand, avails himself of a different type of "fin de siècle" genre or style, one that emphasizes more the *aesthetico-pragmatic* dimension of poetic progress than the emotional aspects of it. In this critical sub-genre, a poet like the Hugo of the *Préface de Cromwell* has a much more palpable, societal goal. The aim of this brand of criticism is to help oneself, as well as others, to transcend old, false tastes. The reason such a transcendence is necessary, according to Hugo, is that old taste ("le vieux goût") does not merely consist of formal or aesthetic elements, which, for him, can never be the sole raison d'être of the work of art, anyway. Taste is also composed of ideological and political elements. It is this second characteristic or dimension of the state to be overcome that Hugo will call somewhat sarcastically, "the tail of the 18th-century that still drags into the nineteenth." He then hastens to add,

> But we young men who have seen Bonaparte will not be the ones to carry it over.

In his opinion, the only way to advance or progress in literature is to abandon old social rules as well as old artistic models, which made up this earlier false taste. The saving grace of the progressive artist is to follow the "the general laws of nature," as was seen in chapter three. Thanks to Hugo's use of the noun "laws," in a place where Madame de Staël would doubtless have used a more metaphysical term such as "heroism" or "enthusiasm," one suspects that literary advancement for Hugo was narrowly linked to the concept of real, objective social progress on a political plane. Hugo's "fin de siècle" criticism represents, therefore, a sort of mixed genre, halfway between the essentially sentimental writing of the earliest Romantics—in which group are included Goethe, Shelley, Byron, Chateaubriand, Lamartine, and Desbordes-Valmore—and a third kind of criticism I shall now sketch out.

The third variant of "fin-de-siècle" criticism, whose evolutionary paths I am now tracing from the end of the eighteenth century to the end of the nineteenth, is one which can properly be considered *aesthetic*. The aesthetic form of this cross-genre, "fin de siècle" criticism was practiced by Symbolists like Mallarmé and Verlaine. Earlier, I evoked the relationship between Verlaine's particular poetic discourse and the broader critical idea of progress in art, when I cited the former's "Art poétique." There I noted his insistence on the need for an *otherness* of "skies" and "loves" in the new kind of poetry he advocated. One would do well, however, to consider three other telling verses from the same poem/manifesto which appear to have cemented this relationship. In considering these lines, one needs to determine the nature of the fixed aesthetic points or states which Verlaine wanted to surpass or transcend.

Here are the verses in the order found in his poem:

> 1) "Fuis du plus loin la Pointe assassine"
> Flee furthest from the murderous barb.

This line proscribes any use of humoristic barbs or clever wit such as one discovers traditionally in epigrams. Verlaine's critical idea is to avoid stylistic formulae, which, by definition, are derived from traditional practice. Although they seem at first glance to be mere embellishments, they also allow a poem to unfold like reasoned argumentation, complete with a precise and unmistakable conclusion. Verlaine and other Symbolists were, of course, much more interested in suggestion and nuance than in specific meaning and expression. Going beyond or "fleeing" the stylistic constraints of conventional genres and fixed forms represented, therefore, a tangible kind of progress to such poet/critics.

> 2) "Prends l'éloquence et tords-lui son cou."
> Grab Eloquence and wring her neck.

In other words, the progressive poet should avoid worn-out rhetorical patterns and predetermined figures of speech. S/he instead needs to seek out novel lexical collocations, preferring, for example, uneven rather than even numbers of syllables in poetic verses. Eloquence is, by definition, like Hugo's "old taste," and has to be abandoned like an old mistress (or, perhaps, wife in Verlaine's case!) to whom one must do violence. Transcending these constraints is *critically* equivalent both to being an "original" poet and to "progressing" in the literary domain.

> 3) "O qui dira les torts de la rime!"
> O who shall state the errors of rhyme!

That is to say, poets must be extremely careful in choosing their rhyme schemes. They should not settle for a facile musicality, one lacking in true suggestivity. They should instead search for *new* music that can evoke feelings and thoughts still unarticulated by previously-tried sound patterns.

Verlaine proposes thereby what, in essence, is his critical articulation of stylistic procedures which poets who want to write well should follow in order to make aesthetic progress. He does not insist on the need to change one's mental and/or moral disposition and behavior, as was the case in Madame de Staël's type of criticism. Nor is it a question of rallying poets around a cry to future political engagement, as in the case of Hugo. Verlaine is engaged rather in an effort to modify the artistic habits and techniques of his fellow poets so as to bring about an eventual improvement in the aesthetic effects this new poetry, this poetry of the *New-because-Other*, has on its readers.

Mallarmé exhibits a similar aestheticism in his own "fin de siècle" criticism. In his "Crise de Vers"(1893), for example, we find the following allusion to the end-point or destination to which I alluded earlier:

> We are witnessing, as this century's finale, not as with the last century's, great upheavals.

In this passage, Mallarmé underscores the culmination of a period that, just like the other writers we have studied, he himself wished to transcend. Yet, no sooner has he expressed a view of the passage of time so highly reminiscent of that voiced by other "fin de siècle" critics than he suddenly adds a qualifier to reassure readers of his complete indifference vis-à-vis the real world,

> These upheavals take place far away from the public arena.

To Mallarmé, this other incarnation of "fin de siècle" criticism, it is therefore of little concern that the poet's person diminish with respect to the value of his or her work. No longer interested in either the personal, emotional, moral, or societal dimensions of the artist, Mallarmé sacrifices the latter's being for the future of the work alone. To quote from him once again:

> The pure work implies the elocutionary disappearance of the poet who gives up his initiative to his own words ... putting thereby the perceived breathing back into an ancient lyrical breath or the enthusiastic personal direction of the phrase.

The circle from one end of the nineteenth century to the other is thereby completed. For Madame de Staël, great poets flee their sentimental emptiness to attain the perfection of art. For Mallarmé, on the contrary, a great work is constructed only when it "empties" itself of the presence of any conscious being. And in between these two extremes, Hugo unites the divergent tendencies of his century, creating a curious kind of hybrid "fin de siècle" criticism, half sentimental, half aesthetic.

To conclude this section, which has sketched out the specific historic transformation and intertwining in France of "original" poets into "progressive" critics, I can now summarize the distinctive characteristics of the genre or style of modern literary criticism just examined:

> 1) It presupposes the possibility of some type of progress, either *subjective* or *objective*, in the literary domain.
> 2) It is consciously and deliberately opposed to an older aesthetic thought to be worn-out.
> 3) It functions both as program and proscription.
> 4) More often than not, it takes on apocalyptic tones, as if not only literature depended on it, but also the World itself.

These traits make it possible for us to relate the development of this brand of aesthetico-critical thought to the rise of critical pluralism in four important ways. For "pluralism" in its relation to the field of criticism (as defined throughout this book) refers to the modern tendency to accept as bona fide, useful, and acceptable interpretations precisely those readings of texts that set out to:

> 1) go beyond, in some fashion, that which has already been stated or done before;
> 2) situate themselves in opposition to earlier analyses;
> 3) exclude other possibilities by their very existence and;
> 4) couch, more often than not, their language in a peculiar contemporary Western discourse that makes of openness, of pluralism, the salvation not only of art, but more generally, of humankind itself.

In Wayne Booth's words, most every modern poet and/or critic thus "claims to offer life as against death,"[21] with each new aesthetic or interpretive gesture s/he makes. Such gestures, and the beliefs subtending them, obviously depend on the simultaneous acceptance of the twin doctrines of progress and originality. They presuppose, moreover, that positive, human and artistic value is generated by the purposeful search for them both. To understand how much these nineteenth-century beliefs have continued to influence the thought and practice of poet/critics writing during our century, I shall now turn to two exemplary cases from even more recent (French) literature.

Two Modern Types of Progress

For critical progress to occur, some form of movement, either real or conceptual, must take place. One has to go somewhere from some place, presumably *forward*. In describing the modern view of critical progress, it might therefore be of great heuristic value to modern readers to examine the different ways twentieth-century poet/critics have dealt with the general topic of movement, particularly as it pertains to various notions of progress. The fact is that writers throughout Western literary history have devoted their creative energy to the depiction of several kinds of voyages. Sometimes these voyages are undertaken by writers themselves, while in other instances, fictional characters do the actual wandering within the narrative. From the allegorical, epic adventures of heros found in works by Homer, Virgil, Rabelais, Fenelon, and Swift, to the metaphysical, sometimes drug-induced journeys of a De Quincey, Baudelaire, or Huxley, travel occupies a special place in the creation of a number of important literary works.

With the advent of Surrealism, however, movement of different types becomes the basis for a genuinely new poetics. Indeed, it would not be an exaggeration to suggest that the perceptual discoveries made during so-called aleatory movements, and that the fortuitous lexical and thematic collocations produced by the graphic meanderings of their "automatic writing" style, constitute the very foundation of much Surrealist literature. The kind of trip that comes to be especially worthy of the Surrealist poet's attention is psychic. I refer here to the type of mental voyage which—in the opinion of many of these poets, at least—ends at the source of thought itself. By attempting to reach through poetic representation that which was firmly believed to be the ultimate seat of artistic creation, i.e. the unconscious, the Surrealists were among the first to turn this cerebral quest into a poetic principle or method, not just a temporary brush with some inspirational Muse, as it was for certain Romantics.

To the extent that these quests, like any other, imply a movement towards something, it will be assumed that, on the conceptual level, a relationship exists between them and the notions of literary originality and progress. This is hardly unreasonable, since all artistic originality or progress presupposes some kind of movement from one state to another, one which, presumably, represents improvement, or, at least, a figurative step in the "right direction." The reason it is important to examine these differing treatments of motion, therefore, is that, ultimately, they both shed light on literary pluralism, on the modern aesthetic tendency to seek novelty and difference, at all costs.

Now, ever since Baudelaire proclaimed the need to travel "anywhere out of this world," in his famous prose poem of the same title, modern poets have frequently created characters or narrators whose principal relations to their respective texts have involved either movement itself or, at least, the concept of movement. The entire project known as Futurism, initiated by the Italian, Marinetti, was, in fact, based on the radical poetic exploitation of motion in all its possible thematic and stylistic manifestations. One understands then why speed, color, typographical experiments, and the suppression of capital letters, punctuation, and verb conjugations should have figured as prominently as they did in futurist works, which include not only poems, but also painting and architecture. These innovations seem to constitute a dramatic rejection of any and all vestiges of Romantic theory and practice for the purpose of creating a forward-looking, so-called futuristic type of originality.

But questions about just *where* all these poetic works and characters are going, and *why* they are doing so, are crucial ones to which it appears few critics have cared to respond. One exception, Sima Godfrey, has suggested that literary modernity itself, at least as it may be defined within a certain French tradition begun by

Baudelaire, manifests itself in the narrative form of an open invitation to travel. This invitation, extended by a poet to the reader, takes the form of a textual voyage that "can promise only a movement—with no fixed destination—'bien loin d'ici' [another allusion to one of Baudelaire's many "travel" poems]."[22] This modern aesthetic propensity to move, or to represent movement, lies at the very base of literary pluralism. What I wish to ask here in regard to two major modern poets of motion is whether their fictional travels have a fixed destination or not. Where, in other words, are modern writers in general trying to go, and what do they hope to find once they get there? The implications of the answer to this question will help us complete our historical understanding of the relationship between various literary quests for originality and the rise of critical pluralism.

The two paradigmatic figures to whose works I shall direct my attention are Henri Michaux and Louis Aragon. The reason I have selected these two poets is that one continually finds in their writings a fascination for a kind of perpetual motion. The latter serves as a guiding thematic principle to their works. In the post-face to *Mes Propriétés/My Properties* (published originally as a separate volume in 1929, becoming in 1935 the second section of *La Nuit remue/The Night moves*), Michaux, for instance, puts forth the idea that for him, writing was above all else an effective means of attaining better health. He writes, "For hygienic purposes, perhaps, I wrote *My Properties*, for my health."[23] Unlike Kafka, Rilke, and innumerable others, for whom the desire to write derived from some profound ambition or need to create literature, Michaux actually set out to cure himself of his anguish over his all-too-human condition through artistic expression.

In addition, concerning a rather surprising thought he finds in Kafka's journal, Michaux avers that for Kafka

> the essential thing in his life [was] to write, a way of residing better with his pain. For me, no. I always hesitated to continue writing. What I wanted was to be cured, as completely as possible ... [24]

From Michaux's vantage point, writing appears to have been a therapy, an actual attempt to cure himself of his existential uneasiness, not simply a means by which to live or cope with some inevitable, fundamental unhappiness endemic to all writers. Unfortunately, the precise steps he took in his writing to bring about this cure were, to my knowledge, never really made clear elsewhere in his work.

In any case, if Michaux did not act merely out of a deep-rooted need to write, this was mainly because he did not wish to accept any specific identity qua poet. Unwilling to conform in any sense to those techniques or rules that might by thought of as "normal," he admits to suffering from an "incapacity to conform."[25] The conformity in question includes both poetic traditions and conventions, as well as personal behavior patterns. In a word, Michaux does not care to be classified or pigeon-holed in any manner whatsoever. His originality is consciously radical and totalizing. One might even say that he wishes to be original *for* originality's sake and thereby constitutes a telling example, if not the "best" example, of the kind of contemporary artist to which the Romantic poetic legacy gave rise. Above and beyond anything else he hopes to accomplish as a professional "artist," Michaux forever wanted his work and his self to be *different* from what everyone thought they were beforehand. "Progress," to him, meant constantly seeking to be *other*.

As a result, he never ceased to stress motion of different sorts throughout his work. This deliberate emphasis on Michaux's part suggests the dynamic conception of his own identity, his radical originality. To a certain degree, one is tempted to explain his reluctance to conform by citing his incessant peregrinations throughout the world. Relying on his biography, one might mention Michaux's departure from his native Belgium as a sailor at the age of twenty-one as unmistakeable "proof" of his lack of desire to remain fixed for any length of time at a particular place, or in a specific state of mind. After all, this departure signalled the first of what were to be many long trips (both figurative and literal) in his life. Tracing the various stages of his artistic evolution in this fashion, one could indeed note a common thread that would link his personal philosophy to his multi-dimensional approach to artistic production. Always eager to explore unfamiliar territories and media, Michaux was apparently as much at ease with writing poetry as he was with doing drawings or paintings.

Some of the early Surrealist linguistic games and experiments also intrigued him, as did his own mescaline-induced experiences. Drug-taking, and the concomitant illusions of motion drugs are often said to produce, may well serve to explain, biographically, his fascination with movement. But if, instead, one brackets such extra-textual considerations as irrelevant to his actual artistic production, one realizes that motion in and of itself became for Michaux (and, by extension, many other modern writers) the actual thematic basis for a whole new, and decidedly modern, poetics, one that a recent critic calls a "poetics of motion."[26] Irrespective of any historical connection to his real life, Michaux's poetics represents a kind of twentieth-century version of the Parnassian ideal of Art for Art's sake, a version that I could call "Motion for Motion's sake." Based on the desire to break away from any preestablished forms or methods, his poetics revolve around a fundamental inability to accept any aesthetic status at all. For whatever historical or psychological reasons, Michaux the artist/poet was someone who, quite simply, refused to accept the "stagnation of outer reality."[27]

Early on in his career (1927), he even wrote a prose piece in the collection *Qui je fus/Who I was* titled, "Je ne peux pas me reposer"/"I can't rest,"[28] as if to drive the point home to us, so to speak. Forty years after making this first statement on the matter, he shall reiterate the sentiment in these words:

> I am one of those people who loves movement... Movement as disobedience, as altering.[29]

In this respect, Michaux also resembles a would-be descendent of the Symbolist tradition. It is ironic that a poet like him, who tried so assiduously to escape any and all classification, must here, at least, be seen as typical of earlier poets such as Baudelaire (in texts like "Le Voyage," "L'Invitation au Voyage," or "Any where out of the World," for example), or Mallarmé (in "Brise marine")[30] who always seemed uneasy with their present situation. Nevertheless, one must not forget that these poets tried to cure themselves of this uneasiness by their imagining being someone, or somewhere, else.

While Michaux shares with these and other earlier poets this sustained sense of a tension between *here* and *there*, or *now* and *then*, one should not conclude, however, that writing for Michaux was in any way an act of returning to, or imitating, some model for the purpose of transcending it. "Objective" progress in literature was far less important to him than his own "subjective" progress. The poet, in Michaux's opinion, cannot expect, nor should s/he want, to work on any given technique, form, etc. so as to arrive at some aesthetically pleasing, static whole. This is the sense in which any comparison of Michaux to the Romantics is unjustifiable. Romantic poets were greatly concerned with originality, to be sure, but mostly worked from within certain conventions and forms, which they subsequently re-worked and renovated. Once again, we must remember the relative hesitancy and formal conservatism with which late eighteenth- and early nineteenth-century poets embraced the then-nascent ideal of "original" poetry: "Sur des pensers nouveaux faisons des vers *antiques.*"

The genesis of art as Michaux saw it was instead the result of a sort of mystical and fortuitous event, a "state of grace" similar to what Breton in his *Manifeste du Surréalisme* called precisely by this very term, an "état de grâce." In Michaux's terms, poetry was essentially "a gift of nature, a grace, not work. Just having the ambition to write a poem suffices for it to die."[31] From this point of view, any individual who *wished* to write poetry was doomed to failure, according to Michaux. For one must not consciously try to construct a poetic text, but should instead let one's words come together according to spontaneous lexical and thematic affinities. Here one is reminded of Mallarmé's oft-quoted "feux réciproques," and of Breton's "mots qui font l'amour," which take away the actual control of their flow and concatenation from their author, just as in the case of Michaux's words. In this respect, Michaux's critical articulation of any objective progress made by him qua writer resembles the *aesthetic* type of "fin de siècle" criticism we saw above.

Of course, Michaux also believed that such laissez-faire artistic construction led him to an exploration of his own inner feelings, to subjective progress. Subsequently, it led him to a better personal management of certain existential problems. As he contends in another work:

> I write in order to wander through my self. Painting, composing, writing: wandering. Therein lies the adventure of being alive.[32]

Unconvinced of the possibility of immobilizing his or any other person's being through the use of language, and, moreover, uninterested in doing so, he, like Montaigne, is thus content to paint "le passage."[33] He knows that he is constantly "en difficulté," but he refuses to state just wherein this difficulty lies. The fact is that stating the location or nature of this place runs absolutely contrary to the very conception of human life in flux that he attempted so deliberately to represent.

The implied emphasis on perpetual motion also helps to explain Michaux's choice of what I shall call transitional or transitory titles for many of his later works: *La Nuit remue/The Night moves*, *Lointain intérieur/Far away interior*, *Ailleurs/Elsewhere*, *La Vie dans les plis/Life in wrinkles*, *Passages*, *Moments*, and *Face à ce qui se dérobe/Facing that which slips away*, to mention only the most obvious. It would be a mistake, however, to assume that this motion is ultimately directed towards any particular place. This is an important point. For, while it is true that Michaux does seem to focus in, on occasion, on an object or character such that he can be said to be "centralizing"[34] it, he does so only temporarily. He prefers instead to move on quickly to the next object, or to the next state of being of an object. We are not dealing here, as will be demonstrated presently in Aragon's texts, with an idealistic writer. He is not someone who, by artistic means, purports to make objective progress. He does not pretend to arrive at some cerebral destination, some supreme source or seat of thought where all oppositions and contrasts cease to exist, like Breton. When reading

Michaux, one realizes that the motion to which he alludes both permits and comprises the largest part of his literary production.

In the final analysis, then, the "poetics of movement" he proposes underscores the equivalence that exists in the mind of many modern writers and critics between progress, originality, and the will-to-difference. This conceptual equivalence is the fundamental assumption which has generated the rise of literary pluralism. As both theorist and practitioner, as poet/critic, Michaux was simply seduced by "the magic of motion."[35] Yet, for these same reasons, some might find it difficult to accept that Michaux was ever really a poet at all, at least, in any traditional sense of the word. Surely, a "true" poet would have tried to accomplish more than articulate his own existential transitoriness and concomitant malaise for all the world to read. Surely, he would have wanted to "progress" aesthetically by seeking to be more "original," formalistically or even thematically speaking.

The one work by Michaux that might be considered exceptional in this regard (both by the vast majority of critics, and by Michaux himself)[36] was the collection *Un certain Plume*. *Plume* is exceptional because it seems to contain texts that are more conventionally "poetic" in tone and form than so many other of his writings. In qualifying this text as a more traditional type of literary work, my intention is to speak of this poet's practice rather than to pose again the rather bothersome question of what poetry itself is. Once again, my aim is to illustrate another significant aspect about the historic link between his new kind of poetics and the modern rise of literary pluralism.

When one turns to the text, "Plume voyage," from this early collection, however, one can see that if Michaux had ever thought of himself as a "poet," it must have been here. By now it should be obvious that within the context of Michaux's poetics the title of this prose poem could be read almost as a tautology. That is, any personification of this poet's pen ("plume"), through the capitalization of this noun, would perforce travel, since the constancy of that dynamic state is, by all accounts, precisely what induced him to raise his own *plume* in the first place. Even so, the text illustrates neatly the intimate connection between Michaux's poetic exploitation of motion, and his very real uneasiness with the phenomenon itself. Throughout the narrative, Plume's actions encounter obstacle after obstacle. Unable to send back an inedible root served to him in a restaurant, for example, he walks out and looks for a place nearby to sleep. Finding no one around to offer him a bed, he is obliged to travel on foot all through the night.

Then he runs into a problem on a train. When the conductor sees him board, he shouts out to our unfortunate hero:

> So you think that they've been heating this locomotive for the last three hours and attached eight cars in order to transport a young man your age ...[37]

Excusing himself once more, Plume gets off the train, only to meet this same inter-personal inflexibility elsewhere. Plume's activity in reality is thereby nullified and frustrated at every possible turn. He makes no *progress*. From the opening line—"Plume can't say that people care much about him during his travels" (a cruel understatement)—to the final paragraph,

> But he says nothing... He thinks about the unfortunate souls who can't travel at all, while he travels and travels continually,

Plume cannot do anything at all, except dream.

For the purpose of clarification, let me emphasize here how, in this respect, too, Michaux has created a character who reminds us of Baudelaire's poetic universe. One of the latter's most famous creations, "L'Etranger," is a fictional character whose very identity also seemed to depend completely on his unconnectedness to the ordinary world. As in the case of Plume, Baudelaire's stranger is never really described, and like him also, appears utterly unattached to "normal" facets of life. All he appears able to accomplish is to dream about what *passes by*: "the clouds which pass by ... over there ... the marvellous clouds!"

The most characteristic topos of Michaux's cosmos, therefore, is in fact an *a*-topos: a never-ending accent on movement, on change, on *difference*, in a word, in every possible sense and direction. While this quintessentially pluralistic gesture in the name of difference is often depicted, thematically, as an excursion into the external world, it just as often leads Michaux back into a description and narrative development of an internal, oneiric domain. It thereby exemplifies the modern aesthetic impulse to seek a more and more radical originality, one that has less and less to do with any privileged origin or past source of aesthetic value at all. Yet, the progress his work makes can only be measured critically in terms of the amount and types of movement portrayed. There is no pretense on his part of having progressed to a *better* place, truth, or poetic form. Instead, all one can say is that he has merely progressed, that is, he has "gone forward."

In Louis Aragon's work we discover much of the same thematic concern with motion. Indeed, at the height of the early Surrealist period (1920-24), he published one of the first major collections of so-called automatic texts under the title, *Le Mouvement Perpétuel/Perpetual Motion*. Because automatic writing itself, as a practice, is perhaps best understood in terms of a pen that never stops moving across the page (or, as one might say, a *plume qui voyage*), I need not insist on the appropriateness of Aragon's choice of title for this kind of artistic work. But what should be noted is a significant detail found in the center of the frontispiece to the collection used for the original edition.[38] Surrounded by the words "mouvement" and "perpétuel," which form a mandala-like pattern around it, is the following phrase: "Voir au dos la pensée"/Turn over for the thought. Remembering what I hinted at above about the absence of any clearly articulated final destination for Michaux's thematic treatment of various movements, one can already see just how Aragon's "poetics of movement" might differ significantly from the latter's. No longer is one in the presence of a Motion-for-Motion's sake aesthetic, for Aragon evidently believes that somewhere behind, or underneath, his constantly shifting point of view lies a specific *thought*.

This represents a small, but notable difference from Michaux's stance. At least two conclusions can be drawn as a result. First, from the beginning of his career, Aragon seems to have been convinced that perpetual motion was not an end in and of itself. It did not necessarily connote personal, subjective progress, since it was directed not solely at a resolution of his own inner conflicts. It was also meant to lead to the attainment by writers and their readers of a particular knowledge or thought, to objective progress. A second conclusion drawn from this frontispiece concerns the knowledge needed to find the mental origin of these extraordinary texts: If one wants to find the thoughts underlying these automatic poems, one has to go *behind*, or *back* to, them, presumably into the mind of "their" author.

Going "backwards" to an origin, however, cannot help but remind us of the earliest Romantic poets and theorists, of how they conceived of their own brand of originality. At first, most of them were reluctant to move ever onwards and forward when sitting down to write new works. Unlike Michaux, they were somewhat more conservative, and tried to change the literary framework they inherited, not utterly destroy, or reject it out of hand. One thus gets the immediate impression that Aragon shared much of the essential poetic theory which, by his time, was already a hundred years old.

Although Aragon agreed that determining some of the unconscious impulses at work behind his particular use of language might take a long time, he did still hold firmly to his critical belief that this determination was at least theoretically possible. Commenting on the poem "Bouée"/"Buoy" for example (one of the more accessible texts from *Le Mouvement Perpétuel*), Aragon admits that forty-two years had to pass before he realized how the particular grammatical games he put in play in the poem represented the real "reasons" behind it. In reference to one of the more peculiar verses, he explains:

> The poem is made entirely out of a kind of perpetual hesitation towards the grammatical form; it is in this way that a *translation tone* intervenes ... by which is meant the *pre*-translation tone ... as when, for instance, the possessive adjective is generally suppressed [in the poem], so as to be replaced by the genetive

of the personal pronoun: *A child once gave up* not *his soul*, but
the soul of himself.

In fact, had he not happened upon another poem by the Russian poet
Lokman, in which a similar linguistic game was at work, he may
very well (according to him) have remained ignorant of this
"secret."[39]

It is on this level then, that the two exemplary poets I am
discussing are perhaps most at odds. If one were really capable of
deciphering even a few of the unconscious catalysts behind a given
poetic construct, sooner or later one would be forced to espouse the
idealistic, nineteenth-century notion that the writing process has a
teleological dimension to it, a dimension beyond that of its being
"merely" therapeutic for the writer. From this angle, readers, too,
stand to gain from their experience of the literary work. Comforted
in the knowledge that what one is reading—however bizarre on the
surface—has an intelligible backside to it ("au dos la pensée"), one
can continue reading in the hopes of reaching a specific end.
Objective progress for all, in other words, is possible in spite of the
profound formal originality of the literary text.

Instead of being swept up by a flow of images of transition in
order to witness primarily the human condition (Michaux), one can
thus read Aragon for the added "advantage" of *getting somewhere
else.* To express this critical difference more succinctly, Michaux
wrote so as to seek out what he and we readers did not know, and
what he believed we *could not* know. At best, Michaux held out
hope for subjective progress, for himself, if not also for others like
him. Aragon, on the other hand, wrote in order to learn what he and
we readers did not *yet* realize, in order to edify everyone in the
process.[40] Aragon's idealism thus seems more appropriate to the
nineteenth century, with its optimism and strong belief in both types
of progress than to the twentieth century.

Both writers were in this fashion naturally attracted, albeit for
different reasons, to a thematics of motion. Their modern "quests"
for originality often thematized the critical notion of progress in
exemplary ways. In his novel, *Le Paysan de Paris*, for example,
Aragon raises the Surrealist predilection for aleatory movements up

to the level of poetic principle. Although it may be objected that
prose cannot be used to embody any "poetic" principle, one must
recall that such generic distinctions were, by and large, irrelevant to
the Surrealists. In any case, by rejecting the historical divisions
between light and dark, truth and error, as misleading indices of
reality, Aragon decided in this work to give free rein to the
intermittent perceptual errors made by his senses. His aim was to see
what happened as he walked the streets of Paris. He exclaims, "I no
longer want to restrain myself from the errors of my fingers, from
the errors of my eyes."[41]

The reason he no longer wished to restrain himself lies in his
desire to create a mythology of modern life. He describes this
mythology as a "a living science that engenders itself and commits
suicide" (14). Since the mythology he wants to write must consist of
a more complete picture of reality than has been previously given,
he will insist on expanding the field of acceptable data to include
false or erroneous perceptions recorded while wandering. The new
reality thus garnered is multi-faceted, *pluralistic*, one might say, and
assumes the plural form of RE-A-LI-TE*S* (68); that is, a larger
Surreality.

Consequently, behind the constant stylistic variations and
perpetual motion of the narrator in this book, Aragon implies that
these heterogeneous peregrinations are not mere thematic reflections
of the world as it is, nor of his *own* experience of it, as Michaux
seemed to suggest. Through the use of such movement, as well as of
the apotheosis later in the book of his radium-fingered mistress,
Error (135), Aragon succeeds instead in actually transforming the
many mistaken perceptions to which he fell prey during his walks
into

> curious paths towards a *goal* that nothing can reveal [to him], except
> for them [these errors] (my emphasis 13).

This goal or telos, noted earlier in *Le Mouvement Perpétuel*, thus
returns to the fore as the principal aim of Aragon's poetic
production. Paradoxically, it is a *backwards* goal, like that of the
early Romantic poets examined earlier. Yet, his goal was even more

modern. For him, the work of art is, ultimately, less a fortuitous juxtaposition of various narrative situations and stylistic devices than a deliberate retracing of the steps made by an ever-mobile perceiver. And while these steps lead both him and his readers to a certain destination, this destination can only be *recovered*, curiously enough, at the perceiver's point of departure.

In this manner, objective progress can indeed be made by writers themselves, as well as by readers, according to Aragon. This explains why many years later in his *Je n'ai jamais appris à écrire/ I never learned how to write*, Aragon will continue to say, "I still believe that one thinks on the basis of what one writes, and not the reverse."[42] Our general knowledge and understanding of the world stands to increase with every "good" new text written. It also sheds some light on Aragon's great admiration for Samuel Beckett's works, which he contends

> *begin without end*. Do you understand? I mean that even the last word of each one of them is the first. That the path explored begins from where it ends. (147)

In conclusion, the idea of perpetual motion was for Aragon, (and, by extension, many other modern inheritors of Romantic poetic theory) primarily that of the writing process itself. "Error," understood both in terms of perceptual mistakes and in the strict etymological sense of *wandering*, becomes personified in his work as the principal goddess in the pantheon of his modern mythology. She is the guide who leads modern writers into those grey areas of their psyches for the dual purpose of giving them new insights into themselves, as well as of providing their readers with, by definition, "original" poetic images. Aragon's method of writing is based on a constant *errance*, a pluralistic quest for heterogeneous "mistakes," scriptural differences that, in time, would allow him to determine *a posteriori* what he was actually feeling and thinking when he first sat down and picked up his pen.[43] His particular originality contributes to our collective critical belief in the subjective and objective progress to which his writing gives witness.

By the same token, Michaux shared with Aragon both the rejection of most prefabricated writing models and a disdain for any preconception of what he was about to write. He, too, underscored motion of various forms and types throughout his life and work. Yet Michaux sought more a resolution of certain human internal conflicts than a discovery of some "pure" collective thought which would ground his texts. To this extent, he believes in subjective progress, but has little concern for the possibility of objective progress. It might also be argued that his artistic productions were somewhat less "intellectual" than Aragon's, even though they most certainly contained equal, if not superior, emotive force. I am not contending, of course, that Michaux himself was any less intellectual than Aragon, but rather that the careful deciphering and reconstitution of *some thing* before, behind, or below his work would appear to have played only a small role in its production. Therein, no doubt, lies one of the main reasons why he is harder to place definitively in any particular literary tradition than his Surrealist counterpart. After all, how does one categorize critically, except partially, a corpus that seeks to move in every possible direction, to break out of any and all preestablished molds? In the final analysis, this resistance to classification may very well constitute the surest sign possible of a truly modern poetics of motion, and of Michaux's ultimate importance to the contemporary literary scene. For many poets and theorists of our time seem to want to move further and further away from stylistic conventions and epistemological models, ever more intent on asserting their radical originality. Their success in escaping such critical constraints remains, however, to be proven by more astute readers than I.

Trans-historical Reasons for Critical Progress

The literary and intellectual history examined in the last two chapters (and the first three parts of this one) explains a large part of the story behind the rise of literary pluralism. Yet, such an examination fails to address certain *trans*-historical factors which form three other sources of pluralistic sentiment in the domain of criticism. By "trans-historical," I mean factors which, although surely exacerbated in our time by the particular historical nexus of concepts and practices found throughout the nineteenth and twentieth centuries, have always had a strong effect on exegetical thought. Readers and critics alike have always sought, and will always seek, to produce different interpretations of the same works of art for, at least,[44] three other reasons that will probably never cease to interest any and all future critics. My task in the remainder of this chapter is to investigate more closely these three reasons, factors, or sources: *epistemological*, *socio-pragmatic*, and *psychological*. I intend to demonstrate how their interaction with the specific historical changes studied earlier has rendered pluralism the pervasive force it is in contemporary literary studies.

Beginning with the first of these trans-historical sources, one must come to grips with the fact that twentieth-century theory and criticism have essentially reified the nineteenth-century's conceptual fusion of literary originality and progress we earlier saw operating in France's exemplary "fin de siècle" criticism. Epistemologically speaking, the reification, hyperemphasis, or over-idealization of these concepts, has occurred because of the persistent belief that all interpretive stances imply a deliberate choice of one set of critical criteria, assumptions, frameworks, and methodologies over others. The belief in the inevitability of fundamental, irreconcilable differences between one reading and another, between one interpretation and another, represents one of the final pieces of the conceptual puzzle I have sketched out across the last two hundred years or so.

As it happens, Anglo-American criticism may well be the big "culprit" in this reification, to the extent that some of its most influential voices have made of pluralism the sine qua non of its very self-definition. In 1953, R. S. Crane, for instance, stated one of the central pluralistic tenets of the so-called "Chicago school" when he emphasized that criticism was

a collection of distinct and more or less incommensurable "frameworks" or "languages" differing widely on "matters of assumed
principle, definition, and method."[45]

At much the same time, European phenomenologists, too, added
their own voices to the growing consensus concerning the centrality
of pluralism in critical thought. A thinker like Maurice Merleau-
Ponty, for example, set himself the critically important,
epistemological task of determining how we know that we are
(correctly) perceiving things. For him, any perceived thing, say, a
literary text, cannot be considered

an ideal unity in the possession of the intellect, like a geometrical
notion, for example; it is rather a totality open to a horizon of an
indefinite number of perspectival views which blend with one another
according to a given style which defines the object in question.[46]

Merleau-Ponty's strain of thought, like that of R.S. Crane, represents
an approach to texts that is permeated by much the same pluralistic
sentiment articulated earlier in the century by the American
philosopher, William James, as was seen in chapter two.

Once this sentiment became an article of faith, however, as it
appears to have done, the proverbial flood gates (of critical practice)
were theoretically opened. No longer could one ask the question of
whether interpretive consensus was feasible because one
automatically had to consider the point moot. When structuralist and
post-structuralist criticism came to the fore in the sixties, seventies,
and eighties, there was thus no longer even a trace of doubt vis-à-vis
the epistemological import of pluralism in the critical arena.
Everywhere it was assumed that pluralism was/is a fact of critical
life, primarily because of irreconciliable differences in
methodological approaches. In 1973, for instance, Stanley Fish did
not hesitate to define both literature and, by extension, its study as
an

open category, not definable by fictionality, or by a disregard of
propositional truth, or by a statistical predominance of tropes and
figures, but simply by what we decide to put into it.[47]

A few years later, Susan Horton echoed this generalized attitude towards interpretation when, in her 1979 book, *Interpreting Interpreting: Interpreting Dicken's "Dombey,"* she stated:

> Different ways of structuring texts, different conceptions of parts and wholes, the different needs of readers, and misreading of parts of a text produce different interpretations.[48]

In 1983 Paul Armstrong added his voice to this growing consensus when, in an influential *PMLA* article, he advanced the idea that

> Psychoanalysis, Marxism, phenomenology, structuralism—each has a different method of interpretation because each has a different metaphysics, a different set of convictions that make up its point of departure and define its position in the hermeneutic field.

With this as his given, he then immediately emphasized that

> To embrace a type of interpretation is to make a leap by accepting one set of presuppositions and rejecting others.[49]

And in her recent book on contemporary literary theory and pluralism, Ellen Rooney, too, underscores the same fact. We find this fact over and over again in different forms, probably because it commonly serves to justify a pluralistic view of interpretation. It involves the naturalness and inevitability of choosing one set of textual criteria over others in the earliest stages of critical readings. According to this view, different choices of textual criteria cannot help but lead various readers to different interpretations. Quoting from a manuscript of Gayatri Spivak, Rooney writes:

> However pluralist its demeanor, American liberal masculism (alias humanism) will never declare that it is merely one of many plausible *choices* [my emphasis].[50]

All of these voices, so characteristic of our time, eclipse the possibility of interpretive consensus. They function as if the latter were by definition anathema to true critics of literature.

The irony, of course, is that there appears to be a consensus about a lack of preliminary methodological consensus! Since all these voices continue nevertheless to speak one way or another about literary texts, one has to ask what they all hope to accomplish. If, in their quest to be original, to make progress *as* critics, they claim that none of us share any fundamental epistemological assumptions, frameworks, or methodologies, one can only marvel at the audacity, maybe even absurdity, of their (and our!) respective stances. In this regard, Steven Knapp and Walter Benn Michaels are perhaps the most honest (anti-)theorists vis-à-vis this situation when they state that since

> no one can reach a position outside of practice [i.e. avoid choosing one "set of presuppositions and rejecting others,"] ... [T]heorists should stop trying .... The theoretical enterprise should therefore come to an end.[51]

Interestingly enough, however, both of these critics have continued to write texts that, however *anti*-theoretical they may be, will inescapably provide more theoretical fodder, so to speak, to those looking for it. Theory does not disappear just because one says it should. Stanley Fish, perhaps the most powerful voice of them all in this respect, has at least followed his own reasoning to its logical conclusion and realized the fundamentally rhetorical, circular, *non*-progressive nature of his own discourse.[52] Yet, he, too, often acts as if what he discovers in a given text, or about textuality, represents something new under the sun. If any single individual's thought has been taken to lead many people in American academic circles someplace (else) in the last twenty years, it is surely that of Stanley Fish. Thus, in spite of his apparent refusal to attach or associate the specific notion of "progress" to his own work—a refusal shared by many other influential contemporary critics—this has already been done *for* him, through the promulgation and cooptation of his thought into the mainstream of American critical theory and practice.

The empirical question one must ask, then, is whether he and other theorists *have* found something critically new under the sun, or whether they have not. If they have, I would like to recommend that they consider saying so, instead of acting as if they did not believe, on some level, in such essentialist notions as Progress or Truth. If, on the other hand, they have not, we others should realize that reading such criticism represents a contemporary form of intellectual delectation more than edification. Seeing the present state of critical affairs from this less *meaningful* angle might very well temper many of the otherwise heated debates held under the auspices of various academic and professional authorities.

This leads me to consider a second trans-historical factor whose present-day role in the reification of the critical dimension of literary pluralism is particularly important. This factor, *socio-pragmatic*, pertains to the ever-growing professional pressures on critics to act as if their own interpretive originality generated, in and of itself, some type of progress in the literary domain. The fact is that for a long time literary critics have interpreted literature, ostensibly, just because both they and it were *there*. It is hard to imagine what a critic does otherwise. Thus, in his description of "critical reading," Michel Charles defines a literary text simply as being "that which is to be explicated."[53] The theoretical questions of just *what* is there, and of whether any individual text deserves such treatment, are still very much up in the air, however. These questions leave open the possibility of doing a critical reading on, or *to*, any piece of writing whatsoever.

Clearly then, the decision to interpret the same work ever more differently—which is precisely what I mean by "critical plu-ralism"—eschews the problem of *literature* vs. *non-literature*, in order to get more quickly to the task at hand, i.e. "literary" criticism and theory. This collective gesture of ours is made in the name of expediency, for socio-pragmatic reasons that foreclose the stickier issue of literature's specificity. In Charles' words,

> One is interested in resolving the difficulty of a text only when it has sufficient authority (or when one is solicited by an institution *or by the text itself*); inversely, the difficulty gives authority to the text, to the extent that it is capable of escaping modest attempts at critical analysis. It is clear that the University consecrates thereby the existence of a literature.[54]

As a result, critical progress is made nowadays when a text is chosen as a starting point for what will be the forward thrust of the new, original interpretation. The question of why we start *there* (with *Madame Bovary* or *Paradise Lost*) is eclipsed by more "important" considerations.

All texts thus become potentially "open" texts (Umberto Eco's term) whenever we feel that we can draw more intellectual or aesthetic profit and satisfaction from them than before. Once the work's reception is deemed to be incomplete, the current pluralistic mentality invites us to seek out greater satisfaction from it in the name of the larger society to which we belong. In this way, when we approach a given work,

> we open ourselves to it [as much as we open the *text*] as the source
> of an always elusive ultimate satisfaction towards which it promises
> to lead us if we can but get beyond our imperfect experiences of it
> ... [It] becomes emblem of the idea of progress, the *fiction* of
> progress in the real world (my emphasis).[55]

Although we usually think that other readings of the same work are justified on the societal grounds of a collective belief (still) in the progress produced by each new reading, our critical pluralism is thereby little more than a disguise for individual pragmatic motives. We are *not* always open to suggestion when we propose our original analyses. Instead, we often propose alternatives which preclude all others. In no way do our particular alternatives *necessarily* imply a movement "forward" in our appreciation or understanding of a text.

Regarding this last point, one can only sympathize with Robert Crosman, who asks the question of whether readers make or discover textual meaning. Crosman indirectly answers his own inquiry when he affirms that

> it is not mutual tolerance and respect for differences in opinion, but
> an aggressive belief in the exclusive rightness of own's own opinion
> that leads to a physical or intellectual "war of all against all."[56]

Respect for pluralism is implicitly, if not explicitly, advanced, as the primary motive behind what, in fact, turn out to be an individual's practical reasons, needs, and desires for creating yet another reading of a particular work. In the light of our as yet unquestioned faith in the appropriateness of the myths of progress and originality, it thus appears that to serve these individual socio-pragmatic needs our profession has simply decided that "texts *ought* to have plural meanings."[57] Since all of us often want different things from what our society might want, textual meaning is made

> precisely as we [individually] *want* it to be made ... Unanimity is neither possible nor desirable [for] reality is never unequivocal.[58]

For the vast majority of contemporary critics, professional pressures have made time-honored critical questions like "What is literature?," Why is this text worth reading?," "Does this analysis really add anything useful to our knowledge of this work?" well-nigh irrelevant. In today's world, texts are supposed to generate more texts. To be sure, a work that, for whatever essentially idiosyncratic reasons, finds itself used an an examplary instance of literary productivity more often than not merits a large degree of critical appraisal and respect. The author of such a work will be judged to have a certain merit in that s/he helps critics, in their turn, write *more*, though not necessarily *better*. But, this suggests that the principle behind contemporary critical pluralism is a quantitative one, much more than it is qualitative. In fact, in the United States, especially, quality has very little to do with this and other aesthetic matters, as Robert Pirsig admirably showed in hundreds of pages of critical reflection on the subject in his 1974 novel, *Zen and the Art of Motorcycle Maintenance*.

It is also true, as K. M. Newton has indicated, that for American academics, in particular, the socio-pragmatic necessity of the syndrome popularly known as "Publish or Perish" encourages professional critics "to search for new readings of texts."[59] It thereby encourages them to exploit the inherent polysemic nature of any and all texts. The truth, however, is that this textual fact or semantic potentiality "has always existed since the emergence of literature as a separate discourse."[60] It has merely been exploited more fully nowadays, owing to a combination of the historical and conceptual developments discussed earlier, as well as to the socio-pragmatic factors examined here.

So, if one also takes into account the important rise of modern capitalism in the nineteenth century, one understands why the power of any trans-historical socio-pragmatic reason for critical pluralism, such as I am discussing here, has increased significantly within our life time. Modern industrialized societies have, after all, had a much larger practical stake in the *production* than in the *quality* of their respective products. Progress in the arts, as in other realms, has thus come to be associated with objects that, for any number of reasons, give birth to others. Such objects, such "oeuvres d'art," might properly be called self-duplicating. For when these objects come into being, they lead other authors to write in their turn. In this fashion, "original" authors begin to be held more and more in esteem.

So, for a critic like Jacques Derrida, a work is chosen for analysis because it allows him to write *from* it (*à partir de*), not so much *on* it. Walter Benjamin, perhaps better than anyone else, made this crucial point about all modern art-forms. He did so not only in his classic essay on "The Work of Art in the Age of Mechanical Reproduction," that has been cited in an astounding number of contexts, but also in a passage like this one:

> An author who teaches writers nothing, teaches no one. What matters, therefore, is the exemplary character of production, which is able first to induce other producers to produce, and second, to put an improved apparatus at their disposal. And this apparatus is better the more consumers it is able to turn into producers—that is, readers or spectators into collaborators.[61]

This socio-pragmatic reason for critical pluralism could only have grown in importance in the West in direct proportion to the proliferation of industrialization and its corresponding dominant ideology of capitalism.

I thus propose the following equation to describe in reductive terms the historical rise of critical pluralism in the West:

more analysis = critical progress.

By the same token, the rise of aesthetic pluralism throughout this period can be characterized by using a slightly more elaborate formula:

aesthetic originality = *different* literature = aesthetic progress

What these reductions indicate is how much the notions of "value," "worth," and "quality" have practically disappeared from both aesthetic and critical spheres within the textual field we think of as "literature." More and more, "critical progress" is a matter of quantity, not quality. Quantity, in this case, means not only the number of new pages and readings of the same works; it also refers to the theoretically measurable "distance" between what has already been said and what is being proposed, irrespective of the intrinsic worth of the subject broached. In the words of one of the most vociferous opponents of current literary scholarship, Charles Sykes:

> the key [to critical research] is originality, whether that originality is applied to an incredibly narrow sliver of knowledge and whether it has the slightest importance or interest for anyone other than the author.[62]

Politically engaged interpretations have also enjoyed great success in the post-structuralist phase of the development of criticism. Without a doubt, the writings of Edward Said, Theodor Adorno, George Lukàcs, Frederic Jameson, Terry Eagleton, Houston Baker, and Henry Louis Gates, as well as a host of feminist critics like Mary Ann Caws, Carolyn Heilbrun, Elaine Showalter, Nancy Miller, Barbara Johnson, Susan Suleiman, and Naomi Schor include innumerable valuable contributions to the study of canonical and not-so-canonical literature. They have provided us with genuinely new ways of looking at, and learning from, literary texts. But the decision to take either one's own discourse or someone else's (literary) discourse as fundamentally, or predominantly, political should not be taken lightly. A profound knowledge of the relevent history, politics, and sociology is the very least one might expect from a critic inclined to view literature from a political point of view.

To make real critical progress, however, as I think only a select few have, involves more than simply carving out a critical niche by finding something vaguely "political" about a given text. Doing this amounts to little more than an insignificant *distancing* with respect to other texts, a gesture that we have just seen is basically quantitative. If, for instance, one objects vehemently to the description of a woman in a particular novel, or to including that same work in any acceptable canon because its general "politics" are not correct, it is reasonable to ask whether reading a work in this fashion represents anything other than an anachronistic, and essentially false, interpretation. Since we all realize that different societies have different mores, it is not really fair to equate our ideas with those of a different time and place, and to expect everyone to share our point of view on certain societal relations. The numerous Jews who recently objected to the performance of Wagnerian opera in Israel on the grounds that this art form was steeped in the anti-semitic views of its composer were, it seems to me, slightly insensitive to precisely this trans-historical dimension of any and all types of music. The *fatwa* pronounced against Salman Rushdie by fundamentalist Muslims on the grounds of his purported impiety similarly reflects an important misunderstanding of the global (rather than local) literary context in which a work like *Satanic Verses* was written. And finally, Senator Jesse Helms' misreading of Robert Mapplethorpe's photography illustrates once again how one's own political agenda cannot, and should not, be used to judge the inherent value of a given piece of art.

Therefore, (badly) politically engaged critics, like those who condemn the Wagners, Rushdies, and Mapplethorpes of the world, do not fully take into account certain historical and sociological realities. In the process, they often miss the point of various works of art and literature. Admittedly, such individuals are not whom we usually think of as aestheticians or critics. But when they do not detect the type of *progress* which, from their socio-pragmatic or political perspective, they would like to see artists make, they resemble misinformed critics whose readings lack a sufficient breadth of understanding vis-à-vis the totality of the discourse(s) or text(s) considered. They project onto such works either more or fewer of their own socio-pragmatic concerns than what the works can rightfully be said to "contain." Ultimately, then, critical progress can be attributed to a work only when a political reading of it comes to grips with what is politically relevent for the time and place of the chosen discourse itself. That a particular text (critical or more "aesthetic") contains offensive ideas should be of interest to students of literature only when something negative results from the pragmatic manner(s) in which it has been, is, or will be, utilized. And this, needless to say, is precisely the great benefit, and even, originality of some of our best feminist and African-American scholarship.

Thus, any critical progress made by the political critic derives less from the politicization of the text itself than from a more realistic assessment of the positive or negative social practices to which it has given rise. To quote Gerald Graff:

> That an idea has certain political consequences is irrelevent when adduced as an argument against (or for) the idea [...] What underlies such protests is not a theoretical objection to the research in question [or, say, to a particularly odious character in a novel] but a *practical* objection to the way that research is used ....[63]

It is this modern concern for, and appreciation of, the ways texts function under specific social conditions (which Graff calls the "specificity" and "sociological adequacy"[64] of a political interpretation), which have contributed to the otherwise ever-present, trans-historical, *socio-pragmatic* forces behind any and all forms of critical pluralism.

The final factor which increases pluralist sentiment among modern literary critics is *psychological*. The countless number of individual psychological differences, wishes, and drives among critics has always affected the form of the different interpretations they produce. The theoretical articulation of these individual factors has gone on now for some time, at least since the time of Freud.

Several volumes could be written on the relationship between pluralism and current psychological theories. However, for my more limited purposes here, I shall mention only two of the more influential notions in modern psychoanalytic literary criticism. The first is Jacques Lacan's. I refer here to the Lacanian emphasis on the unremitting nature of desire and on the "slipperiness" of the signifier. The second is Julia Kristéva's related notion of "desire in language." Both well-known ideas have gone far in encouraging individual readers to seek out ever more intriguing significations within the fabric of the same well-read works. In both cases, omnipresent psychological differences are shown to ground various usages of language, and ultimately, to promote a pluralistic view of the work properly done by critics and writers alike.

Beyond these individual psychic needs and desires, however, lies the peculiar modern need and will to be different, as was discussed in the previous chapter. The advent of originality and progress as dominant concepts in the modern mindset is the historical factor that exacerbates the feeling among critics and scholars that critical pluralism is appropriate and, in fact, inevitable. What is perhaps most intriguing about this situation is the programmatic fashion in which various contemporary theorists of the reading act have used psychological terms to explain interpretation itself. The debate between Norman Holland and David Bleich during the 1970s is especially instructive in this context, for it centers precisely, if inexplicitly, on the (pluralistic) question of why there are so many readings of the same work.

To a certain degree, the debate between these two critics is a false one. The reason I say this is that the title of Holland's essay—"The New Paradigm: Subjective or Transactive?" cited in my second chapter—suggests that Bleich's model of the critical act of reading is *purely* subjective, rather than transactive, as in Holland's theory. In fact, as the reader shall see presently, both theorists make clear that "correct" critical practice consists of, and depends on, a give-and-take between the reader and something else. The key distinction, however, is that for Holland the "something else" is first and foremost the reader-of-the-text herself, whereas for Bleich, it is instead *other* readers of the text. This distinction is of interest because it restates one of the central problems of critical pluralism that I have been discussin all along: to wit, whether it is acceptable, or indeed, inevitable, to have an ever-increasing number of readings of the same works of art.

In order to examine their debate in more detail, let me first summarize Holland's work. Bleich's work is, after all, to a large extent a reaction to, and refinement of, the latter. In an highly influential, prize-winning *PMLA* article of 1975,[65] Holland contends that whenever we read literature critically, we act much as we do when we "read" ourselves. Just as we seek meaning and/or significance in the works we choose to read, so, too, do we seek some type of unity within ourselves that constitutes our "identity." The identity of each individual reader, which Holland admits is not always stable, but which for most societally-accepted people is nevertheless "relatively fixed," thus re-creates itself "as though it were a *text* [in front of one]" (815).

Furthermore, when each of us reads a piece of literature, this principle manifests itself, as mentioned in chapter one, through three different modalities: 1) we find things we fear or wish most, 2) we derive pleasure from fantasies generated by the experience, and 3) we re-create our lives and life styles at an intellectual or esthetic level (817). It should be recalled that in his "New Paradigm" essay, which appeared a year later, Holland adroitly called this principle underlying every act of critical reading the process of reading DEFTly, i.e. through *d*efenses, *e*xpectations, *f*antasies, and *t*ransformations. What Holland set out to accomplish was to describe, delimit, and systematize in a quasi-therapeutic discourse the pluralistic nature of any act of interpretation. Since we all read DEFTly in *different* manners, depending on our individual psychic natures, we, therefore, find in Holland's work one more powerful and contemporary theoretical justification for critical pluralism.

David Bleich, on the other hand, takes exception[66] to this view on several key points. First, he disagrees that Holland, or anyone else, can ever really arrive at a "full therapeutic definition of each reader's identity" (*SC* 119). He then asks how one can ever really

know whether a particular aspect of a reader's critical response to a
text is a defense, expectation, or fantasy, and doubts whether
Holland's theory of reading is actually different, in any significant
sense, from more traditional psychoanalytic therapy (*SC* 120-22).
The problem appears to lie in the supposed "authority" that inheres
to the theorist/therapist him- or herself. Preferring to ground the
authority or acceptability of a critical act of reading in
"intersubjective negotiation," as do Stanley Fish and Susan Horton,
Bleich explains that such negotiation alone "regulates whether any
experience is considered the same or different among different
people" (*SC* 295).

It is precisely here that I find a connection to the problematic of
critical pluralism. While it does not seem to me particularly
important, from a conceptual point of view, to worry about labelling
a given aspect of critical responses a defense or expectation, Bleich's
insistence on the intersubjective nature of authority does demand
closer attention. For if one decided that interpretive authority lies in
certain privileged texts or individuals—as Bleich would have us
believe Holland thinks—one would have an excellent case for arguing
against unlimited pluralism in the critical domain. If, instead, one
adopts the opposite perspective on the matter, one finds oneself
forced to agree with Bleich when he states:

> The degree to which knowledge [somehow critically "extracted"
> from, or "discovered" in, a text] is not part of a community is the
> degree to which it is not knowledge at all (*SC* 296).

The question, therefore, is whether any objective progress can be
expected from the practice of criticism as Bleich understands it. As
I have already said, progress of any kind implies a usually forward-
moving departure from a given, more or less fixed, point. In
Holland's opinion, critical reading does lead, at very least, to a type
of ameliorative transformation of a reader's self-knowledge, if not
also to a somehow positive development of the sense of individual
identities generally held by that reader's audience. For this to occur,
one obviously has to posit the initial existence of *some-thing* (an
individual's "relatively fixed" identity or sense of self) that can be

thus trans-formed. In Holland's essay of the same title, this new "transactive paradigm" of the interpretive gesture generates a different sort of critical question altogether, namely:

> What can *I* (or you) find operating in *people's relations* to *Hamlet* that will explain why so many different literents [those who respond or re-create literature] from so many different times, places, and cultures can re-create their differing identities from this one set of symbols? (344)

Bleich, on the other hand, refuses to attribute any necessarily positive movement or "progress" to the critical act, as he defines it, because he thinks there is no such *thing* as a self, that can be relied on with *authority*. All of this reminds me, significantly, of my argument in chapter two concerning the non-existence of something called a "literary text." Borrowing the Kuhnian notion of a paradigm change to describe his own "subjective paradigm," Bleich then insists that any "change in paradigm is *not progress toward* anything, but *development from* something" (*SP* 315). From Bleich's point of view, Holland's paradigm is thus the polar opposite of his own. The latter uses an essentially "objective paradigm," that began with Descartes and which "thinks it's getting nearer to Truth" (*SP* 316-18). His comparison of the relative merits of both paradigms leads Bleich to a crucial juncture in his argument, one that, in the final analysis, indicates its theoretical weakness. Referring to a familiar question that underlies countless student complaints that he and others often receive—namely, "Why is it that if my interpretation doesn't agree with yours, I get a lower grade?"—he responds by giving what he firmly thinks is *not* the correct answer. The wrong answer, as it turns out, is the traditional one, i.e. that some interpretations are simply "better" than others (*SP* 332). This response, he contends, assumes the objective paradigm, for what it implies is that some interpretations are "better" because they are so for the supposed critical authority, the teacher, if not necessarily for the individual reader.

But, in fairness to his main target, Norman Holland, one must note that just because Bleich displaces the source of authority from an individual to a more amorphous, if not also far more problematic, collectivity known as the "community," this does not mean that the notion and power of authority itself has been dispelled. Giving the "community" rights and privileges over particular individuals to whom equal rights and privileges have traditionally been awarded (presumably for *some* good reasons) does little to modify the institutional structure which determines the all-important critical questions of acceptable/unacceptable, good/bad, powerful/weak readings. Consequently, Holland is quite correct in claiming that in his pluralistic model of both child cognitive development and, ultimately, of human interpretation in general, the *final* reality of the phenomenal world is neither naively "objective" nor "subjective," but rather the "transaction between the me and what I relate to as not-me" (NP 337). The beauty of Holland's formulation is that it avoids the ontological question of what exactly constitutes either one of these "relatively fixed" poles of me and not-me, and concentrates instead on the functional relationship betweem "them."

Though both psychologically-motivated models come to grips with the reality of critical pluralism, and, indeed, intensify our collective modern belief in the appropriateness of this concept/phenomenon within the literary field, Holland's thus appears to be the more convincing, even though it is less inclusive and less "pluralistic" on the surface. Unlike Bleich's model, it does not depend on a neat separation between objective and subjective critical paradigms in order for it to reconcile itself with the notions of authority and truth. In fact, Holland does not have to discard truth or authority at all, because they act more like structural functions than metaphysical entities in his view. So, where Bleich erroneously criticizes Holland for his misguided faith in "pure" objectivity, and in its corollaries of truth and authority, Holland boldly proclaims that no such absolute is needed for what we might call the "truth function" to operate in society. Critical truth may very well be multiple and variable, he suggests, but a new reading does not triumph because of some intrinsic property of novelty it possesses. Instead, quoting from the autobiography of the physicist Max Planck, Holland states:

A new truth does not triumph by convincing its opponents and making them see the light, but rather because its opponents eventually die (NP 342).

Perhaps the most radical modern psychological theory lending credence to the contemporary faith in critical pluralism, though, is that of René Girard.[67] Inasmuch as Girard's ideas cut across sociological, anthropological, and psychological boundaries, it is difficult to say that his general theory contributes "merely" to a trans-historical psychological disposition that gives rise to critical pluralism. I will, however, limit myself to this dimension of his thought since many of the issues and questions raised by his corpus lie outside of my chosen topic. The main innovation of his theory of interest in this context, the idea of *mimetic desire*, can be shown to pertain directly to the increased modern faith in, and reliance on, pluralism examined throughout my study.

For Girard, all people possess a fundamental psychic drive to imitate, a drive not unlike an analogous human proclivity articulated long ago by Aristotle. What we all seek to imitate is desire itself. Nietzsche and Schopenhauer, of course, had similar notions about our intrinsic will-to-power or will-to-life, but what Girard adds to the debate concerning inherent human drives seems particularly useful—even as a metaphor—to a more complete picture of the critical act of interpretation. In the drive to imitate, Girard identifies a triangular relation between two competing rivals and a third party. That is, in a typical scenario, person X encounters person Y who desires to possess or otherwise appropriate a given individual or object, Z. The desire for Z then becomes a "model," which will be imitated by X all the more because it is being desired by Y.

In terms of critical practice, I translate this to mean that whenever a reader comes face to face with a particular literary text, the desire to read it critically increases in proportion to the desire of an *other* to read it thus. If one considers a classic work like *Hamlet*, one might say that, for Girard, the modern impulse to produce yet another reading of this text has been reinforced precisely because of the existence of a long list of previous readers/"rivals" of *Hamlet*. Sooner or latter in this new interpretation, a "violence" (Girard's term) arises from this very struggle for a position of critical authority over the text. The mimetic drive thus

> meets violence and this violence redoubles the mimesis [...] Each violence is modeled after the first violence and serves as a model in its turn (*CS* 171).

In terms germane to my argument, this implies that every new reading of a text figuratively does violence to all previous ones, although a specific "rival" will usually bear the full brunt of the (critical) attack. When, as in this case, there are no longer anything but "affronted doubles," one need discover (or invent?) only the slightest textual detail or trait in order to complete the rejection of the rival reading(s). In Girard's words, when this occurs

> the least hazard, the lamest sign can draw to itself the fixation of all the reciprocal "hates" on to one of these doubles (*SC* 182).

This process, or system, as Girard calls it, describes in intriguing psychological terms, I believe, what happens in a typical modern-day analysis of a literary work. Unsatisfied with other readings, the critic seeks out his or her place in the interpretive history of a text by singling out specific aspects that either have not yet been noticed, or not yet sufficiently considered. In the process, the rival(s) are pushed aside, as somehow inferior, weaker, less "life-affirming," or even less worthy. These rival readers or readings become thereby "scapegoats" for the new critical approach. Equipped with this justificatory reasoning, the *original* critic destroys the weaker ones, and imposes a new will, a new critical configuration on to the old text. Critical progress is made, and the cause of pluralism is furthered because, for the modern reader, what we earlier called the "fundamental difference" of the text has been restored. A new individualistic system of reading has been instituted within the larger system of literary interpretation, or if one prefers, the larger context of previous readings.

Thus, the progress that a self-proclaimed pluralistic critic can boast of having made consists of showing how the rival critics situated themselves outside of the "proper" system, as foreigners or minorities at odds with the "new" one. S/he "claims to offer life as against death," to borrow Wayne Booth's words again.[68] The paradox, of course, is that the new system includes the old, but with a *proper* difference. Girard writes:

> It is never their difference itself that one criticizes in religious, ethnic, national [and we can add, interpretive] minorities, it is that they do not differ *as they should*, indeed, that they do not differ at all. Foreigners are incapable of respecting "true" differences ... (my emphasis *BE* 34).

It is this very notion of *proper* difference that most undermines the unquestioned modern critical faith in pluralism as methodological principle. This is why Booth is correct in saying that,

> in a curious way, those who call for a multiplication of voices often insist that there is only right way of multiplying (*Critical Understanding* 5).

The institution of literary studies is in this way preserved through what Girard calls the destruction of foreign, undesirable elements. The institution finds itself in possession of a vested interest in a pluralistic model that allows it not only to accept, but even more importantly, to *expect* and *demand* that new readings "cleanse" the impure ones from its system. This individual *catharsis* (Girard's term) is then institutionally sanctioned through an acceptance and promulgation of the latest interpretation, and through the concomitant "sacrifice" of critical scapegoats, which permits a collective institutional catharsis. Without such an underlying conceptual model, which I have metaphorized thanks to Girardian theory, the institution itself risks destruction from within. It risks not knowing on what its always-mobile, always-desiring authority rests at any given moment in its history.

While the rise of aesthetic pluralism studied in chapter three cannot, and should not, be checked, its *critical* idealization must therefore cease. Thinking that original works are "good" just because they are original is groundless. Unless a work's originality is critically evaluated on the basis of tradition and relative worth, it is in fact not being *evaluated* at all. And unless such an evaluation is done against the backdrop of some societally determined value(s), little, if any, genuine critical progress can be attributed to a text or a reading of a text. To express this another way, the question critics must begin to ask, along with Harold Bloom, is the following:

> What happens if one tries to write, or to teach, or to think, or even to read without the sense of a tradition? Why, nothing at all happens, just nothing (32).

NOTES

[1] Bloom, *Map of Misreading*, p. 165.

[2] It bears repetition that the arguments contained in this book should not be dismissed as reactionary gestures *against* literary and/or cultural pluralism. Instead, they constitute a plea for a simple re-consideration of certain fundamental assumptions underlying these cultural phenomena. My re-consideration will hopefully lead to a more modest, even perhaps more honest, appraisal of their real import in our (literary) society.

[3] Jules Delvaille, *L'Histoire de l'Idée de Progrès* (Paris: Felix Alcan, 1910), p. 727.

[4] Murray Kreiger, "The Arts and the Idea of Progress," in *Progress and its Discontents*, ed. Gabriel A. Almond, Marvin Chodorow, and Roy Harvey Pearce (San Francisco & London: University of California Press, 1982), p. 456.

[5] In Jerome Buckley, *The Triumph of Time* (Cambridge, MA: Harvard University Press, 1966).

[6] "The Arts and Progress," p. 460.

[7] In *Madame Bovary*, Flaubert parodied this nineteenth-century social type, i.e. the scientific, or more precisely, pseudo-scientific type, in the character of the pharmacist Homais. Homais was, of course, a profound believer in progress.

[8] In his *Oeuvres complètes*, Philosophie, II (Paris: Albin Michel, 1937), p. 65.

[9] See his *French Romantics on Progress: Human and Aesthetic* (Maryland: Studia Humanistica, 1983).

[10] Quoted in Philippe Lacoue-Labarthe & Jean-Luc Nancy, *The Literary Absolute: The Theory of Literature in German Romanticism*, trans. Philip Barnard & Cheryl Lester (Albany: SUNY Press, 1988), p. 13.

[11] I use the term "poet/critic" to underscore the intimate relationship that has existed between these two professions or practices (often within the same individual) since the end of the eighteenth century. An early case in point is that of the Schlegel brothers, who were not just philologists and critics, but had pretentions as *writers*, frequenting the literary circles of Weimar.

[12] For more on this point, see Lacoue-Labarthe & Nancy, p. 12.

[13] See Robert Nisbet, *The History of the Idea of Progress* (New York: Basic Books, 1980), pp. 5-6.

[14] His increasing fascination with prose poems does, however, lend credence to the idea that had he lived longer, he may well have come to believe in the need for a more and more radical, *formal* revolution.

[15] Ricard was the creator of a short-lived, mid-nineteenth-century French literary journal called *Le Progrès*. He believed that a new kind of literature, integrating science and art, could, and should, be produced.

[16] ed. Jean Hytier, *Oeuvres complètes*, II (Paris: Gallimard, 1960), p. 1022.

[17] I purposely avoid using hyphens in this phrase so as not to confuse this type of criticism exclusively with the short historical period of the end of the nineteenth century, commonly referred to as "fin-de-siècle."

[18] Indeed, in a recent book, Diane P. Freedman uses the term "cross-genre writing" to define the scriptural praxis of a host of modern American feminist poet-critics. See her *An Alchemy of Genres: Cross-genre Writing by American Poet-critics* (Charlottesville & London: University of Virginia Press, 1992).

[19] See Sima Godfrey, "Anxiety of Anticipation: Ulterior Motives in French Poetry," *Yale French Studies*, 66 (1984), 1-26.

[20] This "softness" may very well have been a stereotypical image of femininity used by Madame de Staël to suggest the need for a prerequisite feminization of all great poets.

[21] *Critical Understanding*, p. 220.

[22] Sima Godfrey, "The Anxiety of Anticipation," 25.

[23] *La Nuit remue* (Paris: Gallimard, 1935), p. 203.

[24] Robert Bréchon, *Michaux* (Paris: Gallimard, 1959), p. 206.

[25] *La Nuit remue*, p. 204.

[26] Laurie Edson, *Henri Michaux and the Poetics of Movement* (Saratoga, California: Anma Libri, 1985). Generally speaking, Edson's well-documented conception of this new poetics is similar to mine, but as the later part of my chapter will indicate, her's does not distinguish between two different twentieth-century types of "a poetics of movement" that I take to be manifested by the two poets discussed in the present inquiry.

[27] Virginia A. La Charité, *Henri Michaux* (Boston: Twayne, 1977), p. 93.

[28] Reproduced in Bréchon, p. 137.

[29] *Emergences-Résurgences* (Genève: Skira, 1972), p. 65.

[30] Edson, p. 37, note 11. Edson provides me with this important reference to Mallarmé.

[31] Previously unpublished material quoted in Peter Broome, *Henri Michaux* (London: The Athlone Press, 1977), p. 19.

[32] *Passages* (Paris: Gallimard, 1963), p. 142.

[33] Virginia A. La Charité makes this point on p. 135, note 1.

[34] I am paraphrasing here Edson's strategic borrowing of Baudelaire's term which she takes from his *Mon Coeur mis à nu*. See her *Michaux*, pp. 29-45.

[35] This phrase is a chapter title from La Charité's book.

[36] See his comments during an interview in Bréchon's *Michaux*, p. 205.

[37] Text reproduced in Rene Bertelé, *Henri Michaux* (Paris: Seghers, 1973), p. 151.

[38] Frontispiece reproduced in the following edition of Aragon's collection (Paris: Gallimard, 1970), p. 61.

[39] See his interview with Dominique Arban, *Aragon parle* (Paris: Seghers, 1968), pp. 69-72 for a full discussion of this discovery. This type of purely formal, mechanical "origin" of a poem cannot help but remind us of other famous twentieth century poetic "finds" (*trouvailles*), like Valéry's spontaneous desire to write a poem in decasyllables. This find led, of course, to the composition of "Le Cimetière Marin."

[40] Cf. Michaux's text, "Je ne peux pas me reposer" cited above, Bréchon, p. 137: *C'est dans tout indifféremment que j'ai la chance de trouver ce que je cherche, puisque ce que je cherche je ne le sais./* "It is in everything, indifferently, that I am lucky enough to find what I seek, since what I seek I do not know." The important words missing here, of course, are *pas encore/* "not yet (know)," an adverbial phrase that Aragon implicitly adds to our discussion.

[41] Louis Aragon, *Le Paysan de Paris* (Paris: Gallimard, 1926), p. 12. Further references are to this edition and are placed parenthetically in the text.

[42] Louis Aragon, *Je n'ai jamais appris à écrire* (Genève: Skira, 1969), p. 13.

[43] This writing technique, shared by Breton, allowed the later poet to claim almost thirty years after the fact that his automatic poem "Tournesol" was *really always about* his fortuitous encounter one night with the woman who eventually became his wife. Clearly, for this group of writers, poetry became an authentically visionary activity, much like Rimbaud wanted it to be.

[44] My hesitation in using this qualification is the result of my being neither an expert psychologist, nor a sociologist, nor an anthropologist. It may well be that there are still more trans-historical, deeply *human* reasons for the ever-increasing and willful conflict of interpretations than those mentioned here.

[45] In *The Languages of Criticism and the Structure of Poetry* (Toronto: University of Toronto Press, 1953), quoted by David Richter in his study of Crane in the *Dictionary of Literary Biography*, vol. 63 (1988), p. 91.

[46] In *The Primacy of Perception*, ed. James M. Edie (Evanston: Northwestern University Press, 1964), p. 16.

[47] In "How Ordinary is Ordinary Language?" *New Literary History*, 5 (1973), 52.

[48] *Interpreting Interpreting* (Baltimore: Johns Hopkins University Press, 1979), p. 126.

[49] In "The Conflict of Interpretations and the Limits of Pluralism," *PMLA*, 98, 3 (May 1983), 342.

[50] Ellen Rooney, *Seductive Reasoning: Pluralism as the Problematic of Contemporary Literary Theory* (Ithaca: Cornell University Press, 1989), p. 242.

[51] In their *Against Theory* (Chicago: University of Chicago Press, 1985), p. 30.

[52] I am thinking here specifically of his (typically) controversial piece on "Anti-Professionalism," *New Literary History*, 17,2 (Autumn 1985).

[53] In "La lecture critique," *Poétique*, 34 (1978), 139.

[54] Charles, 140.

[55] Murray Krieger, "The Arts and the Idea of Progress," in *Progress and Its Discontents*, ed. Gabriel A. Almond, Marvin Chodorow, and Roy Harvey Pearce (Berkeley & London: University of California Press, 1982), p. 468.

[56] See his "Do Readers Make Meaning?" in *The Reader in the Text: Essays on Audience and Interpretation*, ed. Inge Crosman & Susan R. Suleiman (Princeton: Princeton University Press, 1980), p. 161.

[57] Crosman, p. 162.

[58] Crosman, p. 164.

[59] *In Defense*, p. 5.

[60] *In Defense*, p. 7.

[61] "The Author as Producer," in *Art After Modernism: Rethinking Modernism*, ed. Brian Wallis (New York & Boston: New Museum of Contemporary Art & Godine Publishers, 1984), p. 306.

[62] Charles J. Sykes, *Profscam* (Washington, D.C.: Regnery Gateway, 1988), p. 107.

[63] "The Pseudo-Politics of Interpretation," in *The Politics of Interpretation*, ed. W. J. T. Mitchell (Chicago: University of Chicago Press, 1983), p. 147 & p. 150.

[64] "Pseudo-Politics," p. 153.

[65] Norman N. Holland, "Unity Identity Text Self," *PMLA*, 90, 5 (1975), 813-22.

[66] He does so in two major publications from which I shall be quoting here. They are: his book, *Subjective Criticism* (Baltimore: Johns Hopkins University Press, 1978), and his article, "The Subjective Paradigm in Science, Psychology, and Criticism," *New Literary History*, 7, 2 (1976), hereafter cited in the text with the symbols *SC* and *SP* respectively.

[67] The list of appropriate related titles by Girard is far too long for me to mention here. For the following discussion, I have relied principally on these two works: *Critique dans un souterrain* (Lausanne: Editions l'Age d'Homme, 1976), and *Le Bouc Emissaire* (Paris: Grasset & Fasquelle, 1982), hereafter cited in the text by the symbols *CS* and *BE* respectively.

[68] *Critical Understanding*, p. 220.

Chapter V
CONCLUSION:
RE-VIEWING PLURALISM AND LITERATURE

> What sets worlds in motion is the interplay of
> differences, the attractions and repulsions. Life is
> plurality, death is uniformity. By suppressing
> differences and peculiarities, by eliminating
> different civilizations and cultures, progress
> weakens life, and favors death. The ideal of a
> single civilization for everyone ... impoverishes
> and mutilates us. — Octavio Paz (1967)

I have now isolated the various factors at work over time which
have contributed most to the rise of pluralism as a preeminent
concept subtending modern literary activity. Because a number of
these factors have always existed, as I suggested in the previous
chapter, it has been necessary to underscore the peculiar historical
nexus between these trans-historical factors and those from the
specific literary history of the West. Without this emphasis on a
combination of heterogeneous factors, one would have been hard-
pressed to understand fully why most of us Moderns have come to
accept pluralism as an article of faith in our collective work as
writers, poets, scholars, teachers, and critics.

What remains to be discussed is whether or not the modern rise
of literary pluralism is, in and of itself, of actual benefit to the
producers and interpreters of literature. As was stated from the
beginning, this issue can no longer be a question of *good* or *bad*,
since few people nowadays are naive enough to be misled by such
culture-specific qualifiers. Yet, one would still like to know whether
the current state of affairs represents a sign of health or decay in the
fields of verbal art and its study. In other words, if, for a moment,
one assumed that literary pluralism as a whole *could*, in one way or
another, be limited (contrary to much of what has been suggested so
far), one would first have to ascertain whether it is necessary, or
even desirable, to attempt to do so. The answer to this question
forms the crux of this concluding chapter. It involves both a re-view
of how we have arrived at the historical, ideological stage where

critics and writers now find themselves, and a small, albeit significant, change in our collective view of the causes and effects of pluralism in literature.

In the final analysis, my study has constituted a kind of theoretical deconstruction of the phenomenon of literary pluralism, one that is analogous to those undertaken by Wayne Booth, K. M. Newton, and Ellen Rooney. The major difference between this book and theirs' is its larger historical scope. An even better way in which to describe this book is to call it a polemic, as long as one keeps in mind what the art critic, Hal Foster, says in his powerful essay against pluralism:

> A polemic against pluralism is not a plea for old truths. Rather, it is a plea to invent new truths, or more precisely, to *re*-invent old truths radically. If this is not done, these old truths simply return ....[1]

What Foster means is this: more of us have to realize the simple truth that very little, if anything, that is currently being produced in literature and literary criticism represents "new truth." Since the nineteenth century, the very concept of truth has been under attack, making the *forms* that different truths assume more important, in most respects, than the truths themselves. This is to say that the signified has gradually receded into our collective memories, leaving only the signifier with which to "play." While we discover or *re-invent*—in the rhetorical sense of "coming upon" (again)—different forms of our societal truths, we must begin to appreciate anew how much these discoveries, re-inventions, or "original" texts and readings depend on the pre-existence of old truths for them to signify anything whatsoever in contemporary society. For only in this manner can one better grasp the inherent limitations of our obsessive dependence on qualifiers like "original," "different," "new," and "progressive." Once one recognizes these limitations, the *re-view* (i.e. recapitulation and reevaluation) of the relationship between literature and pluralism takes on a greater legitimacy, as well as a new urgency.

* * *

In keeping with the same order of topics treated thus far, let me repeat first of all that it is *practically* impossible to restrict what I have been calling "aesthetic pluralism." Outside of totalitarian regimes, and often even within them, in clandestine pockets inhabited by officially condemned "reformist" or "revisionist" zealots, artists and writers possess a certain degree of freedom to express themselves as they wish. Thanks to this freedom, they seek to express themselves in personal, idiosyncratic ways that differ from those of their contemporaries, or from those of their predecessors. This personal difference embodied and created by artists has come to be known as their originality, and is generally seen as a progressive gesture that helps "advance" the cause of all forms of Art.

What happened historically, of course, is that as personal freedoms grew with revolutionary times, the idea of individuality began to spread rapidly. In John Stuart Mill's words,

> During the early part of this [nineteenth] century the doctrine of individuality, and the claim of the moral nature to develop itself in its own way, was pushed by a whole school of German authors [like Goethe and von Humboldt] even to exaggeration .... [In America, Mrs. Warren] had formed a system of society [called Warrenite] on the foundation of the "sovereignty of the individual" ... [which] recognized no authority whatever in society over the individual, except to enforce equal freedom of development for all individualities.[2]

As we saw in chapter three, the aesthetic counter-part of this social doctrine of individuality was the modern quest for originality. This newly-valorized aesthetic concept developed just as quickly as its larger social model-doctrine, individuality. It exhibited a similar historical evolution in that it represented a movement away from earlier forms of repression (social or artistic) to more radical expressions of personal liberty. Freedom and the modern desire for, and expectation of, freedom, thus make any wish to limit aesthetic pluralism an exercise in utter futility. To ask a question like, "Why should there be another novel about adulterous love?" in the late twentieth century is tantamount to condemning oneself to the dustbin of intellectual history. The obvious response to such inquiries is: Since we cannot stop writers and critics from behaving as they do, we needn't bother trying.

Nevertheless, I would like to argue that although we cannot, indeed, *should* not, try to limit aesthetic pluralism—any more than we should try to limit political and social freedoms—we critics should re-think what Bloom calls the "over-idealization" of its consequences. For the question one must ask is the following: What do we as a society, or specifically, as members of a literary profession, expect to gain from an unlimited profusion and multiplicity of artistic and/or critical works? Is the deliberate, even obsessive, modern quest for originality in and of itself beneficial to the production of literature in general, and criticism in particular? I believe that the desire to be a new or original writer and/or critic, *for originality's sake*, is sometimes counter-productive. The reason I think this is that behind the desire to be different one often discovers another greater desire. This other desire, while not always explicit, oftentimes strikes me as utopian. I refer here to the wish to produce a text that in some significant way(s) is different from every other text in existence. Why is this utopian? Obviously because one has to ascertain the extent to which the writer or critic has actual succeeded or failed in the attempt to be *significantly* different. One can be different without this difference really meaning anything much at all. Moreover, a "new" text more often than not serves as a model that, sooner or later, acts as an obstacle, an impediment that needs to be overcome, surpassed, or otherwise, improved upon in its turn. It is as if the more one wanted to create something original, therefore, the more one risked producing the future idol or "scapegoat" (cf. Girard) that will have to be pushed aside, forgotten, or destroyed.

What I am suggesting in this re-view of aesthetic pluralism is that writers might eventually wish to temper their originality impulse, especially when they realize that one person's creative door to a new artistic world is another person's brick wall that has to be torn down. In this sense, any "progress" they hope to make as writers, or to have already made, might be seen more as a provisional step in some direction than as a definitive break with the past. This step is not necessarily "forward," but could also be "sideways," or even "backwards," as was seen in chapter three. The situation of the modern writer and critic that I am trying to reevaluate is here again captured perfectly by John Stuart Mill in another passage from his autobiography. The general subject of this passage is nineteenth-century society as a whole. Mill writes:

> the gradual revolution that is taking place in society and institutions has, thus far, been decidedly favourable to the development of new opinions [or works], and has procured for them a much more unprejudiced hearing than they previously met [...] But this state of things is *necessarily transitory*: some particular body of doctrine in time rallies the majority around it, organizes social institutions and modes of action conformably to itself; education impresses this new creed upon the new generations without the mental processes that have led to it, and by degrees it acquires *the very same power of compression* so long exercized by the creeds of which it had taken the place (my emphasis *Auto* 181).

Commenting in uncharacteristically modest terms on the *lack* of originality in his own extremely influential book, *On Liberty*, Mill then immediately adds a personal note that puts the notion of originality into what I think is a better perspective for modern critics as well as modern artists:

> As regards originality, it [*On Liberty*] has of course none other than that which every thoughtful mind gives to its own mode of conceiving and expressing *truths which are common property* .... [The] book which bears my name claimed *no originality* for any of its doctrines ... the only author who preceded me was Humboldt (my emphasis *Auto* 181-2).

A recent *New York Times* essay makes the same point when its author states that "what begins as rebellion often ends up as a new orthodoxy."[3] In neither case do these two critical voices, seperated by time and place, strive to restrict, limit, or silence advocates and practitioners of aesthetic pluralism. (Neither do I.) But, in both instances, there is a sense among the authors that more modesty, or perhaps more historical relief, is desirable in, at least, the *critical appraisal* of a work's originality.

For certain commonly-shared reasons already examined, and for other more localized reasons that doubtless exist in individual cases, most writers thus simply cannot stop wanting to write differently, to some extent, from their contemporaries and precursors. However, an important issue which could no doubt serve as the point of departure for another book, concerns just what this "extent" is. Since the creative drive itself is not likely to disappear now or in the near future, nobody should think that it must suddenly be exorcised. My point is not that it is somehow inappropriate, unhealthful, or undesirable. Yet, the fact remains that art and literature do not progress as the sciences do. A great piece of literature *dis*places, for a while, other pieces of literature, but rarely, if ever, does it completely *re*place them, as one finds in the sciences. When a scientific theorem, for instance, is found to explain a given phenomenon better than another one, it effectively sucks out the inherent value of the latter. The same can hardly be said of a contemporary Latin American novel like Mario Vargas Llosa's *The Green House* vis-à-vis *Madame Bovary*, however. Given Vargas Llosa's great admiration for Flaubert, it is clear that his own novelistic production in no way negates the aesthetic import of Flaubert's. His novels are quite simply *different*. His *oeuvre* constitutes a body of texts whose popular success nowadays is merely what Mill qualified as "necessarily transitory," even if this success lasts a long time.

Still, this must not be construed as meaning that Flaubert's works are somehow immune to this same transitoriness, for surely they are not, and never have been. In other words, not everyone thinks they are the *nec plus ultra* of verbal art. Unlike scientific progress, which is generally reconstructed by historians of science after the absolute and definitive demise of certain facts and whole systems of facts, literature does not progress by a process of elimination. Its very nature is always elusive, shifting, multifarious, in a word, *pluralistic*, making any isolated instances of deliberate originality a critically problematic issue indeed. When, for instance,

James Joyce set out to destroy certain nineteenth-century novelistic conventions with works like *Portrait of the Artist as a Young Man* and, especially, *Ulysses* and *Finnegan's Wake*, he may have *thought* that he was metaphorically destroying writers like Dickens, Dostoievsky, Trollope, and Balzac. But, in fact, he never did completely succeed in eliminating the works of these writers. After all, they are still being read, and, in many instances, more than his own. His dramatic attempts to be artistically original, constitutive of so much modern aesthetic pluralism, thus failed to represent bona fide aesthetic *progress*, in the scientific sense of the word, in the sense of replacement.

Yet, as it should be obvious by now, this is no cheap shot at Joyce, nor at anyone else. In the final analysis, no writer can or, might I say, *should* claim to progress in literature as one claims to progress in other non-aesthetic fields. Let us, therefore, "allow" poets and other artists to continue seeking to be different, since we really cannot do anything about it anyway. Given that most of their quests for originality are probably "life-affirming" in one manner or other, we have no legitimate reasons for denying them their right to creative acts. Octavio Paz's quote at the start of this final chapter seems, in this respect, completely justified and accurate. But those who work in, and with, literature should, I think, also retain a keener *critical* sense about what *they* are actually accomplishing with all their manifestos, demonstrations, happenings, exhibitions, openings, and publications. They need to keep this keener sense because of the historical shifts from signified to signifier, and from representation to expression, that have rendered the whole notion of aesthetic progress, in a strict scientific sense, non-sensical. As Arthur Danto has written, we no longer have a

> basis for saying that we can now express what we could express badly or not at all before, as we could say that we now can show things we could only show badly or not at all before. So the history of art [and literature] has no future of the sort that can be extrapolated as it can against the paradigm of progress: it sunders into a sequence of individual acts, one after the other.[4]

The conceptual basis on which the various Quarrels between the Ancients and the Moderns rested over several centuries has in this way effectively disappeared. The Quarrel itself has not vanished, in other words, but its foundation has. Let us recall that the larger issue of these debates centered on the question of which society could express itself better, the Modern or the Ancient. "Better" or "worse," though, have no place in contemporary critical discourse. For we intellectuals are supposedly beyond such qualitative labels.

Curiously enough, however, words like "progressive" and "original" still abound whenever contemporaries audiences deal with new works of art, literature, and cinema. Therein lies one of the major paradoxes I have uncovered. If, at present, one does not dare to say that text X or reading X is "better" than text Y or reading Y, then, likewise, one does not have the right, logically, to use (let alone *over*-use, as we do), phrases like "truly different," "path-breaking," "completely original," etc.. Phrases like these are, after all, permeated by a misleading, if not irrelevant, nineteenth-century scientific, positivist notion of progress. A Marxist critic might say that this lexical proclivity towards such qualifiers is the consequence of the latest stage of capitalist development. In such a scheme, one could claim that as capitalism grew, it generated such terminology in order to sell products to more and more customers who became mystified by such over-idealized terminology, never asking themselves what these words really meant. I would not dispute this type of argument.

Regardless of the political ramifications of these words, though, it is incontestable that in most economically-advanced Western societies terminology like this is still rampant. In the United States, in particular, the idea of progress, along with all of its conceptual corrolaries of difference and originality, has not suffered any appreciable loss of prestige or influence at all in the last one hundred years, either in professional intellectual and/or aesthetic circles, or in everyday life. Although it is not always admitted or expressed as such, progress is still very important for Americans, if for no other reason than because of what Robert Nisbet calls "the boundless popularity of the word "progressive.""[5] One need only look around one's own immediate locale to find signs of this illegitimate over-use of such paradoxical qualifiers. In St. Louis, for example, I find the following random sampling of cultural manifestations of our society's conceptual obsession with difference, progress, and, in general, things pluralistic:

— On television, which has turned out to be a particularly fertile semiotic field full of contemporary myths, we are asked to admire the local "Channel 5 *difference.*"

— The NBC Nightly (National & International) News contains a special segment each day called "The Daily Difference."

— In a television commercial for a recently improved cough drop, a character turns to a stranger coughing in a restaurant and says, in apparent reverence to a mystifying quality of the medication, "Try this ... it's *new!*" (the sponsor's emphasis). The ostensible reason to try the cough drop is not that it is, in fact, *better*, but that it is simply "new."

— In another commercial, produced by the Chrysler Corporation, we are first confronted with the words, "Things are Different," and are then immediately shown their latest car model. The third part of the implied syllogism behind this sequence of images is: "Things are Better," meaning that *whatever* difference this car brings is perforce "good."

— And in a third commercial, produced by the fast-food chain known as Arby's, TV viewers do not even have to supply the missing parts of the unsaid semiotic equation, since the commercial supplies the viewers with the absent words at the very end. After seeing Arby's latest creation, another in a long line of fast-food "delicacies," the perplexed TV audience learns from bold letters that "Different is good"! Instead of proclaiming such a patent absurdity, I think it bears noting that, in many instances (perhaps even this one!), "different" is just "different." The question of good or bad differences, especially in these cases, is highly debatable.

— On the side of my neighborhood Shell gas station are found the red-colored letters ETD, which signify, *Experience The Difference.*

— In countless film, art, and book reviews, one repeatedly notices terms such as "radically different," "original," "ground-breaking," and the like used to applaud a given work's quality. The same "catch" words are sought out by inquisitive deans and personnel committees in hopes of validating the quality of a professor's candidacy for tenure.

— Cultural programs at local libraries and museums carry titles like, "A World of Difference" and "Celebrate our Differences."

— Household products as diverse as cereals and detergent display on their respective boxes the terms "new and improved," leading one to wonder why it has taken so long for such improvements to be made and, especially, how long it will take for what is now "new and improved" to become "old and degenerate."

What all of this suggests is that in everyday modern Western life and, *a forteriori*, in the intellectual sphere,

> there is no evident inclination to be thought "unprogressive" .... The often mindless worship of the new in any sphere has behind it, whether consciously or not, a philosophy that by its very nature declares the new or the latest the highest in an ascending progression through time (Nesbit, *History*, 311).

And this, in spite of our supposed lack of belief in such notions as good and bad, better or worse. This disinclination takes the form of critical lip-service to some kind of blindly-open pluralism that would have us believe that every text and every writer has an equal share of our society's respect and appreciation, just because that text or that writer is "different." Yet, the attempt to support the ideal of pluralism in the field of criticism screens us from the fact that "*all* discourses, in the very process of establishing significance, *necessarily* exclude not only some readings, but also some readers."[6] Being "different" is thus *not* in actuality all that is required of texts and writers.

Nesbit is, therefore, correct to imply that (literary) pluralism—based, as it is, on the belief in both progress and on originality—results either from a conscious or an *unconscious* decision to valorize something, say, a text or a textual reading, mainly on the grounds of its novelty and/or difference. As soon as we fully realize our extensive reliance on the notions of progress and originality for aesthetic and critical judgments, it is impossible, however, not to confront another choice we have to make. Either we start acting as if we genuinely thought that certain texts represented progress of some verifiable type, thanks to their original nature (thematic, stylistic, ideological, political, etc.), and *say as much*; or else, we admit that our seemingly universal praise for aesthetic and critical originality is often little more than lip-service to the uncritically accepted dogma of literary pluralism. In principle, we cannot have it both ways.

This is why one must never forget that absolute originality is essentially a contradiction in terms. The only kind of originality imaginable is transitory, one that forms a pragmatic reference point from which to make sense of literary history. The "truth" of a work or an interpretation is always already a re-invented old truth, one without which no societal meaning is possible. No matter how great the modern impulse is—on the grounds of an hypothesized textual originality, to find disunity, chaos, and difference in texts where, in pre-modern times, one preferred unity, order, and identity—*practical* considerations, like deadlines, page requirements, and pedagogical imperatives, always make it impossible not to seek out a modicum of "common knowledge," a common ground, without which any communication cannot take place. Instead of wishing to break *definitively* with an aesthetic or interpretive tradition, one would thus be well advised to recognize the theoretical as well as pragmatic unfeasibility of any such project.

In this way what one finally sees taking shape in this polemic is a somewhat more modest and perhaps more honest appraisal of what writers and critics do while they produce different sorts of texts. Following Eric Charles White's lead, I would contend that perhaps the only legitimate theoretical perspective left to people working in the field of literature is to treat their respective contributions as transitory reference points, necessary ends, and inevitable beginnings to further literary production. Providing us a useful model that deserves to be imitated by poets and critics alike, White adds this significant disclaimer to the start of his book, *Kaironomia: On the Will-To-Invent*:

> Claiming for itself no conclusive preeminence and hoping, in fact, to serve as provocation to further invention, the present essay is meant to be read and enjoyed as dismissable speculation.[7]

As nihilistic and defeatist as this opinion sounds, it does nevertheless take into account, consciously or unconsciously, all that has been shown in the present book as well. For it reveals the extent to which the concepts originality and progress should no longer color or influence to the same extent as before our understanding of pluralism's place in the creation and study of literature. It fully accepts the reality of the transitoriness both of art and of its interpretation. It comes to grips with the fact that criticism does not progress in exactly the same way as do the hard sciences, since the textual knowledge it uncovers or reveals, like all knowledge, can only be significant and apprehensible in terms of what Edward Said in his book *Beginnings* calls "*nomadic centers*, provisional structures always straying from one set of information to another."[8]

To die-hard advocates of pluralism who, by words or deeds, would have us applaud literary work because of its supposed absolute originality, I would therefore wish to suggest that the so-called "gig" is up. Writers, being writers, will in all probability continue to wish to be different from one another, just as professional critics are likely to remain desirous of printing a few more pages. But to imply, as too many still do, that literary production aims mainly at showing the profound ideological commitment of a writer or critic to the contemporary cultural ideal of pluralism is to lose sight of the historical inevitability of such gestures. As critical and doubtful of *meaning* and *tradition* as critics and writers may wish to be, their multiple expressions of theoretical doubt are less a sign of some special contemporary capacity to signify things *differently* than a possible sign of some extra-textual commitment to what is currently known as "political correctness." After all, irrespective of how one writes, or of what one writes about, at some point or other in their poems, novels, plays, or readings, one always means *something*; or else, tragically, one means *nothing* at all. In White's words,

> If the modern suspicion of the desire for fullness, unity, and closure can never finally dispel that desire, if our deep yearning for continuity, coherence, and identity cannot be abolished [as, we have seen, it cannot], then at least *intermittent reliance on received knowledge* should not be forbidden (86-7).

If pressed for a value-judgment, I might admit, then, that literary pluralism is "good," inasmuch as it has never been, nor, apparently, can it ever be, avoided. But saying or thinking this is not the same as insisting that our historical situation as writers and critics is now "better" than before, because of some qualitative difference which pluralism brings to bear on the domain of modern Western literature and its study. It is merely an admission that due to forces far beyond the control of most any individual or society we cannot help but wish to be pluralistic. This is why we may be no more pluralistic as a society than our predecessors were, except in the sense that we *think* we are. We think this way because since the late eighteenth century we have insisted on how individualistic, different, and original our literary works are, and how much these supposed "qualities" (cf. "la qualité *maîtresse*") represent our definitive progress over our precursors. In the twentieth century, the obsession with originality has reached quasi-paroxystic proportions, becoming a veritable fetish in the various European avant-gardes. In her study of this concept in the twentieth-century artistic avant-garde, Rosalind Krauss recalls my earlier examination of Breton and Aragon when she writes:

> More than a rejection or dissolution of the past, avant-garde
> originality is conceived as a literal origin, a beginning from ground
> zero, a birth .... Marinetti emerges as if from amniotic fluid to be
> born without ancestors - a futurist .... The first *Futurist Manifesto*
> functions as a model for what is meant by originality among the early
> twentieth-century avant-garde.[9]

However, as she demonstrates in her subsequent analysis of the artistic figure of the *grid* in works by Mondrian, Albers, Reinhardt, and Agnes Martin, this desired and theoretically radical break from tradition, this birth *ex nihilo*, if one prefers, turns out to be a not-so-original copy of nineteenth-century models. Krauss exaggerates, perhaps, to the extent that from a structural point of view a grid is more likely to be noticed as a repeated feature than would a less geometrically-defined trait, like a color. But her main point should still be taken seriously. For it often happens that with sufficient spatio-temporal relief from the spectacular immediacy of a given "original" artistic object (be it a painting, a poem, or a persuasive critical reading), one starts to see much less how the new object *differs* from others, and much more how it resembles them. This is why she correctly asserts that,

> if the very notion of the avant-garde can be seen as a function of the
> *discourse of originality*, the actual *practice* of vanguard art tends to
> reveal that "originality" is a working assumption that itself emerges
> *from a ground of repetition and recurrence* (my emphasis 18).

The combined discourses of originality and progress, contributing over two centuries to the rise of the contemporary discourse of literary pluralism thereby assume greater social, political, and ideological power than the actual artistic products of which they would seem to be the theoretical and critical manifestations. For precisely this reason, in our time, it is harder to see terms like "copy" and "model,"

> performing in mutual interdependence, since aesthetic
> discourse—both official and nonofficial—gives priority to the term
> "originality" and tends to suppress the notion of repetition or copy

> [...] Both the avant-garde and modernism depend on this repression
> (Krauss 25-7).

Yet, pluralists repress this necessary interdependence at their own peril. Without realizing their own slight misunderstanding of the phenomenon of literary and interpretive invention, they find themselves unable to explain certain critical situations that arise at an alarmingly frequent pace these days. A case in point occurs when what is deemed a *truly* different poem or analysis of a poem turns out—at a later time, or in a different place and society—to lack any semblance whatsoever of that magical quality known nowadays as "originality." In this instance, critics, or even writers themselves discover (as Aragon did) that they were more or less copying someone or something else without realizing it. A situation like this implies that pluralists need to re-view the true meaning of acts like creating a new work, and writing a new interpretation. Their revised view should make clear to them that

> the activity of invention must be founded on the [critical] recognition
> that originality is only the instauration of a new commonplace (White
> 89).

So what seems at first to be a radical difference often reveals itself to be yet another moment in a long chain of related aesthetic events. Unfortunately, however, even this metaphor of a chain is inadequate to describe fully the situation of literature and criticism, since it implies a kind of linearity or positive evolution towards an eventual *telos* that simply does not, and has not existed, at least since Nietzsche declared the death of God. This situation must also be understood as "a *discontinuous* series of [aesthetic and critical] phases between which there is a radical incommensurability" (Danto 25, my emphasis). Without this second historical (or *a*-historical?) perspective on the reality of literature and its study, modern literary practice as it now stands cannot avoid having its values skewed in the direction of the new over the old (or conversely, the old over the new) where no such imbalance should rightfully occur. This explains why the critical enterprise must always move from the "pure

difference" of texts to the linguistic "sameness" of readers'
experiences of texts (and then back again), as was explained in
chapter two. Failing such a balancing act between repetition and
difference, between history and the a-historical, literary pluralism
degenerates into nonsense.

To over-emphasize difference and all of its conceptual offshoots
is therefore equivalent to forgetting the unbreakable historical as well
as theoretical link between the same and the other, the model and the
copy, the old and the new. Eve Tavor Bannet, a recent debunker of
certain aspects of what I call "literary pluralism," indicates an
important paradox in this regard. She points out that when
contemporary texts and critical theories emphasize difference and
criticize sameness to the exclusion of the latter, they essentially self-
destruct. Taking as her specific target modern French criticism,
Bannet underscores an issue that touches many of the critical
questions I have been treating all along in this book. In reference to
what she calls some of the most powerful "pluralist theory-fictions
and fictional politics" at work today (those of Lacan, Barthes,
Foucault, and Deleuze), she writes that due to the idealization of
difference, such fictions actually

> fail to register difference and make everything sound the same.
> Refusing to repeat the always already of the past they end up
> repeating only themselves ... [This] translation of everything into
> [personal] fiction makes French poststructuralist theory as totalizing
> and as totalitarian as the social and ideological structures it sets out
> to contest.[10]

By thinking that everything poets and critics do either is, or *should
be*, different, we place ourselves in what, paradoxically, amounts to
an anti-pluralistic position. The great irony, of course, is that our
slow but sure reification of the concepts of originality and progress,
and our subsequent fusing of them into the monolith we have been
calling literary pluralism can no longer be viewed as anything other
than its opposite, a monism!

What then remains to be done? Should we all voice our utter
discontent with pluralism as it relates to the different spheres of
literary activity? Should we all confess that our novels and poems,

readings and analyses, are really little more than so many trivial words, words, words: words that have been spoken before, discoveries that have been made elsewhere? Of course not. What we need to do is to set instead a more reasonable and safe agenda for ourselves, one that recognizes that pluralism has wrought a disregard, even perhaps a dismissal, of something we used to think of as Culture. Being neither an elitist, nor one to proclaim the irrelevance or insignificance of our "necessarily transitory" modern literary monuments, I do not wish to seem unduly nostalgic for something that, in many respects, never existed anyway. But I do think it is time for us to take to heart a concise formulation of our current critical situation expressed by the art critic Hal Foster. Foster warns that in lieu of "Culture," what we now have is a plurality of "cults" (15). Anyone who sees our modern interpretive condition in these terms will agree that we are not necessarily any better off for it than before. For, being "better off," either aesthetically or critically, as an entire community or society, we must, after all, have recourse to an essential(ist) notion like Culture. Without such a concept, no one can pretend to speak, or even think, of one's literary practice in terms of a more general kind of progress for others within the same community or society. And yet, many still do, most often, unknowingly.

To critique pluralism and its effects on literature, as I have done in the preceding chapters, therefore, is to speak against the immodesty, unjustified pretense, and relative blindness (historical and otherwise) of those who, over the last two hundred years, would have had us believe that anything of literary worth must perforce be of recent creation; or, that, at very least, it must somehow be on the "cutting edge" of criticism and theory. It also entails questioning exactly which differences are meant when difference and originality are evoked in any positive assessment of a particular text. From a common pluralist point of view, for example, earlier forms of literature and earlier readings of "classic" works are frequently dismissed because they are said to contain traces of the lives and thoughts of people in possession of the *wrong* differences, e.g., white Eurocentric males. Just as creative and critical texts have increasingly had to be original or different, so, too—goes the common argument—should they embrace peoples, cultures, and behaviors previously unexamined and unappreciated. In this manner, many modern critical readings seek to demonstrate, more and more, how certain contemporary theoretical and ideological *bêtes noires* are exemplified by retrograde authors and equally reactionary commentators.

I would argue for a more honest appraisal not only of the singularity of our own productions, but also of the "originality" (or lack thereof) of all our predecessors in the field of literature. While wanting to be different is all fine and good,

> To see other periods as mirrors of our own is to turn history into narcissism; to see other styles as open to our own is to turn history into a dream. But such is the dream of the pluralist: he [sic] seems to sleepwalk in the museum (Foster 17).

Ultimately, hyperemphasis on difference can and does lead, then, to its own kind of stagnation and stasis, the very enemy of the most vocal pluralists. In the *un*-self-reflective world of so much literary pluralism, "as anything goes, nothing changes; and *that* is the catastrophe" (Foster 24).

Finally, if we fail to notice how much we still hold dearly to fantasies like radical originality and genuine progress; or how much we still feel—indeed, still have—a need to single out provisionally, at least, the "classic" novel or the "great" interpretation, we run the risk of overestimating the power of pluralism in the field of modern literature. This is why believing in the possibility, or better yet, the necessity, of *temporary* literary absolutes seems a more desirable option to me than the open-ended one provided by unquestioned, untempered pluralism. The phrase "temporary literary absolutes" is an oxymoron, to be sure. Yet, it does seem an appropriate one for our time, just like Albert Camus' modern notion of absurdity. It is appropriate because it underscores how we must accept, at a given time, the "truth" and societally determined value(s) of particular utterances. At the same time, it recognizes the ontological transitoriness of these entities. As Robert Nisbet writes in reference to God, the real danger of ceasing to believe in any absolutes is not, therefore, "that one will then believe nothing; it is that one will believe anything" (351).

My story of "the rise of literary pluralism" is, quite simply then, a history of some of the most important criticism and literature produced in the West over the last two hundred years or so. It is a history of literary modernity itself. This history illustrates the extent to which pluralism has greatly influenced texts composed by modern critics and poets alike, even if they have sometimes been unaware of such influence. As such, it puts us in a better position from which to reject many of our unquestioned contemporary literary beliefs and judgments, especially those upheld by the supposed intrinsic value of difference. It also permits us to reevaluate modern literary texts of many different varieties; that is, to attribute some type of value to them, without being afraid to face the pragmatic consequences of this critical responsibility. May our different *evaluations* of texts, therefore, now begin anew.

NOTES

[1] Hal Foster, "Against Pluralism" in *Recodings: Art, Spectacle, Cultural Politics* (Port Townsend, Washington: Bay Press, 1985), p. 31.

[2] *Autobiography of John Stuart Mill* (New York: New American Library, 1964), p. 181.

[3] Richard Bernstein, "The Arts Catch Up with a Society in Disarray" *New York Times* (Sunday Sept. 2, 1990), sec. 2, 1.

[4] Arthur Danto, "The Death of Art," in *The Death of Art*, ed. Berel Lang, vol. 2 (New York: Haven Publications, 1984), p. 24.

[5] *History of Progress*, p. 311.

[6] Ellen Rooney, *Seductive Reasoning*, p. 61.

[7] Charles Eric White, *Kaironomia: On the Will-to-Invent* (Ithaca & London: Cornell University Press, 1987), p. 9.

[8] Quoted in White, *Will*, p. 86.

[9] Rosaling Krauss, "The Originality of the Avant-Garde: A Postmodernist Repetition" in *Art after Modernism*, ed. Brian Wallis, p. 18.

[10] Eve Tavor Bannet, "Pluralist Theory-Fictions and Fictional Politics," *Philosophy and Literature*, 13, 1 (April 1989), 36.

BIBLIOGRAPHY

This bibliography does not include references to certain well-known works that I have had occasion to quote from in the course of my book's argument. It includes instead only those cited works that one cannot readily recover from many other sources.

Abrams, M. H. *The Mirror and the Lamp.* Oxford: Oxford University Press, 1953.

Aragon, Louis. *Le Paysan de Paris.* Paris: Gallimard, 1926.

———. *Je n'ai jamais appris à écrire.* Genève: Skira, 1969.

———. *Le Mouvement Perpétuel.* Paris: Gallimard, 1970.

Arban, Dominique. *Aragon Parle.* Paris: Seghers, 1968.

Armstrong, Paul. "The Conflict of Interpretations and the Limits of Pluralism." *PLMA* 98.3 (May 1983): 341-352.

Austin, Timothy. *Language Crafted: A Linguistic Theory of Poetic Syntax.* Bloomington: Indiana University Press, 1984.

Bannet, Eve Tavor. "Pluralist Theory-Fictions and Fictional Politics." *Philosophy and Literature* 13.1 (April 1989): 28-41.

Barthes, Roland. *Mythologies.* Paris: Seuil, 1957.

———. *S/Z.* Paris: Seuil, 1970.

Baudelaire, Charles. *Oeuvres Complètes.* Ed. Claude Pichois. Paris: Gallimard, 1975.

———. *Petits Poèmes en Prose (Le Spleen de Paris)*. Ed. Marcel Ruff. Paris: Garnier-Flammarion, 1967.

Baudry, Jean-Louis. "Le Texte de Rimbaud (fin)." *Tel Quel* 36 (1969): 33-53.

Beaujour, Michel. "Short Epiphanies: Two Contextual Approaches to the French Prose Poem." *The Prose Poem in France: Theory and Practice*. Ed. Mary Ann Caws & Hermine Riffaterre. New York: Columbia University Press, 1983. 39-59.

Beehler, Michael. *T.S. Eliot, Wallace Stevens, and the Discourses of Difference*. Baton Rouge: Louisiana State University Press, 1987.

Benedikt, Michael. *The Prose Poem*. New York: Dell, 1976.

Benjamin, Walter. "The Author as Producer." *Art After Modernism: Rethinking Modernism*. Ed. Brian Wallis. New York: New Museum of Contemporary Art & Boston: Godine Publishers, 1984. 297-309.

Bernard, Suzanne. *Le Poème en Prose de Baudelaire jusqu'à Nos Jours*. Paris: Nizet, 1959.

Bernstein, Richard. "The Arts Catch Up with a Society in Disarray." *New York Times* 2 Sept. 1990: B1.

Bertelé, René. *Henri Michaux*. Paris: Seghers, 1973.

Bleich, David. *Subjective Criticism*. Baltimore: Johns Hopkins University Press, 1978.

———. "The Subjective Paradigm in Science, Psychology, and Criticism." *New Literary History* 7.2 (1976): 313-334.

Bloom, Harold. *A Map of Misreading*. New York: Oxford University Press, 1975.

Booth, Wayne. "'Preserving the Exemplar': or, How Not to Dig Our Own Graves." *Modern American Critics Since 1955. Dictionary of Literary*

Biography 67. Ed. Gregory S. Jay. Detroit: Gale Research Press, 1988. 307-317.

————. *Critical Understanding: The Powers and Limits of Pluralism.* Chicago: University of Chicago Press, 1979.

Borges, Jorge Luis. *Labyrinths*. Eds. James Irby and Donald A. Yates. New York: New Directions, 1962.

Bréchon, Robert. *Michaux*. Paris: Gallimard, 1959.

Breton, André. *Les Pas Perdus*. Paris: Gallimard, 1969.

————. *Entretiens*. Paris: Gallimard, 1973.

————. *Point du Jour*. Paris: Gallimard, 1970.

————. *Arcane 17*. Paris: U.G.E., 1965.

————. *Du Surréalisme en Ses Oeuvres Vives* in *Manifestes du Surréalisme*. Paris: Jean-Jacques Pauvert, 1962.

————. *Signe Ascendant*. Paris: Gallimard, 1968.

————. *Manifestes du Surréalisme*. Paris: Jean-Jacques Pauvert, 1972.

Broome, Peter. *Henri Michaux*. London: The Athlone Press, 1977.

Buckley, Jerome. *The Triumph of Time*. Cambridge: Harvard University Press, 1966.

Bürger, Peter. *Theory of Avant-Garde*. Trans. Michael Shaw. Minneapolis: University of Minnesota Press, 1984.

Chapelan, Maurice. *Introduction au Poème en Prose*. Paris: René Julliard, 1946.

Charles, Michel. "La Lecture Critique." *Poétique* 34 (1978): 129-151.

Chklovski, Victor. "L'Art comme Procédé." *Théorie de la Littérature.* Trans. Tzvetan Todorov. Paris: Seuil, 1965. 76-97.

Cohen, Jean. *Le Haut Langage: Théorie de la Poéticité.* Paris: Flammarion, 1979.

Crane, R. S. *The Language of Criticism and the Structure of Poetry.* Toronto: University of Toronto Press, 1953.

Crosman, Robert. "Do Readers Make Meaning?" *The Reader in the Text: Essays on Audience and Interpretation.* Ed. Inge Crosman & Susan R. Suleiman. Princeton: Princeton University Press, 1980. 149-164.

Culler, Jonathan. *On Deconstruction: Theory and Criticism after Structuralism.* Ithaca: Cornell University Press, 1982.

Danto, Arthur. "The Death of Art." *The Death of Art.* Ed. Berel Lang. New York: Haven Publications, 1984. 5-35.

De Man, Paul. *Blindness and Insight: Essays in the Rhetoric of Contemporary Criticism.* New York: Oxford University Press, 1971.

———. "Literature and Language: A Commentary." *New Literary History* 4.1 (Autumn 1972): 181-192.

Delas, Daniel and Jacques Filliolet, eds. *Linguistique et Poétique.* Paris: Larousse, 1973.

Delcroix, Maurice & Walter Geerts, eds. *Une Confrontation de Méthodes.* Namur: Presses Universitaires de Namur, 1980.

Deleuze, Gilles and Félix Guattari. *L'Anti-Oedipe: Capitalisme et Schizophrénie.* Paris: Editions de Minuit, 1972.

Delvaille, Jules. *L'Histoire de l'Idée de Progrès.* Paris: Felix Alcan, 1910.

Derrida, Jacques. *L'Ecriture et la Différence.* Paris: Seuil, 1967.

———. "Signature Event Context." *Glyph* 1 (1977): 172-97.

Dillon, George. *Language Processing and the Reading of Literature: Toward a Model of Comprehension.* Bloomington: Indiana University Press, 1978.

"The Director Who Started a Revolution." *New York Times* 25 March 1992: C6, ed.

Eagleton, Terry. *Literary Theory: An Introduction.* London: Basil Blackwell, 1983.

Edson, Laurie. *Henri Michaux and the Poetics of Movement.* Saratoga, California: Anma Libri, 1985.

Ehrlich, Stansilaw. *Pluralism On and Off Course.* Oxford: Pergamon Press, 1985.

Eichner, Hans. "The Rise of Modern Science and the Genesis of Romanticism." *PMLA* 97.1 (January 1982): 8-30.

Erlich, Victor. *Russian Formalism: History/Doctrine.* The Hague: Mouton, 1965.

Felman, Shoshana. *La Folie et la Chose littéraire.* Paris: Seuil, 1978.

Fish, Stanley. "Anti-Professionalism." *New Literary History* 17.1 (1985): 89-127.

———. *Is There a Text in this Class?* Cambridge: Harvard University Press, 1980.

———. "How Ordinary is Ordinary Language?" *New Literary History* 5 (1973): 41-54.

Foster, Hal. "Against Pluralism." *Recodings: Art, Spectacle, Cultural Politics.* Port Townsend, Washington: Bay Press, 1985. 13-32.

Foucault, Michel. *The Order of Things.* New York: Vintage Books, 1973.

Freedman, Diane. *An Alchemy of Genres: Cross-Genre Writing by American Poet-Critics*. Charlottesville & London: University of Virginia Press, 1992.

Girard, René. *Le Bouc Emissaire*. Paris: Grasset & Fasquelle, 1982.

———. *Critique dans un Souterrain*. Lausanne: Editions l'Age d'Homme, 1976.

Godfrey, Sima. "The Anxiety of Anticipation: Ulterior Motives in French Poetry." *Yale French Studies* 66 (1984): 1-26.

Graff, Gerald. "The Pseudo-Politics of Interpretation." *The Politics of Interpretation*. Ed. W. J. T. Mitchell. Chicago: University of Chicago Press, 1983. 145-158.

Group μ, *A General Rhetoric*. Trans. Paul Burrell and Edgar M. Slotkin. Baltimore: Johns Hopkins University Press, 1981.

Guerlac, Suzanne. "Exorbitant Geometry in Hugo's *Quatrevingt-treize*." *MLN* 96 (1981): 856-876.

Hartman, Geoffrey. "The Use and Abuse of Structural Analysis: Riffaterre's Interpretation of Wordsworth's 'Yew Trees.'" *New Literary History* 7.1 (1975): 165-190.

Hartman, Elwood. *French Romantics on Progress: Human and Aesthetic*. Maryland: Studia Humanistica, 1983.

Henkel, Jacqueline. "Linguistic Models and Recent Criticism: Transformational-Generative Grammar as Literary Metaphor," *PMLA* 105.3 (May 1990): 448-463.

Hirsch, E. D. *Cultural Literacy*. Boston: Houghton Mifflin, 1987.

———. *Validity in Interpretation*. New Haven: Yale University, 1967.

"The History of the OED." *Oxford English Dictionary*, 2nd edition, ed. J. A. Simpson & E. S. C. Weiner. Oxford: Clarendon Press, 1989. XXXXV-LXI.

Holland, Norman N. "The New Paradigm: Subjective or Transactive?" *New Literary History* 7.2 (1976): 335-346.

———. "Re-Covering 'The Purloined Letter'." *The Reader in the Text*. Ed. Inge Crosman & Susan Suleiman. Princeton: Princeton University Press, 1980. 350-370.

———. "Unity Identity Text Self." *PLMA* 90.5 (1975): 813-22.

Horton, Susan. *Interpreting Interpreting*. Baltimore: Johns Hopkins University Press, 1979.

Hugo, Victor. *Oeuvres Complètes*. Paris: Albin Michel, 1937.

Jacob, Max. *Le Cornet à Dés*. Paris: Gallimard, 1945.

Jackson, Robert Louis & Rudy, Stephen, eds. *Russian Formalism: A Retrospective Glance: A Festschrift in Honor of Victor Erlich*. New Haven: Yale Russian & Slavic Publications, 1985.

Jakobson, Roman and Lévi-Strauss, Claude. "'Les Chats' de Charles Baudelaire." *L'Homme* 2.1 (1962): 5-21.

James, William. *Essays in Radical Empiricism & A Pluralistic Universe*. New York & London: Longmans, Green & Co., 1943.

Jameson, Frederic. *The Political Unconscious*. Ithaca: Cornell University Press, 1981.

Jenny, Laurent. "La Surréalité et Ses Signes Narratifs." *Poétique* 4 (1973): 507-520.

Johnson, Barbara. *The Critical Difference: Essays in the Contemporary Rhetoric of Reading*. Baltimore and London: The Johns Hopkins University Press, 1980.

————. *Défigurations du Langage Poétique*. Paris: Flammarion, 1979.

————. "Quelques Conséquences de la Différence Anatomique des Textes."
Poétique 28 (1976): 98-116.

Kearn, James and Ken Newton. "An Interview with Jacques Derrida." *The
Literary Review* (18 April - May 1980): 25-40.

Krauss, Rosalind. "The Originality of the Avant-Garde: A Postmodernist
Repetition." *Art after Modernism*. Ed. Brian Wallis. Boston: Godine,
1984. 13-29.

Krieger, Murray. "The Arts and the Idea of Progress," *Progress and Its
Discontents*, ed. Gabriel A. Almond, Marvin Chodorow, and Roy
Harvey Pearce (Berkeley & London: University of California Press,
1982), 468.

————. "Literary Invention and the Impulse to Theoretical Change: 'Or
Whether Revolution be the Same.'" *New Literary History* 18.1 (Autumn
1986): 191-208.

Kristéva, Julia. *Polylogue*. Paris: Seuil, 1977.

————. *La Révolution du Langage Poétique*. Paris: Seuil, 1972.

Kuhn, Thomas. *The Structure of Scientific Revolutions*. Chicago & London:
University of Chicago Press, 1962.

La Charité, Virginia A. *Henri Michaux*. Boston: Twayne, 1977.

Lévy, Sydney. *The Play of the Text: Max Jacob's 'Cornet à Dés.'* Madison:
University of Wisconsin Press, 1981.

Lacoue-Labarthe, Philippe & Jean-Luc Nancy. *The Literary Absolute: The
Theory of Literature in German Romanticism*. Trans. Philip Barnard
and Cheryl Lester. Albany: SUNY Press, 1988.

Little, Roger. "Rimbaud's 'Sonnet.'" *Modern Language Review* 75.3 (July
1980): 528-533.

Margescou, Mircea. *Le Concept de Littérarité*. The Hague: Mouton, 1974.

McFarland, Thomas. *Originality and Imagination*. Johns Hopkins University Press: Baltimore, 1985.

Merleau-Ponty, Maurice. *The Primacy of Perception*. Ed. James M. Edie. Evanston: Northwestern University Press, 1964.

Metzidakis, Stamos. "Barthes' Image." *Neophilologus* 71 (1985): 489-495.

————. "Graphemic Gymnastics in Surrealist Literature." *Romanic Review* 81.2 (January 1990): 211-224.

————. *Repetition and Semiotics: Interpreting Prose Poems*. Birmingham, AL: Summa Publications, 1986.

————. "Semiotic Analysis of Iconic Features in Literature." *Semiotics 1985*. Ed. John Deely. Lanham, MD: University Press of America, 1986. 336-345.

Michaux, Henri. *Emergences-Résurgences*. Genève: Skira, 1972.

————. *La Nuit remue*. Paris: Gallimard, 1935.

————. *Passages*. Paris: Gallimard, 1963.

Mill, John Stuart. *Autobiography*. New York: New American Library, 1964.

Mitchell, W. J. T., ed. *Against Theory: Literary Studies and the New Pragmatism*. Chicago: University of Chicago Press, 1985.

Mortier, Roland. *L'Originalité: Une Nouvelle Catégorie Esthétique au Siècle des Lumières*. Genève: Droz, 1982.

Newton, K. M. *In Defense of Literary Interpretation*. London: Macmillan Press Ltd., 1986.

Nisbett, Robert. *History of Progress*. New York: Basic Books, 1980.

Oxford English Dictionary. Ed. J. A. Simpson & E. S. C. Weiner. Oxford: Clarendon Press, 1989.

OULIPO: La Littérature Potentielle. Paris: Gallimard, 1973 ed.

Richards, I. A. "Poetic Process and Literary Analysis." *Style in Language*. Ed. Thomas A. Sebeok. Cambridge: MIT Press, 1960. 9-23.

———. "Variant Readings and Misreading." *Style in Language*. Ed. Thomas A. Sebeok. Cambridge: MIT Press, 1960. 241-252.

Richter, David. "R. S. Crane." *Modern American Critics, 1920-1955*. *Dictionary of Literary Biography* 63. Ed. Gregory S. Jay. Detroit: Gale Research Press, 1988. 87-97.

Riffaterre, Hermine. "Reading Constraints: The Practice of the Prose Poem." *The Prose Poem in France: Theory and Practice*. Eds. Caws, Mary Ann and Hermine Riffaterre. New York: Columbia University Press, 1983. 98-116.

Riffaterre, Michael. "Describing Poetic Structures: Two Approaches to Baudelaire's 'Les chats.'" *Structuralism*. Ed. Jacques Erhmann. Garden City: Anchor Books, 1970. 200-242.

———. "Hermeneutic Models," *Poetics Today* 4.1 (1983): 7-16.

———. *Semiotics of Poetry*. Bloomington and London: Indiana University Press, 1979.

———. "Syllepsis." *Critical Inquiry* 6 (Summer 1980): 625-638.

———. *Text Production*. Trans. Terese Lyons. New York: Columbia University Press, 1983.

Robbe-Grillet, Alain. *Projet pour une Révolution à New York*. Paris: Editions du Minuit, 1970.

Rooney, Ellen. *Seductive Reasoning: Pluralism as the Problematic of Contemporary Literary Theory*. Ithaca: Cornell University Press, 1989.

Rosenberg, Karen. "The Concept of Originality in Formalist Theory." *Russian Formalism: A Retrospective Glance: A Festschrift in Honor of Victor Erlich*. Eds. Robert Louis Jackson & Stephen Rudy. New Haven: Yale Russian & Slavic Publications, 1985: 162-172.

Said, Edward. *The World, The Text, The Critic*. Cambridge: Harvard University Press, 1983.

Schauber, Ellen, and Ellen Spolsky. *The Bounds of Interpretation: Linguistic Theory and The Literary Text*. Palo Alto: Stanford University Press, 1986.

Schor, Naomi. *Breaking the Chain*. New York: Columbia University Press, 1985.

Scott, David. "La Structure Spatiale du Poème en Prose: D'Aloysius Bertrand à Rimbaud." *Poétique* 59 (1984): 295-308.

Seamon, Roger. "Poetics Against Itself: On the Self-Destruction of Modern Scientific Criticism." *PMLA* 104.3 (May 1989): 294-305.

Sykes, Charles J. *Profscam*. Washington, D.C.: Regnery Gateway, 1988.

Terdiman, Richard. *Discourse/Counter-Discourse: the Theory and Practice of Symbolic Resistance in 19th-Century France*. Ithaca: Cornell University Press, 1985.

Todorov, Tzvetan. *Critique de la Critique*. Paris: Seuil, 1984.

———. *Théories du symbole*. Paris: Seuil, 1977.

———. "Three Conceptions of Poetic Language." *Russian Formalism: A Retrospective Glance: A Festschrift in Honor of Victor Ehrlich*. Eds. Robert Louis Jackson & Stephen Rudy. New Haven: Yale Russian & Slavic Publications, 1985. 130-147.

Tynianov, Juri. "De l'Evolution Littéraire." *Théorie de la Littérature.* Trans. Tzvetan Todorov. Paris: Seuil, 1965. 120-137.

Valéry, Paul. *Oeuvres Complètes.* Ed. Jean Hytier. Paris: Gallimard, 1960.

White, Charles Eric. *Kaironomia: On the Will-to-Invent.* Ithaca & London: Cornell University Press, 1987.

Zinn, Howard. *A People's History of the United States.* New York: Harper Perennial, 1980.

INDEX OF NAMES CITED

self-destructing, -
deconstructing 52, 73, 246
self-reflexive 178
sentimentality 113
sincerity 113
"sign" 142-143
social class 134
society, French 137, 143
Socratic ideals 142
"soft" discipline 54
sonnet 74, 79, 82 , 89-90,
93, 129, 136, 138, 150, 153,
176, 178, 180
"state of grace" 183
strangeness 110
"stream of consciousness"
novels 153
Structuralism -ist 4, 16, 21,
22, 26, 29, 45, 51-53, 72,
148, 167
sublime 137
suggestion or nuance 187
Surrealism, -ist 129, 139,
140, 142-154, 190-191, 194,
199
surreality 151-52
syllepsis 149
Symbolism, -ist 117, 129,
136, 146, 151, 153, 172,
180-190, 195
syntactic structures 79, 138
syntax 137
Taste 178
tautological 80, 81
telos 245
"temporary literary

absolutes"248
"text itself", or "in and of
itself" 44, 45, 46, 47, 49, 50,
51, 73, 87
textuality 79
theater of the absurd 132,
153
Three Unities 108
topoï 108
Tradition, 109, 112, 141
transcendence or
"transcendent essence" 28,
29, 48, 114, 146, 185, 187-
88
trans-historical 87, 172,
204-224
            , epistemological
205-209
            , socio-pragmatic
209-215
            , psychological 215-
224

transitoriness in literature
236, 242, 247
            -in originality 241,
242
            -ontological 248
transnational 172
translation (*translatio)* 95,
108
Truth 23, 178-79
Truth vs. truths 232, 241,
248
uncanny 89

Lightning Source UK Ltd.
Milton Keynes UK
UKOW040059210313

207933UK00001B/4/P